Northern Links

Northern Links

A Duffer's Unforgettable Journey through the World of Canadian Golf

KENDALL

PENGUIN

VIKING

VIKING

Published by the Penguin Group

Penguin Books Canada Ltd, 10 Alcorn Avenue, Toronto, Ontario, Canada M4V 3B2
Penguin Books Ltd, 27 Wrights Lane, London W8 5TZ, England
Penguin Putnam Inc., 375 Hudson Street, New York, New York 10014, U.S.A.
Penguin Books Australia Ltd, Ringwood, Victoria, Australia
Penguin Books (NZ) Ltd, cnr Rosedale and Airborne Roads, Albany, Auckland 1310,
New Zealand

Penguin Books Ltd, Registered Offices: Harmondsworth, Middlesex, England

First published 2001

1 3 5 7 9 10 8 6 4 2

Printed and bound in Canada on acid free paper ∞
Text design and typesetting by Laura Brady

CANADIAN CATALOGUING IN PUBLICATION DATA

Kendall, Brian
Northern links

ISBN 0-670-88884-2

1. Golf—Canada—History.   I. Title.

GV985.C35K45 2001   796.352'0971   C2001-900569-5

Visit Penguin Canada's website at **www.penguin.ca**

For SHARON

For SHARON

CONTENTS

FOREWORD

I'M STILL NOT CERTAIN WHY I STAYED away almost 30 years from a game I had loved passionately as a kid. I know I never stopped believing that in so many ways golf is the most rewarding of sports, and I fully intended to one day make my way back. It just took me a little longer than I expected.

Like many of my generation, I was first drawn to golf by the exploits and charisma of Arnold Palmer, who did more than any other player to popularize the game. Suddenly golf, until then largely a pastime of the rich or at least the solidly middle class, became fashionable even in my working-class suburban neighbourhood. My friends and I began saving our allowances to buy clubs, one at a time, from Canadian Tire, and we would gather on summer evenings to smack balls around the open field at the end of our street. Eventually, whenever we could afford it, we took our games onto the nearby public course, where the green fee, as I remember, was $8.

Then, with impeccable timing, just as the game was taking off in Palmer's wake, there came a hero whom Canadians could proudly call our own. George Knudson, destined to become our greatest professional golfer, emerged from Winnipeg's St. Charles Golf and Country Club to thrill us all with a string of victories on the PGA Tour.

After seeing him on newscasts or watching him Sunday afternoons on our old black-and-white TV, I would go out and try to emulate his cat-like walk on the fairway and that impossibly sweet swing he had perfected over countless hours of practice, the stroke even Ben Hogan said was one of the finest he'd ever seen. Next to my favourite movie actor, Steve McQueen, Knudson seemed to me the coolest man alive. His hair cropped short in those days, he wore tinted glasses over light-sensitive eyes and was never, except during his swing, seen without a cigarette in his mouth or carefully cupped in his right hand against the fairway breezes.

Most intriguing of all, Knudson, like McQueen, perpetually wore a thin enigmatic smile, as if he were in on a joke or a secret the rest of us could never begin to understand.

When I was 16, I stopped playing the game. I've since discovered that many golfers quit around this age for other pursuits: girls (or boys), part-time jobs, higher education, other sports. Still, I never lost interest in golf, and in particular I continued to follow George Knudson's progress in the sports pages.

The decades passed and still I didn't return. I always said I'd come back when I had the time to get serious again about the game, the way I was when I was a boy. But one thing or another always intruded, and time slipped away.

At last, in a burst of mid-life inspiration, I hit upon the idea for this book. I'd begin a journey through the world of Canadian golf that would, I hoped, reignite the passion I felt for the game when I first began. Over the next two summers, I'd try my damnedest to catch up and make up for all the precious years I had lost.

It was a dream assignment, one every golfer in the land might envy. I would enjoy the privilege of playing alongside the incomparable Marlene Stewart Streit at the scene of the triumph that started her meteoric rise five decades ago. At the Banff Springs Golf Course, among other celebrated layouts, I walked in the giant footprints of Stanley Thompson, our most revered golf course architect. Senior golfers Bill Hardwick and Doug Robb inspired me with the stories of how they made their mid-life dreams come true on the European Senior Tour. In Yellowknife I fought swarms of blackflies to compete in the famous Midnight Classic. I met and marvelled at Steve Johnston, our own King of Aces, who ranks third in the world with an astonishing 47 holes-in-one. One autumn I explored the length and breadth of Cape Breton, the ruggedly beautiful isle that is fast remaking itself into the country's hottest golf destination. And on a sweltering August afternoon, I carried the bags alongside the kids at the historic Hamilton Golf and Country Club, one of the few courses in Canada that still supports a caddy program.

There were still more memorable rounds played, fascinating Canadian golfers (both famous and obscure) met, insights gained and lessons learned. But by far my biggest discovery, even if it's one I strongly suspected all along, was that once golf has you in its velvet Vardon grip it never lets go.

And that I was a fool for letting 30 years pass before teeing it up again.

CHAPTER 1

IN GEORGE WE TRUST

"OKAY, LET'S SEE YOU HIT ONE," Ben Kern said, walking to where I stood on the practice range.

Even though I'd just finished stroking four or five shots I regarded as reasonable efforts, my confidence melted under the professional gaze of the man thought by many to be the country's top instructor.

A 7-iron in hand, I set up toward a pin about 150 yards distant, breathed deeply, swung and . . . whiffed!

I felt like burying myself in the nearest bunker. My first significant shot of the season—in truth, the symbolic beginning of my entire *Northern Links* adventure — and all I'd caught was air.

Kern smiled encouragingly at me from under his wide-brimmed straw hat.

"Don't worry about it."

"I guess you make me nervous," I said, knowing how lame that sounded the moment I said it.

"Sure," Ben answered soothingly. "Try again."

Together with eight other golfers of wildly varying skill levels, I'd come to Devil's Pulpit, a course of national renown set in gently rolling countryside about 25 miles northwest of Toronto, for a clinic with Kern, the Pulpit's director of golf. A former PGA Tour player, Kern had tutored many of Canada's top stars, including Lorie Kane and David Morland IV. What he had imparted to them, and what he was attempting to introduce to us, were the teaching principles painstakingly developed by his good friend and mentor, the late, great George Knudson.

Venerated by his peers as a true authority on the mechanics of the swing, Knudson possessed a technique so fluid and pure that other golfers on the PGA Tour often stopped to watch in envy when he practised. "There was poetry in the way George swung a golf club," Kern told me. "There aren't too many players who never lose their swing, not even once. But George was always confident when he walked onto a golf course that he had exactly what he had the day before."

My fondest hope was that the months ahead would lead me to recapture the enthusiasm I felt for the game back in the days when George Knudson was busy inspiring an entire generation of Canadian golfers. What better way to begin than by trying, as best I could, to absorb the swing theories of my boyhood idol?

Though I didn't realize it yet, Knudson would seldom be far from my thoughts during my travels across the country. Everywhere

I went, people told me stories of an incredible shot they had once seen him make, or talked of how much his success had meant to them as Canadians. More and more, I found myself wondering about the nature of a man so obsessed with the intricacies of the golf swing that even on his deathbed he could talk of little else. Soon his story, and the memories it brought back to me, became part of the journey.

In getting to know Ben Kern, both during the clinic and in subsequent conversations, I would learn about one of the most significant collaborations in Canadian golf. Tall and trim, soft-spoken and elegant in manner, Kern has been the keeper of Knudson's flame ever since his friend's death at the age of 51 in 1989. During our clinic, he tried to explain a swing theory that Knudson himself admitted to taking 15 years to fully understand and another 10 years to learn how to properly communicate to students.

Knudson could — and often did — talk for hours about how the swing motion is governed by nature and physics, about how the laws of centrifugal force, motion and inertia all factor in.

To his credit, Kern knew he had to dumb all that down a little during the clinic, especially for the novices among us. Essentially, he explained, George Knudson believed that the swing motion should involve the entire body, that rather than manipulate the club head through impact, as other instructors might suggest, the golfer must allow it to travel on an uninterrupted path determined by the natural motion of the body from backswing to follow-through. "You have to give up control to gain control," Knudson advised, convinced that if the golfer starts in a balanced position and finishes his swing still in balance, not a whole lot can go wrong in between.

A relaxed, Zen-like state of mind is another key component of the Knudsonian philosophy. He stressed that successful golf is tension-free golf, although this was a mental state the precariously high-strung golfer only rarely managed to achieve himself. "You don't play golf to relax, you relax to play golf," he preached.

Naturally, I knew that producing a swing anywhere close to Knudson's own flawless model would require an almost super-human effort. Neither I nor, I strongly suspected, any of my fellow students in the clinic had the time, patience or, most important, the ability to pull it off.

Ben Kern wisely understood this and was perfectly willing to adapt his instructions on an individual basis. During the time he spent with me, he adjusted my grip and reminded me to stand more erect in my stance.

"When learning to swing, never do anything at the expense of balance," Kern emphasized repeatedly to the entire class.

Though adaptable, Ben made it clear that a wholehearted embrace of Knudson's theories was the surest path he knew to a radically improved golf game. "George was a genius," he said with the zeal of the converted. "He understood more about the golf swing than any man alive."

More than a decade after his death, Knudson's legend grows larger with every passing year. His instructional video still sells briskly across Canada and his book, *The Natural Golf Swing*, written with Lorne Rubenstein in the final months of his life, has become a collector's item among students of the game.

"George truly believed that he could change the way the game is played," Kern told me. "He felt he could make it more graceful and even more fun. After he retired from the tour, that was his mission, to show people that they were going about it all wrong.

"The sad thing is, George had really only just started spreading the word when he passed on."

THE MAN VOTED THE Canadian Professional Golfers Association's player of the twentieth century spoke of the golf swing with the same passion that other men might speak of a breathtakingly beautiful but elusive woman. "My great love is swinging a golf club," George Knudson once said. "The competition is secondary. I could have an orgasm in swinging a golf club to the ultimate."

As a boy, George attended art classes at the Winnipeg Art Gallery and briefly considered a career as a commercial artist. Instead, he made the golf swing the expression of his artistic longings.

"I want to paint pretty colours with a golf club," he waxed eloquently at the height of his fame. "I want people to blow their minds when they watch me play. I want to make them feel the same way they do when they go to a concert or a gallery. I want to paint pictures, birds and sky and trees. I want to play great music. . . ."

The quest that would consume his life began at Winnipeg's St. Charles Golf and Country Club, where he worked part-time from the age of 10, cleaning and repairing clubs, caddying and playing every chance he got.

George would be on the course so early in the spring and so late in the fall that he had to wear high rubber boots in the mud. The growing boy didn't smoke, drink or chase girls, thinking only of golf. "If ever I went to a movie on my day off, I played 54 holes before I hit the movie house," Knudson recalled. "The pro ran an indoor golf school at Portage and Main in the winter, and I worked at that, too."

He spent hours poring over the photographs in Ben Hogan's *Power Golf*, then modelled his own swing after that of the most admired ball striker in the history of the game. Years later, on the

5

PGA Tour, George would drop everything to watch Hogan play or practise. From the master he learned that a wider stance helped create harmony throughout the swing. He also put in a hard year and a half learning to emulate Hogan's perfectly balanced finishing position. Soon Knudson's fellow pros began to joke that he looked more like Hogan than Hogan himself.

Following a teenage career that saw him capture the Manitoba and Canadian junior championships, Knudson turned professional in 1958, moving east to Toronto to become the assistant to Bill Hamilton, the head pro at Toronto's Oakdale Golf and Country Club. For the next three seasons Knudson played sporadically and without success on the PGA Tour, earning just $240 in 1960. Finally, he emerged from the pack to notch his first victory, the Coral Gables Open, in December of 1961.

George won again at the Portland Open in 1963, and then at the Fresno Open the next year. I was 12 in 1964 and by then Knudson's name resonated for me and most Canadians. That summer, for the first time, I began searching the sports pages for the golf results even before checking the progress of Mickey Mantle's New York Yankees in the pennant race. While chasing golf balls around the back field, I imagined I was George Knudson fighting it out with Arnold Palmer at the Masters. In 1965, when *Maclean's* put George on its front cover, the image went up on my bedroom wall next to a full-colour action shot of Gordie Howe, my wintertime god.

Playing for Canada at the 1966 World Cup in Tokyo, Knudson became the idol of two countries when he turned in the low individual score, an achievement that earned him a lucrative contract to wear the golfing apparel of a Japanese clothing manufacturer.

From the start, Knudson was a ball-striking virtuoso of such strict intellectual purity that he would almost rather win pretty or

not at all. Of his eight PGA Tour victories, easily the most personally satisfying was the 1967 New Orleans Open, where he edged Jack Nicklaus by a single stroke.

"Don't give me another ball, I've done it all now," George marvelled to himself after he'd strung together a dozen or more brilliant shots to clinch the win. One in particular during that stretch, a 2-iron around a tree, surprised even him. "I didn't know I had the shot in my bag," he said years later. "The only greater moment I could imagine would be winning the Canadian Open with the same degree of skill."

Knudson was indifferent to the cheers of the crowd and even to the admiration of his peers. All he craved was the personal satisfaction of knowing he'd come as close as humanly possible to controlling a golf ball's flight.

And yet despite the countless hours Knudson spent labouring and thinking about his golf swing, it was his fate to rarely feel even remotely satisfied with his efforts. The man regarded as the premier ball striker of his generation believed in his heart that he had only ever hit one truly perfect shot— a 5-iron to a green in Japan during the 1966 World Cup. George remembered that during that single swing his whole body, his entire being, felt as if it had literally "exploded."

Having experienced it once, George Knudson made the pursuit of still more perfect golf shots — ideally an unlimited succession of them—his personal Holy Grail. To build up his physical stamina for the challenge, Knudson, who as a young man packed a mere 140 pounds on his five-foot-ten-inch frame, proceeded to increase his body strength 25 per cent by adhering to a rigid routine of weightlifting and running exercises.

George also consulted sports psychologists, discovering things about himself and his golf game he had never even imagined.

Dr. Richard Lonetto of the University of Guelph had Knudson play the challenging Glen Abbey course with his eyes closed on full swings. George shot 67 and realized that he didn't need to see the ball, provided that his address and form were impeccable.

In his book Knudson observed, "It's amazing how quickly you can learn if you're in balance, and how much of a one-piece motion the swing really is."

BEN KERN FIRST MET GEORGE at Toronto's Islington Golf Club during the 1967 Ontario Open. Leading the field during the final round, Ben, then a collegiate star at New Mexico State University, looked up after hitting a superb iron shot onto the 16th green to see Knudson, who wasn't playing in the tournament, studying him from the gallery. George stayed with him right through Kern's loss in a thrilling playoff. Afterwards, Canada's premier golfer came up to congratulate the younger man on his play.

"That meant a lot to me, I can tell you," Ben remembered. "Having George Knudson tell me that I looked good out there took away a lot of the pain.

"It's funny what sticks in your mind," Kern added with a smile. "My most vivid memory of that first meeting with George is that he was wearing street shoes so highly polished they gleamed. He seemed . . . big time."

Knudson made a habit of quietly following the progress of promising young Canadian golfers — although always with a critical eye. Sandra Post, our most successful professional women's golfer, who twice won the LPGA championship in the U.S., recalled how Knudson turned up to watch her play a Toronto tournament shortly after she had captured the 1968 LPGA.

Clearly unimpressed by her golf swing, Knudson started to walk off the course in silence. "But, George," Post called after him in disappointment, "I've got a great short game!"

Knudson was at the height of his fame then, a time when, as an anonymous obituary writer remembered, "the sweet swing that was his trademark paid dividends when the cheques were passed out on the late Sunday summer afternoons."

He thrilled me and every Canadian golf fan by starting the 1968 season with back-to-back wins at PGA Tour events in Phoenix and Tucson, as rare a feat then as it is now for anyone not named Tiger. In Phoenix, Knudson said, "I hit the ball so close to the hole I couldn't miss." The next week in Tucson, he started the final round four strokes off the pace, then birdied five of the last seven holes for a magnificent 65 and a one-stroke victory.

Telegrams of congratulation poured in from fans across the country. I can remember clipping a newspaper report of the civic reception held for him by the City of Toronto when he got home.

But what I never read in the papers at the time was how the strain of playing for the jackpot on successive Sundays had taken a heavy toll on his nerves. George sat out long stretches for the remainder of the season. Still, he won $71,000 in official prize money to finish in 17th place on the PGA money list.

Even as a boy, George had been wound so tightly that he had to eat by himself because he couldn't sit still through family dinners. Later, after a miserable round on tour, he'd punch his right hand through the hotel room door.

A big part of the problem was that he desperately missed his wife, Shirley, and their three boys. Each week away from them on tour edged him closer to the boiling point. To relieve the stress and the tedium of life on the road, Knudson turned to alcohol, often drinking to excess. Booze also helped dull the pain during flare-ups of the back miseries that plagued him off and on for years.

The era when Knudson starred on the tour was a more innocent time, when reporters generally kept an athlete's personal life private. That's why I can still remember how astonished I was in 1967 when I read a profile of George in the old *Canadian Magazine* that revealed, for the first time, his fondness for alcohol. The author of the article, the late Paul Rimstead, himself a notorious drinker, had travelled to Augusta, Georgia, to cover Knudson's performance in that year's Masters.

During a liquid bull session with a group of reporters that included Rimstead, Knudson practically dared him to reveal the truth about his drinking. "I don't care if people write the truth about me — as long as it is the truth," he declared.

I'm still struck by Knudson's honesty in revealing a secret that reporters might otherwise have kept silent about until after his death. Most who knew him believe that his drinking problem, which he eventually beat, hastened the decline of his game.

TODAY, KNUDSON IS BEST remembered by his fans for a tournament he didn't win, the 1969 Masters, where he tied for second with Billy Casper and Tom Weiskopf, a shot behind George Archer. He played the final six holes two under par, the best of any of the contenders.

"I got the feeling that week that I belonged," George said later. "I experienced every emotion I could, and when I came down the home stretch, I had everything under control emotionally."

If only he had putted better. George Archer took at least a dozen fewer strokes on the greens in winning the tournament.

But that was typical. Figures gathered by IBM during Knudson's years on tour usually showed him first or second in accuracy off the tee, and 127th or so in putting.

Though no one, with the possible exception of his hero Ben Hogan, wielded a golf club with the artistry of George Knudson, in the end that wasn't enough to secure his place alongside Hogan, Bobby Jones, Jack Nicklaus and Arnold Palmer in the pantheon of the century's greatest golfers.

Perhaps it was the beauty of the colours he painted with his swing that blinded him to the need to give putting and chipping, the all-important "short game," the attention it demanded. Knudson won eight times on the toughest golf tour in the world, yet his contemporaries agreed that if he had learned to putt he would have won two or three times that many. Jack Nicklaus labelled him "a million-dollar player with a ten-cent putter."

The plain truth was that putting bored Knudson. Pushing a ball along a manicured carpet with a tiny pat struck him as an unimaginative and even potentially unnecessary labour. As he said in 1974, "My philosophy was, and still is, that if I develop the swing I want, why worry about chipping and pitching?"

Of course, no one, not even George Knudson, could ever achieve that level of perfection. And though he didn't necessarily regret the attempt, he did admit that neglecting his short game cost him dearly in fame and fortune, and possibly even in personal gratification.

With his usual candor, George said, "I got what I deserved."

KNUDSON AND BEN KERN MET up again when Ben was invited to play a tour event in Houston in 1968. For a college kid,

Kern did remarkably well in making the halfway cut. But he
putted poorly and returned to the clubhouse downcast over his
performance.

"George made a point of stopping to give me a few words of
encouragement," Ben recalled. "He told me to take a look at all the
good golfers who wouldn't be around for the final rounds." As they
spoke, Bob Charles, who won the 1963 British Open and the 1968
Canadian Open, walked out the door, finished for the tourney.
"Suddenly," said Ben, "I realized I wasn't doing so badly after all."

The son of Austrian immigrants, Kern grew up in Vancouver
and then Toronto. At the age of 14, he started caddying at the
Mississauga Golf and Country Club, just west of Toronto, where
his brother Fred was the club's assistant pro. The next year Kern
played his first round of golf.

A duffer could easily get sick with envy hearing the story of
Kern's meteoric rise. After scoring something like 107 his first
time out, Ben never again shot over 100. Within a couple of
months he broke 90, and by the end of the summer he had shot a
round in the 70s. Kern went on to become the first Canadian to
win All-American ranking in U.S. intercollegiate golf before
turning professional and earning his PGA Tour playing card on
his first try at the age of 23.

Knudson took Ben under his wing from the moment the
young Canadian joined the tour full-time in 1970. Though
George generously offered Ben advice about his swing, the rookie
usually went away scratching his head in puzzlement over the
message his friend was trying to convey. In those days, before he
had learned to properly verbalize his swing thoughts, Knudson
spoke in a type of cryptic code, leaving it to the listener to deci-
pher his meaning.

Ben told me about a practice round they played together in

Tucson, after which Knudson invited him to the bar for a drink.

"You're not giving yourself much of a chance at the beginning," George said to him.

Ben didn't know what he meant. Did he mean at the beginning of Kern's time on the tour, since this was his first season? Finally, he realized that Knudson was talking about the beginning of his swing, specifically his starting position.

"You know when a white man comes up to the Indian and the Indian always puts up his hand and says, 'How'?" George continued in those less politically correct times. "Well, a starting position is like an Indian putting up his hand and saying, 'Chance.' For you to have a chance, you have to have a perfect starting position."

That was all the explanation George gave. Ben didn't know if he was talking about his alignment, grip, posture or the whole package. And he was too shy and overawed by Knudson to ask. Ben told me he was afraid of looking like a dopey kid.

Despite Knudson's encouragement, Kern never prospered on the big tour. He played for six years, until 1975, with official earnings of just $49,518. Not that it was all a disappointment. Ben was the low Canadian in the Canadian Open for three years, represented Canada in the World Cup and walked away holding seven competitive course records throughout North America.

In the end, the same crucial flaw that kept George Knudson from immortality drove Ben Kern from the tour. "I couldn't putt worth a damn," he said. "I was a good enough putter to be a star in university, but not nearly good enough for a tour player."

In 1976, Kern changed direction, quitting the tour to become first an assistant pro and later the director of golf at the prestigious National Golf Club, just north of Toronto. From there he moved on to Devil's Pulpit in 1996.

"I KNOW NOW I BELONG, that I can win a major," Knudson said after his near-miss at the 1969 Masters.

"But I may never get another chance," he added prophetically.

Increasingly debilitated by his back troubles, George would enjoy only two more tour wins — the Robinson Open in 1970 and the Kaiser International Open in 1972. Soon he regularly missed cuts, and even when he opened a tournament with a low score, his fans back home braced for the inevitable blowout round that would drop him out of contention. His winnings plummeted from $74,366 in 1972 to $10,166 just two years later.

Yet he continued on the tour, though only part-time, until 1978. "I cannot see myself doing anything else," Knudson said stubbornly. "I love to strike the ball. I'm fascinated by the technique."

When he finally conceded that he could no longer compete with the world's top players, George turned to teaching, an occupation that afforded him endless hours to focus his thoughts on the composition of the ideal golf swing. He started his own golf school at the National Golf Club, later moving his operation to the nearby Buttonville Golf and Country Club.

"It was at the National that George started formulating his teaching theories," Ben Kern recounted. "I found myself hanging on his every word. By that time I felt like I was really starting to know what George was all about. I knew that in his understanding of the swing he was head and shoulders above everyone else. Everything he said made such perfect sense to me."

After writing down his thoughts, George would bounce them off Kern. He knew that if he couldn't make his concepts clear to a fellow professional, the average player would never be able to grasp them. George quickly became so absorbed in the process that he would often phone Ben late at night to sound him out about a new idea.

Although an active participant in their development, Kern stressed to me that he should in no way be considered a co-creator of Knudson's theories.

"All the ideas were George's," he insisted. "You couldn't for a minute give swing advice to George Knudson. By that point he had it all so clearly imprinted in his mind that he wouldn't have taken advice from Ben Hogan or anyone else. All I did was help him try to communicate his message. We would talk about things like what should be taught first—the grip, hand formation or whatever. George kept rewriting and rewriting his organizational thoughts."

Like a brilliant yet overly cerebral professor, Knudson fumbled through his first teaching clinics, struggling to find the words to get his message across. Afterwards, students asked Kern to explain in layman's terms what George had told them. Ben constantly urged his friend to be more obvious in his explanations.

In those early days, Knudson, the consummate perfectionist, demanded more of his students than many of them were willing or able to give. Like many gifted athletes, he was mystified when other people failed to pick up on things as quickly as he had. "George wanted his students to enjoy the thrill of hitting a ball the way he knew it could be done," Ben explained. "He couldn't understand people who were happy just to go out there and not embarrass themselves. He would say, 'Well, why even bother?'"

In the last years of his life, Knudson relaxed enough to enjoy teaching even casual students of the game, earning a reputation as a forebearing coach. Following his inevitable induction into the Canadian Golf Hall of Fame in 1985, he focused his energy on first his instructional video and then his book, *The Natural Golf*

Swing. The latter became the basis for a CPGA training manual that was distributed to every teaching professional in the land.

Most exciting of all, Knudson looked forward to resuming his playing career on the lucrative Senior PGA Tour when he became eligible on his 50th birthday in 1988. But those plans were set back when he was diagnosed with lung cancer in June 1987. Knudson, who had been trying to break his addiction to cigarettes for 30 years, took the news stoically.

"Hey, I smoked those things," he told his friend Lorne Rubenstein. "Who was I to think that cancer wouldn't get me?"

Only then did he manage to shake himself of the nicotine habit that I had thought made him look so cool back in the days when he stalked the fairways in triumph. With the natural optimism of a man who often said he fully expected to one day shoot 18 birdies during a round of golf, Knudson endured radiation and chemotherapy treatment, then worked hard to get himself back into shape.

When the cancer went into remission, Knudson finally took his crack at the Senior Tour. In the last spring of his life, he teamed with Johnny Pott in the Legends of Golf tournament in Austin, Texas. Combining for a four-under-par 276, the partners took home $5,000 each.

"I'm still a long way from where I could be, but spiritually I'm motivated," George said. "I want to get back out and kick a few butts."

It wasn't to be. The cancer returned and spread to his brain. Near the end, when he would have been far better off resting in bed, Knudson undertook a cross-Canada promotional tour for the instructional book of which he was so proud.

Even as the hours ticked down to his final breath on January 24, 1989, he was still talking golf. Kern vividly recalled

Knudson, so weak he could barely sit up, going on for hours about his swing theories during one of their last visits, as if he felt the need to drive home his message as hard as he could while he still had time.

"It was very important to him that I was absolutely clear about what he was saying," Ben told me. "He was counting on me to help get the word out."

CHAPTER 2

MIDNIGHT MADNESS

"DO YOU BELIEVE THIS GALLAGHER character?" Roland Gagnon asked sourly. "Every decent hotel room in town has been booked for weeks and now I find out he refuses to share. Insists he has to have his own room. Jeez, almighty!"

The chairman of the Yellowknife Golf Club Midnight Classic and I were in the middle of an introductory lunch in historic Old Town, a colourful tumble of wooden shanties, bush plane operations, native art galleries and restaurants hugging a rocky peninsula that juts into Great Slave Lake. The cellphone bringing the unwelcome request from John Gallagher, the zany, motor-mouthed Toronto television sportscaster recruited to serve as master of ceremonies, had been ringing almost nonstop since we sat down to eat.

Gagnon could only wonder if this was to be just the first annoying request of a soft and complaining southerner who couldn't make do without his creature comforts. After all, Yellowknife was the kind of place where, in the mining camps outside of town, men still bunked a dozen to a cabin. And it wasn't so many years ago that golfers hereabouts toted shotguns in their bags for protection against bears and other fearsome beasts that lurked on the bog and tundra of the only golf course in Canada's most northerly city.

Organizing a golf tournament of world renown was a sometimes nerve-racking task even for someone of Roland Gagnon's considerable experience.

A big man in his late fifties, with a pink complexion, spectacles and a handsome head of jet-black hair, Roland was a retired federal employee ("I didn't actually work," he liked to joke. "I worked for the government.") active on the national council of the Elks, for whom he had organized major curling bonspiels and other events held in Yellowknife. In this, Gagnon's first crack at a golf tournament, a freelance assignment separate from his duties for the Elks brotherhood, the Midnight Classic would enjoy its greatest success ever. A record 384 adventure-seeking golfers were gathering from as far away as Australia for the right to boast of having played under the midnight sun.

The Midnight, as it's most often called, is held every year on the June weekend closest to the longest day of the year, the summer solstice, when the sun merely glances off the northern horizon at the start of a new day, producing a brief twilight before quickly regaining its strength.

The tournament began back in 1962 as a marathon for golf-mad miners, bush pilots, surveyors and other sturdy Yellow-knifers. Starting Friday night, participants literally golfed till they dropped. No stopovers between rounds were permitted. Food and drink had to be gulped on the run, clothes and shoes changed on the fly, and nature's call answered behind a rock between shots. Caddies, kept constantly busy dousing players with mosquito bombs, worked in eight-hour shifts.

In 1970, Yellowknife's own Sandy Hutchinson became a local folk hero after playing a record 171 holes during 35½ hours of continuous golf.

No one was ever likely to beat that. The next year the Midnight switched to the nine-hole stroke-play format still in effect today. Beginning Friday morning and continuing through the weekend, shotgun starts send flights of golfers off every three hours. The tournament's top prize, awarded to the player carding the lowest nine-hole score, is usually a trip for two to Edmonton. Prizes are also given based on gross and net scores for each tee time.

After lunch, thoughts of John Gallagher put aside and his high spirits restored, Gagnon blasted his vehicle's air-conditioning for the drive to the golf course, about three miles to the northeast of town near the airport.

It was like a sauna outside, the thermometer topping 30 degrees Celsius under a cloudless subarctic sky. For at least two days of the past week, Yellowknife had been the country's hot spot, an occurrence sufficiently rare to promote considerable comment and unabashed civic pride. In a harsh land of climatic extremes, the heat wave might last for weeks. But then, come the depths of the pitiless winter, temperatures plummet as low as –56 degrees Celsius and darkness drapes the city for all but four hours of the day.

Our drive through the capital of the Northwest Territories took us out of Old Town and into the new Yellowknife of office highrises, shopping malls and modern hotels. All the amenities of civilized society—fast-food joints, video and convenience stores, a two-screen cinema and even a stylish no-smoking coffee shop—appeared to be in place, albeit rather sparsely scattered throughout the 10 square blocks or so of the often bleak downtown core.

Named after a group of native Dene whose copper knives inspired the explorer Samuel Hearne to call them "Yellow-Knives," the city saw its first white settlers with the discovery of gold in 1934. Almost overnight a rough boom town of gambling dens, bordellos, log-cabin banks and bars that never closed sprang to life. When the first mines dried up in the early 1940s, Yellowknife dwindled to almost a ghost town. It was the discovery of rich new veins of gold in 1945 that finally secured the settlement's future.

Today, the shafts of Con Miramar anchor the community of 17,500 at opposite ends, the mining giant's 1,200 miles of tunnels burrowing for treasure beneath the city itself and even far out into the ancient bedrock under Great Slave Lake.

What most surprised me during my short time in Yellowknife was the impressive cultural diversity of a city this far north. A young Rastafarian cabbie with luxuriant dreadlocks drove me in from the airport after my 750-mile flight from Edmonton.

"Yeah, mon, YK be a good place to make me money in the summer," he said in his Caribbean singsong. "But you bet I be quick back home when it snow."

Yellowknife's citizenry, most of whom have been drawn to the north by high-paying jobs with the mine or the territorial government, includes South Americans, Vietnamese, Pakistanis, Africans, Indians, Arabs, Americans, at least one seasonal Jamaican, as well

as Canadians from every province. Dene and Metis compose
another 15 per cent or so of the population.

A vast wilderness starts at Yellowknife's doorstep and reaches to
the roof of the world. Just to the south of all that, Gagnon turned
onto a dusty sideroad leading into the golf course parking lot.
There, in keeping with the great northern tradition of refusing to
take anything not life-threatening too seriously, we were welcomed by a club sign featuring a raven with a golf ball clenched
firmly in its black beak.

Three times the size of the common crow and protected by
northern law, ravens are just one of the unique hazards at a golf
course renowned for its quirks. Swarms of the cunning and quick-
eyed creatures swoop from the sky to steal hundreds of golf balls
every year — as many as 300 from the driving range alone. No
one knows why the ravens want them; maybe it's their idea of
sport. But the threat of larceny is so persistent that local rules permit golfers to replace stolen balls without penalty.

The clubhouse of the Yellowknife Golf Club stands in stark
contrast to the country club palaces of the south. Perched on an
outcropping of bare rock, it's a sprawling, unprepossessing clapboard affair furnished with worn carpeting, rickety tables and the
type of plastic-covered chairs most often found in company cafete-
rias. There are washrooms and a small snack bar, though no room
for a pro shop, which has been crammed into a trailer out back.

This is actually the second clubhouse in the golf club's short
but colourful history. The first was the fuselage of a DC-3 that
crash-landed at the nearby airport in 1949. Offered the carcass
for the moving, the membership hauled their prize to a position
near the first tee and in the process earned themselves what
must surely rate as the most novel clubhouse in the annals of
Canadian golf.

Ambitious plans were made to turn the cabin of the aircraft into a comfortable lounge, with a shower installed in the tail section and a bar in the cockpit. But the practicalities of the renovation soon dampened enthusiasm. Before long the downed bird was taken away and replaced by the current building, a donation from the local gold mine.

As Roland and I climbed the clubhouse stairs, a deafening mechanical roar assaulted my senses. Looking up, I saw the gleaming silver belly of a large passenger jet passing no more than 400 feet overhead.

"Yup, that can rattle a golfer," Roland said, amused by my startled reaction. "Especially when they remember how we got our first clubhouse."

Every day dozens of aircraft make similarly thunderous descents into the busy terminal beyond the golf course fence.

Once inside the clubhouse, Gagnon said his goodbye and turned me over to Trevor Maywood, Yellowknife's head pro. A trim, intense 39-year-old of medium height with blond hair flattened by the heat and his golf cap, Maywood had recently been recruited from the club in Salmon Arm, British Columbia. Trevor, a bachelor, jumped at the opportunity in Yellowknife, describing his new posting to me as one of the rarest opportunities in Canadian golf.

"You'll find golf up here to be a different experience," he solemnly promised. "You might even say that this is golf in its truest sense. It's more extreme here, maybe more like the game was in its earliest days."

Together we walked out into the sun's harsh glare onto a large wooden deck flanking one full side of the clubhouse. There, for the first time, I gazed upon a golf course unlike any my innocent southern eyes had ever seen.

Beneath a shimmering haze of heat and dust, fairways not of lush and fragant grass but of loose and shifting ankle-deep sand extended like a desert to the horizon. No artfully shaped water hazards, flower beds or the other fripperies of modern golf course design were anywhere to be found. Instead, thin stands of scrub spruce and pine, patches of spongy caribou moss, random out-croppings of reddish grey granite and artificial-turf greens, each encircled by a heavily irrigated ribbon of natural grass no more than two yards in width, provided the few splashes of colour.

No one in Yellowknife is fool enough to believe they've built the world's prettiest golf course, but club members take consider-able pride in all they've accomplished since the June day in 1948 when together Sandy Scott, manager of the local Hudson's Bay Company, and John Anderson Thomson, a surveyor and mining engineer, scrambled over rocks and hacked through the bramble to lay out the nine-hole course. Against all advice, the club's founders even optimistically planted grass seed in a land where turf stubbornly refused to grow. They dug a deep well and through the summer watered and patiently fertilized the fairways. But only a handful of widely scattered and now long-dead green sprouts ever appeared.

The putting greens, or "browns" as they were called, were of sand that was rolled and pounded down, and then saturated annually with 400 gallons of heavy bunker oil to provide at least a semblance of smoothness. After putting out, players were required to sweep away all ball- and footmarks with the aid of chained and weighted coco mats. The most envied member of any foursome was the scorer, whom club rules exempted from mat duty.

In those days the frontier crept right onto the golf course. Golfers armed themselves against the threat of black bears who, while making their way to the town's garbage dumps, gathered in groups to frolic on the strange oily surfaces of the greens. Before departing, they often clawed out the putting cups, carrying them away as souvenirs.

"Wolves had a different approach to the game," wrote George Erskine Inglis, another founding member, in a 1968 article for *Canadian Geographic*. "The red pin flags were the objects of their attention. The wolves would jump up and literally tear the coloured triangles to shreds in snapping efforts to satisfy their curiosity. Our golfing ladies were kept busy replacing the flags."

Despite the obstacles, such was the enthusiasm for golf among Yellowknifers that volunteer springtime work parties were always well attended, all winter-weary hands eager to get the most from a season lasting at best from mid-May to mid-September. An added incentive for participants was a $5 rebate off the $15 paid in annual dues.

In 1993, the golf club entered its modern era with the installation of three experimental artificial greens. The upgrade thrilled the membership, and by 1995 the remaining six had been converted.

SOON TREVOR MAYWOOD AND I were joined on the clubhouse deck by two local men eager to get in a final practice round before the tournament's start the next morning. One of them, a lanky fellow in his mid-twenties, took a 7-iron out of his bag and set up on the artificial turf mat of the first tee, which is set on the deck's surface.

Small mats of artificial turf, about 6 by 10 inches in size, hung on strings from both their golf bags.

"They're for hitting from out in the sand fairways," Maywood whispered. In the old days, golfers would use their hands to sculpt themselves a kind of sand tee, or they dug down into the fairway sand to reach wetter, firmer soil to hit from. The turf mats came into use about 10 years ago. "They're a big improvement," Maywood said. "The mats guarantee a good lie every time."

The starter hole is a 150-yard par three, straight out from the tee. The first golfer suffered the disadvantage of a stiff, jerky swing. But his shot was on line and looked good, if just a little shy of the green. It'll bounce on, I thought. Instead, his ball died a sudden death in the sand about 10 yards short.

"You can't count on fairway bounces here," Maywood told me. "You have to go for the green every time."

The second golfer, a few years older and a more gifted athlete than his partner, did exactly that. Using an 8-iron, he skyed a lovely shot that arced steeply before touching down about 10 feet from the pin.

Ready to call out "Good shot," I instead watched in silent amazement as the ball bounced a dozen feet straight up in the air. An eight-foot bounce followed that, and then a five-footer, followed by a rapid series of ever-smaller hops before the ball finally exhausted itself and curled to a stop about five feet from the cup.

"Look, I know what you're thinking," Maywood said, turning to me, a note of challenge in his voice. "But I guarantee you that once a player makes a few adjustments to his game, he'll enjoy the experience of playing here. The people of Yellowknife have as much fun as golfers anywhere."

Indeed, Yellowknifers are so enamoured of the game that in recent years the club's 500 or so permanent members have increasingly had trouble booking tee times. The problem became so acute that the governors finally decided to undertake the course's most dramatic improvement yet—a $1.2 million expansion from nine to 18 holes. The bulldozers and crew of Centaur

Products of Calgary, the same firm that installed the original nine artificial greens, were on site throughout my visit, out of view from where Maywood and I stood on the clubhouse deck, but busy nonetheless raising the dust that hung suspended like a shroud over the entire golf course.

I had to admire Trevor Maywood's obviously unfeigned enthusiasm for his new posting. It could only have been a major shock when he first set eyes on the weathered clubhouse and dusty fairways. Certainly most pros wouldn't consider Yellowknife a dream posting.

Golf on the edge of the northern frontier has a way of quickly getting under the skin of even a hardened professional. Maywood's immediate predecessor, a local legend named Conan Donahue who could whack a golf ball farther than anyone in these parts had ever seen, still sounded wistful about his old job when I caught up to him several weeks later at the United States Golf Academy in Plymouth, Indiana. Donahue was working as an instructor there after having moved on from Yellowknife.

"How is everybody?" Conan eagerly inquired. "Boy, I miss the old gang at the club."

Donahue was 16 when his family moved to Yellowknife from British Columbia in 1987. Before long he won a reputation as one of the town's leading young hellraisers, a standing that has a definite cachet in a community constantly fretting that it might be growing too darned civilized.

"My first thought when I saw the golf club was, Man, this is ugly!" he recalled. "I had a really hard time getting used to playing on it. Back then, they hadn't even started using the little turf fairway mats."

After working at the course part-time and during summer vacations, Conan left to attend a two-year program at the San

Diego Golf Academy. In 1998, armed with his teaching certificate
and a business degree in course management, he returned home
for a year as the club pro.

That summer Donahue became known as the Flying Swing
Doctor when he made the long journey to Holman, an Inuit village about 300 miles inside the Arctic Circle on Victoria Island,
to conduct a clinic for the townspeople and compete in the annual
Billy Josse Memorial Tournament.

The burly Yellowknifer awed locals by booming drives as long
as 350 yards into the never-setting sun. About 20 to 25 people
turned out for the clinic, a number Donahue considered more
than respectable in a community of only 400. Most were Inuit
who had never played before.

Donahue then went out and cleaned 61 other contestants in
winning the three-day, 27-hole tournament named after the local
Hudson's Bay Company agent who had stubbornly extended the
borders of the game to the really remote north.

Billy Josse, a Scotsman and confirmed golf addict, used to pass
Holman's endless winter hours practising his putting on his living
room floor. Come the brief summer thaw, Josse planted flagsticks
and gleefully chased balls across the tundra. At first the townspeople
thought he was crazy. Then a few got interested and tried the game
themselves. Before long, Josse never lacked for company.

When Josse died in 1980, his friends formed work teams to
build a nine-hole golf course in his memory. The annual memorial tournament started soon after.

"Actually, the layout up there isn't all that bad," Conan told
me. "It's a short little course cut through what they call tundra
turf. And believe me, tundra turf is a lot easier to hit a golf ball off
than anything you'll find in Yellowknife."

The Holman course is just one of several throughout the north that have sprung up like Arctic wildflowers in recent years. By any measure, they're crude, substandard layouts. But the fact that they're there vividly illustrates the game's booming popularity.

Donahue viewed the blossoming of northern golf as all perfectly natural. "Think about it," he said with rising enthusiasm. "Sure, the winter up there is longer. But once the warm weather does come, you can golf almost around the clock." Conan told me he had actually heard people in Yellowknife say in all seriousness that they have the perfect climate for golf.

Donahue wasn't certain what his future in golf might hold, but the 28-year-old wasn't ruling out the possibility of one day reclaiming his old post as Yellowknife's head pro.

"It's the people and the atmosphere of the place," he said, the wistfulness creeping back into his voice. "I teach here at the golf academy, so you know I see a lot of golfers. But I've never met anyone who loves the game as much as the people back home."

YET APPARENTLY EVEN THE golf fanatics of Yellowknife have their limits. So fierce was the heat reflected off the sand fairways the afternoon of my first visit that no more than a staunch handful of players ventured out to play nine.

In preparation for the tourney's start the next day, I laboured mightily over a single large bucket of balls at the driving range while overhead a cackling swarm of ravens mocked my efforts. The damn birds had it right. I knew the best I could hope was that I wouldn't humiliate myself too badly once the action started.

That evening, trying to walk off my pre-tournament jitters, I went back to explore Old Town, the city's birthplace. I wandered past the Bush Pilot's Memorial, a stone pillar erected in tribute to the peerless airmen who opened the north, and past B&Bs and the offices of float plane, fishing and tour boat operators. When a snarling husky barred my entry to one of the last laneways, I beat a hasty retreat to a bare-plank table at the locally famous Wild Cat Café, a squat log cabin as rough-hewn as the original 1930s diner of the same name.

Early the following afternoon I made my way back to the golf course, there to find the tournament's star attraction, John Gallagher, a microphone in his hand, basking in the sun on a bench by the first tee. Beads of sweat glistened on his forehead beneath a flourishing crop of hair implants carefully coiffed into a medium-high pompadour. Immaculate in an all-white ensemble of short-sleeved shirt, shorts and golf shoes, Gallagher would occasionally nod to a cameraman and then rouse himself to conduct a brief interview with a likely looking golfer who had just completed his round.

Despite Roland Gagnon's reservations, most members of the golf club I spoke to, especially the younger ones who caught his act on local cable TV, were thrilled that he had agreed to be this year's featured guest. Gallagher, who in his showbiz life most often goes by his surname alone, had recently been the madcap host of a sports talk show on TSN. Turned roving reporter, he was to cover the tourney for the network as well as serve as master of ceremonies.

"Don't you love this heat?" Gallagher asked happily when we were introduced, turning his already meat-red face to better catch the sun. "Who'd have thought you'd get to golf and have a day at the beach all at the same time?"

A mixed bag of celebrities had preceded Gallagher as official host of the Midnight, including then-Governor General Romeo LeBlanc; Edmonton Oilers defenceman Randy Gregg and his wife, Olympic speedskater Kathy Gregg; and Canadian

Football League great Jackie Parker. Almost always in the past, the featured guest had taken the ceremonial first golf stroke when the shotgun signalled midnight on the opening night of the tournament. Gallagher, however, had declined the honour, his social calendar already full.

Sitting beside him on the clubhouse bench was a young and attractive brunette, a representative of the local cable TV company, whose weekend assignment was to show Gallagher and his two-man crew the local highlights. In a few hours they would be off on a fly-in trip to a fishing lodge. Also gleefully anticipated by Gallagher was an intensive crawl through the town's raunchiest bars.

Gallagher had played his nine holes that morning. "Shot a 69," he said breezily. "In just nine holes! I'm a lousy golfer but that's ridiculous. Best ball, that's what this event should be. I love best ball."

Inside the clubhouse, things were getting rowdy as the weekend-long party shifted into gear. Some tournament participants have been known to get so drunk that when they finally start playing they don't care whose ball they hit. Locals I talked to laughed the shenanigans off, explaining that it was all in keeping with the fun-loving spirit of the club's founding fathers. Before the long opening night was through, every garbage can on every hole of the course would overflow with empty beer and liquor bottles.

Trevor Maywood suddenly appeared from out of the fog of cigarette smoke. "There's someone you have to talk to," he said firmly. "Nathan Zoe, a big friendly Dene kid who practically lives here."

Maywood told me he had never seen anyone take to the game so quickly as the 14-year-old, who had only been playing a year.

"I'm surprised you didn't bump into him yesterday. He usually parks himself beside the first tee in case anyone wants a game. If he's not there, he's sure to be at the practice range. I saw him down there a few minutes ago."

I left the clubhouse din and walked to a picnic table close by the range, where I sat and watched a husky, dark-skinned boy dressed in blue jeans, sneakers and a red T-shirt boom shot after shot 240 yards or more down the range. Seeing him set up so deliberately, completely focused on each swing, made me think of George Knudson's boyhood practice rituals in Winnipeg.

Taking aim at a giant flagpole that stood in front of the St. Charles clubhouse 500 yards away, Knudson would swing for hours on end, hitting balls until his hands bled. Young George loved practising so much that he could hardly wait to get to the range, preferring his time there to actually playing. Only once was he talked into playing without a warm-up. But disgusted after mis-hitting his opening drive, George turned around and headed straight for the range. Knudson made it a rule to practise at least one hour for every hour he spent on the golf course.

Like most young golfers, Nathan was in love with hitting it long. Grabbing on to his driver with a baseball-style grip, he cranked up and slammed each shot with every ounce of his strength. Not once while I watched did he reach into the bag for an iron.

Later, after I'd introduced myself, he sat with me on the picnic table and talked about his passion for the game.

"I used to play soccer, baseball, shoot pool, all that stuff," he said, his broad face breaking into a thousand-watt grin. "But now I've given it all up for golf. Everyone says it's all I can think about. You know, I think they're right."

"He has the *look*," Conan Donahue would say of Nathan. It

was Donahue who first enlisted him in the club's junior program. "He's an unbelievable natural athlete," Conan enthused. "But more important, I've never seen anyone so anxious to learn."

Nathan got started in the game after his father, who doesn't play, gave him a golf bag he'd won in a raffle. The money for his first set of clubs came from working at odd jobs. The slightly unorthodox baseball grip, which he had so far refused to change despite considerable prodding, was taught to him by a family friend during his first visit to the practice range.

Every day Nathan spent hours poring over golf magazines for tips. "My putting was horrible," he confided. "Then I read this magazine article. Keep your head down—that's the key." The club's better players, wondering if they had a budding Tiger in their midst, eagerly offered the boy their counsel and made a point of playing a round with him whenever they could. Like Conan Donahue before him, Trevor Maywood personally tutored him at least once a week.

Nathan's immediate ambition was to get around the nine-hole course in under 40 strokes. He complained that he still couldn't sleep at night for thinking of a missed birdie putt that had robbed him of his goal.

Looking out over the rolling dunes of the driving range, Nathan sighed happily and said, "If I had a home to build, I'd build it right here." In the meantime, he had his sights set on the next best thing—landing a job at the club for the following summer.

"If he stays this keen, if he gets some breaks, maybe gets a college scholarship, Nathan can go as far in the game as he wants to go," insisted Trevor Maywood.

"I want to be the first native Canadian on the PGA Tour, to make all the Dene proud of me," Nathan said. His hero is Notah

Begay III, the first full-blooded American Indian to play on the PGA Tour, whose name means "almost there" in Navajo.

Failing that, he felt certain he'd enjoy the life of a club pro. "Maybe one day I could take over here in Yellowknife," Nathan said hopefully, adding his own name to a growing list of aspirants.

NATHAN PRACTISED ALONGSIDE me as midnight drew closer and I took my final warm-up shots. He'd have happily spent the rest of the night hitting balls at the range, but soon an uncle would arrive to drag him home.

Finally, it was time to head to the second tee, my starting point for the shotgun start. A short walk from the clubhouse, this was considered a prime slot, I'd been assured by Roland Gagnon, one that would save me a potentially long and undoubtedly weary trek back in at the end of the round.

A start at any but the first hole would have pleased me just as well. Cursed by a severe case of first-tee jitters all through these early months of my return to the game, I felt immense relief at not having to hit my first shot under the drunken scrutiny of the increasingly rambunctious clubhouse crowd, which by now had spilled out onto the deck by the first tee. Raucous laughter and thunderous rock music followed me out across the sand.

Waiting on the second tee were my playing partners for the night. I introduced myself to Dan, a local mining engineer, and his friends Jim and Nancy, a married couple who had lived in Yellowknife a few years back and had returned on vacation. Like Dan, Jim was a mining engineer. All three appeared to be in their mid-thirties.

My partners began dousing themselves with heavy mists of

Deep Woods Off, a precaution I had already taken back at the range. Blackflies, although only active about two weeks of the year, arrive at more or less the same time as the tournament. Seasonal swarms of mosquitoes were also buzzing like Messerschmitts on the prowl.

Horror stories abound about past participants who had been all but driven from the course by the pests. This year, though, as long as you remembered to spray on the Off every half-hour or so, the situation remained tolerable. "It's the heat," Dan pronounced, snapping the cap back on his spray can. "The heat wave has killed off most of them. This is the lightest year for bugs I can remember."

Also gathered on our tee was a second foursome that would follow us off. Included in this group was an undertaker from Australia, John Scott, a solid eight-handicapper who had the distinction of having travelled farther than anyone else to play in the tournament. I had just introduced myself and asked him to meet me later for an interview when the starter's gun sounded.

Yellowknife's second hole is a straightaway 382-yard par four. Dan teed up first and stroked a long bomb down the heart of the fairway. In the eerie demi-light of a subarctic midnight, we just barely managed to follow the flight of his ball. The expression "Sounded good" would accompany at least half our tee-shots for the next hour or more while the sun began its rise.

Jim went next and also hit a good one—not quite as long as Dan's, though just as straight.

"You're up, Brian," someone said.

I placed my Titleist on the tee and tried to shut out the small gallery gathered around me, focusing only on my pre-shot routine. I picked out a spot about 225 yards down the fairway and imagined myself swinging through the ball toward the target and beyond. I bent just slightly from the waist. "Proper posture is proud posture," George Knudson preached.

I swung my driver and laced a low shot that crested at a height of about 15 feet before coming to earth with a single skip and thudding to a halt in the sand about 180 yards down the left-hand side of the fairway.

Not great, but I'll take it, I thought, breathing easy again as I put my club away and hurried after Nancy to the forward tee.

Enthusiasm ran high after Nancy, who had taken up the game the previous summer, short-stroked her ball up the middle. My partners jumped into their electric cart and sped off down the fairway. I picked up the rear, keeping up as best as I could in the deep sand, a pull-cart in tow.

When I'd located my half-buried ball, Dan drove up to offer advice on how to place the mat of artificial turf for my next shot. "Dig it right down into the sand and wiggle it around a bit to make certain you've got a good level spot," he suggested. "If you just lay the mat on top of the sand, you'll misjudge your swing for sure.

"Don't worry, you'll get used to it," he called back, steering the cart toward his own ball, another 50 yards farther on.

I surveyed my second shot carefully. Finally, I decided on a 7-iron, the club I felt most comfortable with. A better golfer would have opted for a 5-wood or a long iron. But after a passably decent tee shot, I hesitated to do anything rash.

Digging my feet into the sand, I waggled, swung and, despite Dan's warning, completely misjudged the mat's placement, topping the ball badly. The Titleist skipped once on a nearby patch of caribou moss and landed about 70 yards away in a small grove of spruce trees just off the fairway.

I stalked unhappily into the woods, where I discovered my

ball buried beneath a tangle of twigs and pine cones. Two shots later I had extricated myself and was back on the fairway. Two more shots, a pitch and a passably decent chip, put me on the kidney-shaped green. Two putts got me home in eight.

"A snowman!" I groaned as we made for the next tee. Already I feared what further horrors the night might bring.

The four of us chatted and waited impatiently for about 10 minutes before the group ahead finally moved out of range. Because of the tourney's record number of entrants, play proceeded at a crawl throughout the night. Golfers all over the course, at least those sober enough to notice, ground their teeth in frustration at the delays.

Jim and Nancy remembered Yellowknife fondly from their time in the city almost a decade before. In the years since they'd moved on, Jim's job as a mining engineer had taken them to postings throughout North and South America, and finally to their current home in Oakville, Ontario.

Their vacation plans included a weekend with their two kids out at Dan's cabin on a wilderness lake. More than anything, though, it was the golf that had drawn Jim back. The 15-handicapper recalled the days when he was a Yellowknife club member as some of the best times of his life. While it was true that other golf courses boasted grass fairways and greens, this place had always had something special, at least for him. Jim and Nancy's entire vacation had been planned to allow them to play alongside their old pal Dan in the Midnight Classic.

But just an hour later and only two holes farther along in our round, Jim had already decided that the old chestnut was true — you can't go home again.

The artificial greens, in particular, were driving him to distraction. He'd make what looked like an excellent approach shot, only to watch his ball ricochet off the green's concrete-hard surface and into the sand. When putting, he had absolutely no idea of how to read the turf's funky twists, curves and undulations.

"The greens are a joke," he grumbled loudly. "It's like playing mini-golf."

Jim stubbornly insisted that the pounded and oil-slicked "browns" still in play his first time around at the club provided a truer test of a player's skill.

Of all the golfers I met in Yellowknife, Jim stood alone in this preference. Club members, especially the better players, quickly adjusted their games to the artificial greens. The key, they said, was learning to hit approach shots high enough, and with sufficient spin, so that the ball would land softly and hold the green with a minimum of bounce. Mastering the vagaries of the new greens when putting merely required a little patience. Golfers soon came to appreciate the unfailing fairness of the man-made surfaces.

In fact, it wasn't long before the club's lowest handicappers complained that putting on the artificial greens was too easy. When plans were drawn up for the expansion to 18 holes, the new surfaces were designed much larger (an average of 3,600 square feet compared to 2,800) and with more twists.

My own performance was brutal. I never seemed able to manage more than two good shots in a row. The turf mat was a novelty I couldn't quite get the hang of. Almost always I misjudged the arc of my swing, topping the ball. Two or three times, in frustration, I discarded the mat and used my hands to dig down to firmer sand to hit from. I felt myself caught in every golfer's worst nightmare of hopelessly trying to escape from a sand bunker without end.

While on my knees pawing in the sand, I recalled a story I'd come across in my research about the day in 1949 when Stanley Thompson, the most esteemed of all Canadian golf course architects, visited the Yellowknife course. After a tour, the designer of such classic courses as Alberta's Banff Springs and Cape Breton's Highlands Links was approached by one particularly enthusiastic founding member.

"What do you think, Mr. Thompson," he inquired, "of digging a few sand traps here and there?"

Astonished, the great man took a long time before answering. "I think," he said finally, "your golf course is one complete sand trap."

By the sixth hole, we were already exhausted. Since any ball hit on the fairway seldom skipped more than a dozen feet, the course played far longer than the posted 2,899 yards. We all reeked of bug spray and were covered from foot to golf cap in a thick, greasy layer of dirt. We had started out more than three hours before. The endless waiting at every hole got even worse as the night wore on.

None of us could fathom how or why the old marathoners had done it: constantly swatting away swarms of blackflies and mosquitoes as they golfed around the clock, dropping as many as 15 pounds of body weight before even the hardiest of them finally wore out.

The novelty appeal of playing on a sand course had long since worn off. Twice I helped my partners push their electric cart out of the deep fairway grit. The constantly circling ravens mercifully left us alone, but the sand swallowed at least six of our golf balls. Fortunately, unlike northern golfers of old, we had come well supplied. Golf balls were once so scarce locally that golfers kept small bottles of specially mixed white paint to brighten the scarred covers between rounds.

The story is told of the Yellowknifer who charged into the

bush in pursuit of a bear who had stolen one of his precious golf balls. After a noisy struggle, the golfer emerged triumphant, his ball slightly chewed but still in playable condition.

We were like soldiers of the Foreign Legion on an arduous mission, constantly bucking up one another's spirits. When Nancy, who had been riding a cart all night, said she didn't know if she could make it through, the rest of us cajoled her into pressing on.

At the 456-yard seventh hole, known as Sahara, I hit what by any reasonable standard was no better than a decent drive. Yet from the Hallelujah Chorus that rose from the dusty throats of my new friends, you would have thought I had blasted it 250 yards straight down the pipe.

"Wow, sweet shot, Brian!"

"Brian, killer poke!"

"You da man, Brian!"

As we rode, pushed and trudged our way through the sand, we couldn't help wondering why on earth the club's governors had decided to invest $1.2 million on a new nine. No matter how busy the course had become, the usual reason given for the expansion, surely the money would have been better spent improving the existing layout. Scientific breakthroughs in the development of grasses that are stronger, more resistant to extreme temperatures, drought and humidity had by now convinced almost everyone that turf fairways could be successfully cultivated at the Yellowknife course. Further evidence was seen in the glowing health of the thin ribbons of heavily irrigated turf that already surrounded the greens. The project would be difficult and it definitely wouldn't be cheap. But with a combination of a deep soil bed, a sophisticated sprinkler system and one of the new strains of super grass seed, it almost certainly could be done.

The greening of the Yellowknife course was something still being considered by the club's governors. Another possibility often talked about was the construction of a combination clubhouse–conference centre financed in co-operation with local tourist operators, particularly those in the growing business of luring tourists north in the winter to view the Northern Lights. The project could conceivably become a year-round source of revenue for the golf club, with the profits pumped back into golf course improvements.

"It'll all happen—the clubhouse, grass, the whole nine yards," insisted Dan, the only resident Yellowknifer among us. "There's a lot of money in this town. The mining company or somebody else will put up the cash for the turf. You wait and see."

By this point Dan was getting a little touchy at all our criticism of his home course. Like many Yellowknifers, he preferred to view his club's shortcomings as all part of its eccentric charm.

When the foursome behind us caught up to our group on the ninth tee, I asked the Aussie undertaker how he was enjoying his round.

"Gawd, mate!" he sputtered in reply. "This is bloody disgusting. Listen, if you really want to know what I think call me tomorrow—or later today, I guess that is," he went on in a rush. "I don't know where I am with this constant, bloody daylight. I'll give you some quotes!"

After putting out on the ninth, we painted on smiles and posed for a group photo taken by a commercial photographer camped on site for the night. Having started our round on the second hole, we still had one more to go, the par-three first. The clubhouse party roared on at fever pitch as we climbed the stairs to the teeing area. Framed by an open screened window, a sweaty young couple necked frantically, oblivious to our presence on the deck below. As I pulled out a 7-iron and prepared to hit, my ball tottered on its tee to the crash of acid rock.

I wanted so badly to end the night on a positive note. I swung through and watched my shot soar on line toward the green. For the briefest moment I thought it would make it. With any kind of a bounce, it surely would have. But the ball died another sudden death in the sand about 10 feet short.

A chip and two putts later, I followed my partners into the clubhouse to hand in our cards and slake our thirst with beer. Though almost four in the morning by now, the party showed no sign of slowing down. It all seemed surreal to our bleary eyes. The blanket of cigarette smoke. The deafening noise. Couples danced frenetically around our table. Almost everyone in the room was under 30 and roaring drunk. The older club members had long since left, leaving the party to the youngest members and their friends.

Nancy sat tallying our scores. "Hey!" she shouted to me over the din. "You got a 65!"

My score would prove to be almost double the 34 carded by the local golfer who won the tournament.

"What the hell," I said with a weary shrug. "At least I beat Gallagher."

BACK AT MY HOTEL, DRAPES drawn tight against the sun, I slept until noon. After breakfast, I telephoned John Scott, the Australian who had agreed to an interview. Scott was staying across town at the home of his friend, golf partner and fellow undertaker Roland Gosselin.

The two had met the year before at a convention of funeral directors in St. John's, Newfoundland. At Gosselin's urging, Scott timed a vacation in Yellowknife to include their participation in the Midnight Classic.

The Australian was in the shower when I arrived. Gosselin, a strong-featured man with a disarmingly boyish smile, took the opportunity to show off some of the Inuit art and other northern artifacts that decorated his comfortable home.

"Can you guess what this is?" he asked, brandishing a narrow white bone just over two feet in length.

I admitted I had no idea. "It's the penis bone of a walrus," he said, chuckling happily at what was obviously an old gag. "Now you know why you've never seen a photograph of a female walrus who isn't smiling."

Gosselin had pulled out all the stops for his friend's visit. He hired a bush pilot to fly them into a remote arm of Great Slave Lake for an overnight fishing trip. Scott, who had never fished before, started by catching a six-pound lake trout. Minutes later he took an eight-pounder. Then, after an exhausting 25-minute battle, the Aussie hauled in a massive 31-pound lake trout, which ranks as a trophy fish even in these parts. Gosselin and I were watching a videotape of the trip when Scott joined us.

Scott clapped his hands and chortled loudly at the video replay of his Hemingwayesque struggle with the great fish. Compact and athletic-looking, with blond hair and bright, sparkling eyes, Scott was as gregarious as his host, giving the lie to any notions I might have had about humourless funeral directors.

The 51-year-old recalled that flying over the northern bush

was "exactly how I expected, how I hoped, Canada would be. It'll always be like a perfect picture postcard in my mind."

Like many Australians, Scott, a divorced father of two, was an inveterate world traveller. His successful funeral operation in the Victoria State town of Kyneton financed two and sometimes three overseas trips a year. And whether he travelled for business or on pleasure, he always took his golf clubs.

He had golfed around the world, from Fiji to Europe to North America to the Australian outback. But of all his golfing adventures, he said, none was as disappointing as Yellowknife's Midnight Classic.

"For a starter, mate, it was definitely the worst course I've ever played on. The only one I can think of that was even comparable is a dustbowl of a course I once played in Kalgoorlie, a mining town in western Australia."

He paused for a moment, remembering. "But, no," he continued with conviction, "Yellowknife was definitely worse than that."

Like me, Scott had trouble adapting his swing to hit fairway shots off the turf mat. Finally, by about the seventh hole, he gave up in disgust and hit his remaining shots from the sand.

"It was also the slowest game of golf I've ever played," he complained. "Over four hours to play nine holes, for God's sake! And what the hell kind of tournament lasts just nine holes?" Scott demanded, on a roll now. "That's not a tournament. That's a gimmick."

When the Australian finally paused for breath, he noticed that Roland had grown uncharacteristically quiet, a wounded look in his eyes. It was Gosselin, only a casual golfer himself, who had urged his friend to play in the tournament, feeling certain he would enjoy the unique experience of golfing at midnight in what was, after all, an internationally famous event.

"No, no, Rollie," Scott said quickly, worried that he had hurt the feelings of someone who had gone to so much trouble on his behalf. "This has been one of the best vacations of my life. You know that, mate. But this man is asking about the golf. And the golf here stinks. I would never play this course again. Not if you paid me."

NEVER AGAIN. NOT IF you paid me. Looking over old clippings from the files of the *Yellowknifer*, a local weekly newspaper, I found that these are comments typical of disappointed golfers who come from often great distances to compete in the Midnight Classic.

Just as typical, however, is the outspoken enthusiasm of the diehards who sign on year after year, many of them Yellowknifers or former residents of the city. What these golfers share is the pioneer spirit, the gumption and grit that built the community and the golf course in the first place. Yellowknifers know their course is far from perfect, but as they endlessly repeat, "Where the hell else can you play golf 24 hours a day?"

For outsiders, arriving with the right attitude makes all the difference. John Gallagher, who charmed even tournament chairman Roland Gagnon, was one visitor who fitted in brilliantly.

"Everything about Yellowknife was so different," he told me later, revving into his trademark machine-gun delivery. "At the end of your round, you take your golf shoes off and the sand is just pouring out. And those little mats you carry around to hit from: I saw worse rugs on Toronto Mayor Mel Lastman's head. But, seriously, I loved them. You're guaranteed a great lie every time. And with my game, that's a very serious consideration.

"Hey, I was treated like a king. I had dinner at the Wild Cat

Café. What a place that is. I ordered the venison, moose and caribou combo."

Maybe what contributed most to Gallagher's enjoyment was that unlike other golfers who sometimes take their games a little too seriously, he had long ago accepted his shortcomings and could view his score of 69 with equanimity.

"I'd go back in a second," said Gallagher, eagerly putting in his bid for a return engagement. "All they have to do is ask."

CHAPTER 3

MAGNIFICENT MARLENE

LIKE MOST CANADIANS OF A certain age, even those with only a casual interest in the game, I already appreciated Marlene Stewart Streit's status as a genuine legend of Canadian golf. Not a few historians rank her the outstanding player this country has ever produced—man or woman—and that's including George Knudson.

But knowing the general outline of someone's fame is not nearly as fascinating as seeing firsthand its power to enthrall. "That's Marlene Streit," the whispers began from the moment she walked into the clubhouse restaurant of Toronto's Lambton

Golf and Country Club, a private course Marlene, although an honourary member, hadn't visited in years. The presence of a celebrity in the room was palpable. People stared, mesmerized.

"God, you look great, Marlene!" an elderly man called from across the room after we sat down at our table. "I bet you go out there and break par today."

Marlene nodded graciously and smiled in his direction.

"Do you know him?" I asked.

"No, I don't think so," she whispered back, worried he might overhear. "If I ever met him, it must have been years ago."

On and on it went. All day long there was a buzz in the clubhouse and around the course because the great Marlene Stewart Streit was on hand. The club pro emerged from his office to tell Marlene what a thrill and an honour it was to have her there. The course starter, a cherubic fellow who had been a Lambton fixture for years, fussed unashamedly. "Marlene, you really have to come more often. You know how much we all love to see you."

On our way out to the first tee, a groundskeeper at first hesitated, then shyly approached to ask Streit for an autograph. "I've followed your career since the sixties," he said. "I think you're just terrific."

In truth, Streit would have preferred to play our round of golf at her home course, York Downs Golf Club, which is much closer to where she lives north of Toronto. But determined to set an appropriate scene for our first meeting, I finally sold her on Lambton, in the city's west end. It was at Lambton in 1951 that the then 17-year-old Marlene bested another giant of Canadian golf, Ada Mackenzie, and went on to capture her first championship of significance, the Ontario Ladies Amateur.

Though not so obvious then, it soon became clear that Streit's victory at Lambton marked a symbolic passing of the torch from

Ada Mackenzie, who had dominated the first half-century of women's golf in Canada, to Marlene Stewart Streit, who would even more completely own the next.

After Lambton, Marlene never looked back. Before the summer of 1951 was through, she'd taken both the Canadian Close (Canadians only) and Open crowns. Named that year's winner of the Lou Marsh Trophy as Canada's outstanding athlete, male or female, Marlene became the country's newest sporting sweetheart, the equal of Olympic figure skater Barbara Ann Scott in her popularity. Still ahead lay an unparalleled career that would include victories in every major world championship in women's amateur golf and culminate, in January of 2000, with Streit's being named the Canadian Ladies Golf Association's female amateur player of the century.

THE LAMBTON GOLF AND COUNTRY Club Marlene first knew had seen some changes over the years. Where once a stately Victorian-style clubhouse dominated the landscape, a concrete bunker of the Bauhaus school now stood. Numerous alterations had also been made to a lush ravine course that leads golfers down to the Humber River and Black Creek plain and then, beginning at the 15th hole, back up the hillside for the finishing holes.

Since Lambton first opened in 1903, four of golf's premier architects, A.W. Tillinghast, Harry Colt, Donald Ross and Stanley Thompson, have all contributed to its design.

But it was as the home course of yet another immortal, George Lyon, the golfer credited with making ordinary Canadians take notice of the game, that Lambton first made its mark. Only Streit herself would ever surpass Lyon's record in national and international competition, which included an Olympic gold medal for golf in 1904. So far-ranging was Lyon's reputation and that of his home 18 that the story was told of a Canadian tourist in New York who asked a newsboy if he knew the location of Toronto. "Yessir," the youngster replied immediately, "Toronto is done located about seven miles from Lambton."

When our time was called, Marlene strode briskly to the red tee of the opening hole, a straightaway 325-yard par four. A small crowd of Lambtonites looked on in reverent silence.

Even now, at age 65, her appearance still recalled the teenage gamine who first stole fans' hearts. Despite a lifetime in the sun, Marlene's face, framed by a visor and a neck-length shock of grey hair, was remarkably unlined. And two children and almost five decades later, her barely five-foot-tall frame remained girlishly trim.

Streit stood over the ball, her feet set wide apart, and drew her club back in a sweet, natural swing that ended with her standing on tiptoes after a sharp pivot and a long, textbook follow-through. The ball stopped rolling about 200 yards distant, straight down the middle of the fairway. With a short, satisfied nod, Marlene strode off after her ball.

"Keep up or pick up," she called after me, laughing.

The same flawless swing had been on display almost since the first day Streit picked up a golf club. Born on a farm in Cereal, Alberta, Marlene moved with her father, mother and baby sister to the picturesque southwestern Ontario town of Fonthill in 1940. There, on the main street, the Stewarts settled happily into a two-storey, seven-room house.

Growing up, Marlene sometimes clerked in her father's electrical appliance store, which he ran out of the main floor of the family home. More often she was free to skate and ski in winter and play softball with her friends in summer. Gifted in all sports, Marlene most enjoyed the rough and tumble of the games preferred by the boys.

When she was 12, the gang began riding their bikes to nearby Lookout Point Golf Club to caddy for pocket money. Club members kidded her that she wasn't much bigger than their golf bags, but Marlene thought this was the easiest money she had ever seen. Big spenders might tip as much as $2.50 a round.

Soon the little girl with chestnut-coloured curls became a club favourite and Fonthill's golf course began to feel like a second home. The club pro, Gordie McInnis, a stocky, gentle man, took her under his wing, paying Marlene to do odd jobs in the clubhouse and to shag balls when he practised. As an extra reward, he would let her hit a few and give her a lesson.

That was all it took to get Marlene hooked on golf. "It was love right from the start," she told me at Lambton. "I just knew this was the game for me."

Attracted by Marlene's enthusiasm, McInnis strove to give her a solid grounding in the fundamentals: grip, stance and posture, the total knitted together in the fluid rhythm of her swing. He kept his instructions to her simple, as he did with all his students, no matter how advanced. McInnis believed that at heart golf was really a very basic game.

"Smoothness, rhythm and balance, Marlene," he told her over and over again. "That's all you need."

Although she played a round only once a week when the club permitted caddies time on the course, Marlene spent hours every day hitting balls on the practice range. Saturday afternoons during the off-season found her pounding still more balls into a canvas net at one of the two winter golf schools McInnis ran in St. Catharines and nearby Thorold. Coupled with her studies, golf left Marlene time for hardly anything else, though she did somehow manage to budget the hours to play in her high-school bugle band.

In 1949, when Marlene was 15, she entered her first tournament, the Ontario Junior, held at the tough Ladies' Golf Club of Toronto, which was founded by Ada Mackenzie in 1924. She shot 104 to finish third. The next year Marlene placed second in the same tourney with a round of 90.

Despite a steadily improving game and a handful of victories in minor events, Marlene arrived at Lambton for the 36th annual Ontario Ladies Amateur in late June of 1951 a virtual unknown. Certainly she was given little chance of advancing far in the match play event. The year before, after managing to qualify for the tournament, Marlene had bowed out in the first round.

No one, possibly not even Marlene Stewart, realized how far she had come since then. Qualifying with ease in the 18-hole medal round, Marlene then ran off two convincing victories to set up her semi-final match with Ada Mackenzie, the tournament's defending champion and the wonder woman of Canadian golf since long before Marlene was born.

The 59-year-old Mackenzie, though not quite the player she had once been, was still a dominant force on the women's scene. She had won her first of nine Ontario Ladies' titles in 1922. As well, Mackenzie had taken six Canadian Close and four Canadian Open championships, and twice reached the semi-finals of the U.S. Women's Amateur. Born into old Toronto money, Mackenzie was an imposing yet beloved figure who started the Ladies' Golf Club to give women a home where their golfing needs would always take priority over those of the few men allowed severely limited playing privileges.

A white-hot competitive fire and the ability to concentrate totally on the job at hand were the hallmarks of Mackenzie's game. After having once been distracted by the gallery during an important match, she never forgot the advice given to her by a more experienced player: "If you must regard the gallery, Miss Mackenzie, regard them as cabbages. It helps amazingly."

Mackenzie's mere presence in the field was enough to give most young golfers the shakes. She was also dead-on her game, having started the week at Lambton by shooting the low score in the medal round.

After we had putted out on the first hole, I asked Marlene how she felt before the start of their match. "Your nerves must have been a mess," I suggested.

Marlene raised an eyebrow in surprise, as if the question had never before occurred to her.

"No, not really," she answered unhesitatingly. "I was a little nervous, but I always am before I hit my first shot. If anything I felt inspired by Ada Mackenzie. If you wanted to be anybody, you had to beat her."

Besides, Marlene *knew* she could beat Mackenzie, because she already had. The year before at the Canadian Ladies' Open in Winnipeg, Marlene had knocked the four-time champion out of the tourney, beating her 4 and 3. At the time, most observers shrugged off her victory as one of those fluke things that sometimes happen in sport, noting that the 16-year-old had herself gone down to defeat in the next round.

Her most vivid recollection of that first victory over Mackenzie was how, after Marlene had closed her out on the 15th hole, her opponent didn't even realize the match was over. "I wasn't going to tell her," Marlene said, grinning at the memory. "This was Ada Mackenzie and I was a wide-eyed girl still in high school. So I followed her obediently off to the next tee. Finally, one of her friends ran up and said, 'Ada, the match is over.'"

It was at that same Ladies' Open in Winnipeg that Marlene first met George Knudson, the golfer whose name is inevitably paired with hers when people speak of the two greatest players, male and female, Canada has ever produced.

Knudson, who was 13 at the time, had been promoted from caddy to clubhouse boot boy at the St. Charles club, the site of the tourney. "You may not know this, but I have cleaned your shoes," Knudson playfully informed Marlene years later.

"I think George was a little surprised that I actually did remember meeting him in the clubhouse shop," Marlene told me. She recalled a skinny, fidgety boy bursting with enthusiasm for the game. "What a player he became— all smoothness, rhythm and balance, all the things I admire most in a golf swing."

Many in the large gallery gathered at Lambton's first tee for the start of Marlene's rematch with Ada Mackenzie were unaware of their history together. Almost all expected the youngster to be overawed by the challenge facing her.

Even when Marlene, who wore the charming tartan cap with a bobble on top that quickly became her trademark, took the first two holes, Mackenzie's supporters remained unconcerned. The defending champion's deficit seemed more a matter of bad luck than anything else. Mackenzie's putt for a half at the first hole actually dipped in and out of the cup. On the par-three second, Marlene's birdie putt hung on the lip. Then Mackenzie's putt for a three hit her opponent's ball and knocked it into the cup as well, giving Marlene the hole.

But Marlene kept it up, taking both the third hole and the imposing par-four fourth, which ever since George Lyon's day had been one of Canada's signature holes, demanding a long drive to the valley floor followed by a perilous approach shot over a stretch of Black Creek that snaked to and fro in front of the green.

The girl was sizzling. Marlene stunned the gallery by running her winning streak to six straight holes. She dropped a lovely putt for a birdie two on the fifth and took the sixth in par. Marlene had played the first half-dozen holes in just 20 strokes, two under par.

Meanwhile, the teenager had crossed over into that special zone of heightened concentration that would be her greatest asset in the years ahead. "I had a kind of tunnel vision," she told me. "I really think that was the biggest reason for my success. I knew how to concentrate completely."

Many who watched her felt certain that like that other great champion Ada Mackenzie, who had to be told the match in Winnipeg was over, Marlene became so absorbed in her own game that she hadn't a clue what was going on around her.

"Oh, I knew," Marlene said with a sly grin. "I saw it all. I just refused to let it enter in."

Though the record shows she was equally adept at stroke play, Marlene's ability to erase her opponent from her mind made her ideally suited for the head-to-head combat of match play. "I've always preferred match play," said Marlene. "To me, match play is the essence of amateur golf. I like the fact that you know exactly where you stand after each hole. That, I think, makes you more determined."

Marlene played only the course, ignoring her partners, believing that if she shot par but they shot better, they deserved to win. Nor did she attempt to be colourful and win over the galleries. Before long, she acquired the nicknames Little Miss Robot and Little Ben, after the cheerless Ben Hogan, for her stoic approach to the game.

When Marlene realized that opponents often mistook her aloofness for rudeness, she began politely explaining to them before matches that she hoped they didn't mind, but she'd simply prefer it if they didn't talk.

"I was young and I wanted people to like me," Marlene remembered, still a little put out at having had to explain herself. "But, really, other than 'good shot' or 'too bad,' what was there to say? I didn't want to hear about what their kids were up to. We could get together and chat about all that later."

What opponents didn't know was that the admitted self-absorption of Marlene's approach to the game helped her control a fiery temper that early on had hurt her ability to concentrate. After Marlene once threw a tantrum at Fonthill, Gord McInnis threatened to suspend the teenager from the club. Marlene, who couldn't imagine a worse fate, soon learned to channel her anger by concentrating on one shot at a time, by willing her mind to stay in the present.

Just how thoroughly Marlene mastered her temper could be seen later that summer of 1951 during the final round of the Canadian Ladies' Open in Montreal. On the 17th green, Marlene faced a 15-foot downhill putt to preserve her one-hole lead over American Grace Lenczyk, a former U.S. and world amateur champion. Just as Marlene readied herself, a *Toronto Telegram* photographer broke from the gallery and took a position directly behind the cup, the flash on his camera set to explode not 20 feet away. Twice Marlene addressed her putt, then pulled back. Finally, the angry shouts of the crowd forced the newshound to back away. Marlene coolly dropped her putt and then finished off Lenczyk on the next hole.

"IT WAS THE ONLY TIME IN my life that I have ever been six holes down after playing six holes," Ada Mackenzie recalled a few years later of the showdown at Lambton. "Still, I wasn't too perturbed. I've played enough golf to know that youngsters can blow up quickly and I was confident that this little cherub was too inexperienced not to be bothered by her lead."

Sure enough, Marlene faltered as the golf course wound its way down into the Humber River valley. From the seventh to the 12th holes, Mackenzie dominated her younger rival, gradually whittling Marlene's lead down to just two holes.

"I felt I had her now," Mackenzie continued her account, "knowing that psychologically she would be becoming desperate as her big lead dwindled."

"Surely," I stubbornly insisted to Marlene, "your nerves had to be jumping by now."

After all, Marlene was still just a kid who had yet to win an important tournament. And this wasn't just anyone on her tail but the inimitable Ada Mackenzie, a tough old boot famous for her closing rallies.

For the second time, the question surprised Marlene. "No, like I told you before," she said, speaking clearly and slowly, as if to a child. "I only get a little nervous before a match, never during.

"Sure, I was six up and then lost a few holes, but so what? I just kept playing my game. Gord always said to me, 'Just play one hole at a time.'"

The name of Marlene's adored coach popped up constantly during our day at Lambton. Though largely unsung, McInnis was regarded by Marlene and his peers as one of the country's top teachers. Cathy Sherk, winner of the 1977 and 1978 Canadian Amateur and the 1978 U.S. Amateur, was taught by him. The eccentric but brilliant Moe Norman also sought his advice.

"Gord just had a great eye," Marlene said warmly. "Without his help, I don't think I would have ever succeeded."

She idolized him from the start. As a teenager, Marlene volunteered to caddy for McInnis just to study his swing, then copied it so perfectly that amateur champion Nick Weslock joshed the Fonthill pro that he ought to charge the girl with theft. Marlene followed at his heels like a puppy, endlessly asking McInnis questions about the game. On weekends, she often babysat the McInnis children. "Every time I turned around I nearly tripped over her," McInnis once joked of his protégée.

McInnis's knowledge and friendship were the rocks on which Marlene built her game. "I always knew that Gord believed in me," she said. "Before every tournament I'd ask him, 'Do you think I can win?' and he would always say, 'Yes, you can.' His confidence strengthened me."

What Marlene appreciated most about McInnis was his ability to keep the game simple. She's convinced that too many coaches unnecessarily confuse their students by overstating the difficulty of the golf swing.

When Marlene was 18, she enrolled in a four-year business administration course at Rollins College in Winter Park, Florida, where she could golf through the winter against top U.S. collegians. The coaches there suggested changes to her swing. Marlene listened politely but always went away confused by what they were saying. "In the spring I'd come home and Gordie would say, 'Aw, you don't need any of that stuff. Just keep doing what you're doing.'"

Marlene joked with me that she'd like to write her own instruction book—or, rather, pamphlet. "I'd call it 'Smoothness, Rhythm and Balance.' It would probably be about eight pages in length and every page would say the same thing, 'Smoothness, rhythm and balance.'"

Marlene adopted the same no-frills approach with the young Canadian golfers she has encouraged over the years. Cathy Sherk, Sandra Post, Dawn Coe-Jones and more recently the rising young professional A.J. Eathorne have all benefited from her tutelage. In the 1960s, Marlene founded the Marlene Streit Awards Fund to help finance the travels of Canadian girls to championships in the United States.

All the demands and pressure put on today's young players by coaches and parents who dream of their kids striking it rich made Marlene grateful at last that her own parents, neither of whom played golf, knew so little about the game.

When she was 15, Marlene shot a hole-in-one at Fonthill's 127-yard second hole. "Well, this was obviously a big deal," Marlene remembered. "But when I rushed home to tell my mother, she just kind of shrugged. After I had stormed up to my room, Mom must have wondered what she'd done wrong. So she phoned Gord and said, 'Marlene told me she just got a hole-in-one. Is that good?'"

Marlene's friendship with Gordie McInnis lasted until his death in 1993. Two or three times a year, right to the end, she would make the 90-minute drive from Toronto to Fonthill to play a round with him and hit a few balls on the practice range while he looked on.

"Seeing Gord always gave me a boost in confidence," Marlene said, her voice softening. "If he said everything was right, I knew it was. Gord was the only coach I ever needed."

UNFLAPPABLE LITTLE MARLENE Stewart put an abrupt halt to Ada Mackenzie's comeback charge on Lambton's par-four 13th hole.

Both players were on the green, lying three. "I was about six feet away and she about five," Mackenzie recounted. "My putt hit the back of the cup, rimmed and the ball stayed out by an inch. This was the putt Marlene had to make. If she missed, I felt she would blow up completely because the pressure had been on her since the sixth hole.

"Well, that youngster walked up to her ball as confidently as though she were on the practice green. She stroked the ball cleanly, followed through beautifully and dropped the putt."

Marlene parred the next two holes for as many wins and the victory. She had covered the match's 15 holes in 66 shots, even par for the distance. In the process, Marlene had outplayed Canada's greatest female player in virtually every aspect of the game. And in the final the next day, when she wrapped up the Ontario Ladies Amateur championship against Grace Currer, the Toronto and District titleist, Marlene would be even better.

What astounded everyone who watched Marlene at Lambton and throughout her career was her uncanny ability to turn three shots into two from within 150 yards of the green. Marlene, who enjoyed complete confidence in every club in her bag, was so particularly deadly with her short irons that after hitting the ball she didn't even bother to watch its flight. She already knew exactly where it was going.

Marlene's pinpoint accuracy was still on display as we made our way around Lambton. She consistently hit her fairway woods as accurately as other golfers might hope to hit their short irons. Off the tee, not a single ball went anywhere other than straight down the fairway.

"That's what the fairway's there for," she said with a shrug and a cocky smile after I complimented her on yet another fine shot.

As a youngster Marlene worked so hard on her game that she developed a three-inch callus shaped like a half-moon on the palm of her left hand. Thrilled to her soul by the very act of hitting a golf ball, she practically lived at the practice range. "I loved the privacy, the peace and quiet of it," Marlene explained. "I'd get lost in myself, losing all sense of time. It was something I never tired of. Even today, I'd rather practise than play."

The countless hours of practice inspired the boldness of Marlene's play in the heat of competition. Because she had already hit every conceivable shot thousands of times at the practice range, what was there to fear?

From the victory at Lambton on, Marlene carried about her an air of invincibility. Her icy calm unnerved opponents, and the incredible accuracy of her shots stripped them of their advantage in size and power.

Almost overnight Marlene Stewart claimed her place among the top amateur golfers in the world. Already dominant in Canada, she made her breakthrough to international stardom in 1953 at the British Ladies Amateur championship in Porthcawl. The 19-year-old shocked Britons with the brilliance of her play in the championship match against Philomena Garvey, a six-time Irish champion.

"We walked in dazed procession, wondering how so young a girl could know so much wonderful golf," wrote Desmond Hackett of the *Daily Express*. "Apart from the immortal Babe Didrickson Zaharias, I have never seen anything so coldly calculated and correct as this child. We have seen a girl who will surely become the greatest-ever woman golfer."

A hero's welcome awaited Marlene in Toronto. Still clutching her trophy, she was met at the airport by the mayor and then paraded in an open convertible through downtown streets lined with 15,000 cheering fans.

By now all of Canada was smitten by the wholesome girl in the tartan cap, who also favoured colourful sweaters and saddle shoes worn with white ankle socks. Though Marlene was all business on the golf course, away from it she was described by one interviewer as "the chattiest, cheeriest, chirpiest kid-next-door who ever snapped her bubble gum in the high-school gymnasium." Profiles and articles chronicling her achievements ran in newspapers and magazines from coast to coast.

Marlene found herself feted at sports banquets, where she was amazed to be treated as an equal among such icons as Lionel Conacher and Jim Thorpe.

"I've always been intrigued by people who are really success-ful," she said to me. "And I liked to ask them, 'How do you win? What do you think about to win?' Almost everyone told me the same thing—be positive, don't think for even a moment about losing. That made a big impression on me."

Then, just when the future seemed so bright, tragedy almost struck her down. On December 17, 1954, while returning home from school in Florida, the airplane she was travelling in crashed into a farm field nine miles short of Toronto's Malton Airport. The impact ripped off a wing and left a huge gash in the fuselage. Marlene and the 22 other passengers scrambled to safety just sec-onds before the plane exploded into flames.

The next day the story screamed out from the front pages. "God spared us," Marlene, pictured by the wreckage, told the *Toronto Daily Star*.

Her brush with death prompted the 20-year-old to seriously consider her future. Though certain she wanted a life in golf,

Marlene also refused to settle for anything less than a fulfilling personal life, which for her meant marriage and children. But for the present her focus remained on scaling the game's heights.

In 1956, Marlene enjoyed a golden summer that saw her take the Canadian Open and Close titles (the fourth and sixth of her career respectively) and capture the biggest prize of all, the U.S. Amateur. Played at the Meridian Hills Country Club in Indianapolis, the tournament featured a thrilling final that pitted Marlene against JoAnne Gunderson, a strapping 150-pound 17-year-old who later became known as Big Momma when she starred in the professional ranks.

Four down after 25 holes in the 36-hole final, Marlene rallied to win six of the last 10 holes. All day Gunderson outdrove her by as much as 50 yards off the tee. But once again Marlene's pinpoint accuracy with every club in her bag more than made up the difference. On the 35th hole, she sank a putt of just over 11 feet to clinch the victory.

"I don't care if I never win anything again," Marlene happily pronounced after capturing the championship she would always consider the high point of her career. "This is the one I wanted to win most of all. It's the biggest thrill of my life, and I was glad to do it for Canada."

Marlene's intense patriotism was another thing that endeared her to Canadians. "I love to play for Canada—that's my biggest thrill," she told me. "What could possibly be more satisfying for an athlete than representing your country?"

That year, for the second time, Marlene won the Lou Marsh Trophy as Canada's outstanding athlete. In the five years since her victory at Lambton, Marlene had singlehandedly put Canada on the map of international golf and now stood widely acclaimed as the most outstanding player ever developed in this country.

Starting around this time, pressure was put on Marlene to leave the amateur ranks and test her skill on the newly formed Ladies Professional Golf Association (LPGA) Tour. Hoping to cash in on her growing fame and photogenic good looks, tour organizers, as well as other players, made persistent overtures. But the nightmare of the airplane crash helped Marlene realize that the last thing she wanted was a life spent constantly on the road as a touring professional.

In 1957, Marlene married John Douglas Streit, a partner in a successful Toronto investment firm. Her husband's financial success made it possible for her to enjoy the best of both worlds, golf and family, even after the birth of their two daughters, Darlene, in 1960, and Lynn, in 1962. Never without domestic help, Marlene could continue to play golf whenever and wherever she desired.

In her mind, Marlene had missed out on nothing by remaining an amateur. She travelled the world from Britain to Norway to Australia and competed against everyone from Babe Zaharias to Mickey Wright to JoAnne Gunderson Carner.

But still, the question has always persisted: How would Marlene Stewart Streit have done as a professional?

Marlene, always so certain of her abilities, of course hadn't the slightest doubt about it. "I know exactly how I would have done," she stated firmly. "I would have been great out there."

Former opponents who went on to play in the professional ranks felt just as certain of a triumphant outcome. "If she had turned pro, she would've needed a truck to take her money to the bank," JoAnne Gunderson Carner said of Marlene. "I've never seen a more competitive golfer."

Marlene's fiercely competitive nature, combined with a natural-born killer instinct, has kept her near the top of the amateur golf world for 50 years. Streit takes no prisoners on the golf course.

"Look, when you're five up, you don't say, 'She's a nice girl. I don't want to beat her too badly'; you want her six down," Marlene once declared. "When I'm two under par, it doesn't matter how far in front I am, I want to be three under."

In 1963, Streit won the Australian Amateur to become the first woman to win the Canadian, British, U.S. and Australian titles in a career. Three years later, Marlene defeated the world's best in capturing the individual honours in the World Team Amateur Championships.

Along the way there have been 11 Canadian Open championships, nine Canadian Close titles and other victories too numerous to mention. Marlene's accomplishments have seen her enshrined in the Canadian Sports Hall of Fame and the Canadian Golf Hall of Fame and made a member of the Order of Canada.

And still the competitive fires burn bright. Even as a senior golfer, Marlene has continued to dominate. She won the prestigious U.S. Senior title in 1985 and again in 1994, the second time against a finalist 10 years her junior.

Tied going into the 18th hole of a playoff against 50-year-old Nancy Fitzgerald, Marlene hit a weak drive off the tee. Only a display of the familiar pinpoint accuracy and her icy resolve saved the day. Using her 5-iron, Marlene placed her second shot within three inches of the pin, then tapped in for the birdie and the title.

"I just got into that little place of mine where I can block everything out," Marlene said of her victory. "I've done that for years."

ON A RAINY FRIDAY AFTERNOON at Lambton in 1951, Marlene didn't lose a single hole in her final match against Grace Currer. She consistently outdrove her opponent by almost

20 yards, and several times set iron shots mere feet from the pin after hitting from angles reporters on the scene described as nearly impossible.

When she sank a long putt to clinch the Ontario title on the 13th hole, Marlene's caddy and Gord McInnis rushed forward and hoisted the young champion on their shoulders while she basked in the applause of the gallery.

"I'm so excited I can hardly believe it's true," the teen bubbled to reporters. "There's the man who deserves all the credit," she said, beaming at McInnis. "I am deeply indebted to him, for he has never taken a penny for the lessons and the help he has given me."

Looking on was defending champion Ada Mackenzie, who would be a faithful friend and mentor to Marlene until her death in 1973.

"This kid," Mackenzie enthused to a reporter, "is the best Canadian prospect I've seen in a long time. She has the temperament to go with her shots. That's something you don't often find. Nothing that little girl does in golf from now on will surprise me."

The next day, photos of a smiling Marlene holding her putter in one hand and her new trophy in the other adorned the sports pages of the Toronto dailies. Headline writers crowned the Grade 12 student the new queen of women's golf and credited her, though this was only her first important victory, with inspiring a wave of public interest in the game.

That summer Marlene burst into the national consciousness by winning 10 of the 15 tournaments she entered. No one in the history of Canadian golf—not George Lyon or Ada Mackenzie before her; or George Knudson, Lorie Kane or Mike Weir later on—has ever risen from obscurity to adulation so quickly.

Judging by our round at Lambton, Marlene's hold over her public remains strong. Several times club members interrupted our progress to request autographs. One man came over to compliment Marlene on her recent performance at the U.S. Senior Amateur championship in Scottsdale, Arizona. In the event she had already won twice, Marlene advanced to the final 16 against women as much as 15 years younger.

Still able to compete at the highest levels, Marlene told me she was proudest of having won national championships in five successive decades. Despite the advancing years, she felt optimistic about extending her winning streak into a sixth decade.

"Why not?" she cheerfully demanded, hefting her clubs into her car trunk. "Now and again the arthritis sets in. But I'm still a threat every time I go out there. Most days I feel like I could play forever."

CHAPTER 4

KING OF ACES

STEVE JOHNSTON REMEMBERED HIS first time as if it were yesterday.

It was a Saturday afternoon when he stood on the elevated 11th tee of Toronto's Whitevale Golf Club alongside his father, a four-handicapper, and two family friends. Steve, just 12 years old and in his first season of golf, looked across the river that cut the valley below to a green about 135 yards distant. A breeze gently ruffled the flag that stood in the dead centre of the putting surface.

His 5-iron in hand, Steve took a single practice stroke, then set and hit a high hooking ball that landed on the front of the green, skipped once and slowly made its way toward the pin.

"That ball's in the hole," Steve's father whispered.

At first Steve didn't quite know how to react; the fact that he'd just scored a hole-in-one barely registered. But the exclamations of surprise and the shocked expressions on the grown-up faces made him realize that something extraordinary had just happened. At his father's urging, Steve raced on ahead to make certain of what they'd all seen, his heart pounding with excitement every step of the way.

The odds against a golfer scoring a hole-in-one on any given tee shot have been reckoned at 15,000 to one. Most golfers, including many low-handicappers, go their entire lives without recording one. And yet for Steve Johnston, Canada's undisputed King of Aces, golf's ultimate one-shot thrill has come to seem almost routine. From his first ace at Whitevale in 1963 to the day this book went to press, Johnston had turned the trick an astonishing 47 times, a total placing him third in the world for lifetime holes-in-one.

When we met in his Toronto office, the handsome, silver-haired 49-year-old, a partner in the international accounting firm of KPMG, could no more explain his good fortune than any of his regular playing partners, who simply call him the luckiest S.O.B. walking the earth. Certainly he's an excellent player — a solid four-handicapper just like his father — but there are untold numbers of golfers out there who are even better and who play far more than the 40 to 70 rounds he manages to squeeze in every year.

George Knudson's hero, Ben Hogan, the most accomplished ball striker in the history of the game, had only four aces in his lifetime. Arnold Palmer, Jack Nicklaus and Gary Player, golf's

"Big Three," recently estimated they had around 17 apiece. Yet there stands Steve Johnston near the top of the all-time list, his total of 47 bested only by the 50 of professional Mancil Davis of Houston, Texas, and the 59 of Norman Manley of Long Beach, California.

Johnston offered no explanations, only theories about why he, above all save two others in the world, should have been so blessed by the golfing gods.

"I've always had a natural hook, which I think helps," Steve told me. "There's almost always some sideways movement on the ball after it lands. I also try to remember the break on the greens, then aim accordingly. And I would definitely categorize myself as an aggressive player. Rather than play it safe, I go for every pin."

Johnston shrugged in apology, aware of the inadequacy of his musings. A natural hook is a common enough occurrence, and virtually every low-handicapper reads greens and attacks the pin. Yet beyond that, how could Steve or anyone hope to rationally explain how a tiny dimpled sphere had so often travelled through space and time from the head of his golf club to the bottom of a distant hole just four and a quarter inches in diameter.

Even in these boom times for the game, when through sheer volume of play more holes-in-one are being recorded than ever before, the phenomenon continues to fascinate. Reports of the most improbable of these "perfect flukes," as golf immortal Harry Vardon described them, frequently appear in newspapers and golf magazines.

In recent years, Canadians have been told the amazing story of nine-year-old Randi Wilson of Seaforth, Ontario, who aced a 103-yard hole on the first swing she ever made on a golf course. "The first hole was great," said Randi of her round, "but the rest of it sucked."

Another child prodigy, six-year-old Jackson Rue from Vancouver, notched two holes-in-one within the span of a year.

At the other end of the age spectrum, a spry 91-year-old Montrealer knocked one in on the fly, tearing out the cup with the force of his blast.

But easily the most heartwarming story was that of Gord Paynter, a 44-year-old comedian and motivational speaker from Brantford, Ontario. Paynter, who has been blind since his early twenties, aced a 184-yard hole at the local Northridge Golf Course after his teenage niece helped point him in the right direction. "All the years I've been playing that course, I've hardly ever been on the green," Paynter said. "I felt like a little kid."

None too surprisingly, Steve Johnston has a story to top them all. He enjoyed the experience of his first ace so much that he went back the very next day and did it again—on the same hole, with the same club and with the same high hook.

This time he didn't run ahead to make certain his ball was in the cup. His father, though in a state of shock, had the presence of mind to hold him back. "My dad said, 'Let's walk together on this one,'" Steve remembered. "That walk with him is one of my most cherished memories. Dad died the next year at the age of 42."

Another difference was that thinking ahead, Steve made certain he was using a golf ball bearing the Campbell insignia. Campbell, like many manufacturers of golf equipment in those days, promoted their brand name by offering prizes to Canadians who scored holes-in-one. Steve had used a different ball the day before, only to be bitterly disappointed when the club pro told him about all the loot he'd missed out on.

A golf bag, a package of balls, bottles of Scotch and rye and a dozen 26-ounce bottles of soda from Canada Dry were delivered soon after to the Johnston home. The delivery man almost refused to hand over the booze when the 12-year-old came to the door and identified himself. He only relented after Steve's mother assured him that her son wouldn't be the one doing the drinking.

In the years ahead, Johnston's prodigious output of aces brought him a pirate's hoard of treasure—clubs and bags, untold numbers of balls, cheese platters, alcohol and a dozen or more commemorative plaques. He has sentimentally held on to many of his prizes, as well as the unrewarded first ball that started his string.

YOUNG STEVE WAS ALREADY shooting in the low nineties the season of his first hole-in-one and rapidly improving. He had two sporting loves, golf and hockey, to which he devoted himself the next few years. In the winter he starred for a succession of top-calibre hockey squads, eventually making it as far as Junior A with the Kitchener Rangers. Come the summer, Steve competed in golf tournaments across the province. He ranked among Ontario's top 10 juniors throughout his teens.

Johnston worked a season as an apprentice pro at York Downs, a private Toronto club, when he was 17. "But I soon discovered that spending my days in the back of a pro shop wasn't nearly as glamorous as I'd hoped," Steve said. By now he had also realized he wasn't talented enough to pursue a professional playing career, even considering his knack for scoring aces.

Steve had racked up 18 of the single-stroke miracles by the time he was 18. Having given new meaning to the expression "shooting your age," he came to be more surprised when he *didn't* get a hole-in-one every two or three months than when he did.

His aces even had a habit of arriving with impeccable timing. Like the day Johnston felt too stressed out to continue studying while writing his final chartered accountancy exams in Toronto. To try to take his mind off his worries, he headed to a golf course where he often played at the time, Westview Golf Club in the town of Gormley.

"I was a mess when I got there," Steve recounted. "But then I aced the ninth hole and I immediately felt a lot better. I mean, how bad can life be when you've just sunk a hole-in-one? All my stress just melted away."

As individual as people or snowflakes, no two holes-in-one ever recorded have been exactly alike. Some are ugly brutes, almost embarrassments, really, that have been banked into the cup off trees or carts, or found the hole after scorching the earth like napalm all the way from the tee. And certainly Steve Johnston has had a few he almost wanted to throw back.

One of his drives got tangled in the flag before finally dropping into the hole. Several have shattered the cup after finding the mark on the fly. The least satisfying of all came a few years back at the Peterborough Golf and Country Club, when Steve's tee shot flew past the green, ricocheted off a rock high into the air and then bunny hopped into the cup from out of the left fringe.

Except for seven or eight of these outcasts, Steve has loved every one of his aces with the tenderness of a father. "The rest have all been what I'd classify as clean," he said. "For me, that usually means a high shot that lands close to the pin and then trickles into the cup. On a few others the arc has been lower after I've hit my tee shot a little thin. But even those have always been on line for the green."

After scoring so many aces, Johnston admitted that the details of most of them tended to blur together. Only the truly outrageous and a few others that occurred in unusual circumstances still stood out in his mind.

One he'll never forget happened a few years ago at the Innisbrook Resort in Tarpon Springs, Florida, where Steve and a few
of his golfing buddies used to vacation every winter. Most of these
friends, having already witnessed at least one or two of his holes-
in-one, were as dumbfounded as Steve by his incredible run of
good fortune. But to a man they were happy for him because he
was such a stand-up guy.

Just one thing bugged them. Whenever Steve put one in the
hole, he barely reacted. They'd be whooping and hollering
and slapping him on the back, but the man who'd done the
deed scarcely cracked a smile. Steve was the most unemotional
fellow they'd ever met, a typical cold-blooded CA, as they often
joked.

At Innisbrook, Steve's foursome was on the tee of a 170-yard
par three when he hit one of his patented high hooks onto the
money part of the green. Though they were almost certain it had
found the hole after a short roll, there remained an element of
doubt since the green had a raised front lip that partially obscured
their view of the area around the pin.

Steve's partner had shanked his tee shot off a tree, well short of
the green. While the two of them looked for his ball, the other
half of the foursome raced their cart on ahead. Grabbing a ball
from his bag, Jim Cochrane, a Toronto BMW dealer, tossed it
about 10 feet past the hole.

"Finally, we were going to get a rise out of Steve," Cochrane
told me when I called him about the prank. "Just once we wanted
to see Steve get excited over an ace. I've actually seen him get
more worked up over missing a putt."

When Steve reached the green, he stopped in his tracks when
he saw a ball, apparently his, sitting several feet from the hole. "You
could tell he was shocked that it hadn't gone in," Cochrane said. "But

even then he refused to give us the satisfaction of a big reaction."

After a moment, sensing that something was up, Steve checked the cup for himself.

"You asshole," he whispered to Cochrane as he reached down to pick up his ball. That night, with his usual good humour, Steve bought the drinks.

Most of Johnston's golfing friends regard him as a walking freak of nature. "Steve, I've only seen two holes-in-one in my life, and they've both been yours!" an old pal told him in amazement. Another friend who had never scored an ace during a lifetime of golf suddenly holed them on consecutive weekends. Could it be rubbing off? he wondered.

"The really scary thing about Steve," Jim Cochrane told me, "is that he could easily have even more aces to his credit. The guy is unbelievably deadly with his irons from about 160 yards in. I've seen him hit lots of tee shots that surprised me by *not* going in."

IF HIS BEST FRIENDS CAN scarcely believe his achievement, imagine the trouble Steve Johnston sometimes has trying to convince total strangers. "That's the reason I don't like to talk about it too much," Steve said. "People look at you like you've just told them you've been to the moon and back."

His 47 holes-in-one and counting have been both a calling card and a distraction in a professional life that has seen Johnston combine his passion for golf with his training as a chartered accountant. In 1992, he founded KPMG's golf industry practice, which specializes in providing golf courses with everything from business plans and feasibility studies to course valuation and site monitoring during construction. More than 400 courses in

Canada and almost 1,000 across North America—including fabled Pebble Beach—have been KPMG clients.

Often Steve is invited to lecture at golf industry symposiums, where the introduction inevitably includes mention of his status among the world's holes-in-one leaders.

"Of course, I get a kick out of the recognition," Steve said. "But I also can't help hearing the snickers of disbelief. I get that almost every time I'm introduced. Forty-odd aces is just too many for most people to comprehend."

Johnston, who has had witnesses for every one of them, doesn't blame people for being sceptical. Even he has trouble believing some of the things that have happened to him on a golf course. For instance, there was the time he collected two aces in the same round at the Lake St. George Golf Club north of Toronto. The odds against that happening are approximately 500,000 to one.

Such estimates are arrived at by insurance companies who provide coverage for hole-in-one contests at corporate and charity tournaments. Prizes go as high as $1 million, but more often range from $15,000 to $25,000. Rather than cash, the top prize is sometimes an automobile.

Steve has appeared as a celebrity guest at more than a dozen charity events, usually asked to stand on the tee of a par three and play closest-to-the-hole with the groups as they go through. But even when he has paid his entry fee for the outing like everyone else, he has never once been permitted to shoot for the prize money. Despite his amateur status, insurers regard him as a kind of professional ringer.

Luckily, Steve golfs in Canada and not in Japan, where he would no doubt receive even harsher treatment from insurers. There the scoring of an ace during a round of *gorufu*, as golf is known, socially obligates the golfer to buy lavish gifts for his playing partners, host a drinking party and plant a commemorative tree near the tee to mark his "joy." Before every round, prudent golfers pay about U.S.$100 for $5,000 in hole-in-one insurance.

Fortunately, an ace in North America traditionally obligates the golfer to nothing more costly than picking up the tab for a single celebratory round of drinks. So Steve swings away worry-free with his deadly high hook, watching his count push ever farther into the realm of the bizarre.

The longest he's ever gone between holes-in-one is three years, which at the time seemed like a long thirsty walk through the Sahara. Usually, they come in bunches. "What I've found is that if I have one early in the year, I'll have two or three before the season is through," Steve said. "It's like I'm zoned in."

BASEBALL SLUGGER REGGIE Jackson once proclaimed that hitting a home run was even better than sex. I wondered if the thrill of putting one in the cup ever diminished for Steve Johnston, who in his area of specialty is an even bigger superstar than Jackson was in his.

"Because I'm so outwardly unemotional, people sometimes think I've grown blasé about it," he answered. "But the truth is that the thrill never diminishes. It's an internal rush that hits you like a shot of adrenaline. I've had so many people say to me, 'I can't believe that went in!' And their reaction has kind of built up in me over the years, so that now even I can hardly believe it when they go in the hole."

Without question the most astonishing—and by far the longest—of all Steve's holes-in-one was number 44, which came on a 325-yard par four at British Columbia's Chateau Whistler. He was still awed by the memory of his prodigious drive from the elevated tee, saying, "All I wanted to do was hit the ball as hard as I could."

Canada's King of Aces paused for a moment of regal reflection.

"Remember, we were 300 to 400 feet above sea level, so the ball does travel a little farther," he continued modestly. "Even so, what do you think the odds were against that ball going in the cup? They must have been staggering."

Go figure.

CHAPTER 5
BANFF SPRINGS ETERNAL

A FULL, FAST-RUSHING MOUNTAIN river slashed the deep green of the valley floor. Towering Douglas firs, magpies flitting noisily among their branches, edged breathtaking views toward Mount Rundle and up both the Bow and Spray valleys. Scattered across the fairway far below, a dozen or more elk grazed in the bronze-tinted twilight.

During two weeks of golf on the Alberta side of the Canadian Rockies, my every arrival at the elevated back tees of the Banff Springs Golf Course's 15th hole renewed my conviction that this must surely be one of the most fabulous vistas in all of golf, if not the world.

A middle-aged Japanese couple, having descended the stairs from the hotel just above, paused to watch as I teed up my ball. Elegantly dressed for dinner, they nodded and shyly smiled in greeting.

"Wonderful, wonderful," the man said softly in halting English, his gaze, like mine, fixed on the dogleg par four that plays across the Spray River on a direct line to distant Mount Rundle.

I took my time to set, breathed deeply and hit a tremendous drive that soared high above the shadowed outline of the mountain, my ball flashing brilliant white as it caught the last rays of the sun and hung suspended as if on a heavenly string above the valley. At last, the ball arced steeply, then began a long, leisurely descent to the distant heart of the fairway.

Never had I hit a shot so sweetly. Drinking in the thin, pure mountain air, I felt proud to bursting. My Japanese gallery applauded enthusiastically.

Though aware my own effort was hardly in the same league, I was reminded of George Knudson's thrilled reaction after he hit his miracle 5-iron to a Japanese green during the 1966 World Cup, the only shot the notorious perfectionist felt he ever hit absolutely truly. Knudson spoke of it as a total emotional, mental, physical, almost spiritual experience. "Give me more of that," he recalled feeling afterwards.

I knew the memory of my shot in this world-famous setting would warm me on winter nights for years to come. Designed by Canada's most revered golf course architect, Stanley Thompson, the Banff Springs Golf Course and the hotel that looms like a fairy-tale fortress on the cliffs overhead have come to symbolize Canada as surely as the beaver, Wayne Gretzky and Niagara Falls.

The course, the first anywhere to cost more than $1 million, has long been included in virtually every ranking of the game's leading layouts, and its most celebrated hole, the par-three Devil's Cauldron, which Thompson set beside an impossibly picturesque glacial lake, numbers among the most photographed in golf.

The southwestern reaches of Alberta hold many of Canada's most beautiful and demanding golf courses. There are the two superb Robert Trent Jones designs an hour west of Calgary at the Kananaskis Resort and two acclaimed new courses, SilverTip and Stewart Creek, on opposite sides of the Bow River Valley close to Canmore. A three-hour drive to the northwest of Banff is the Jasper Park Lodge Golf Course, another Stanley Thompson gem.

Though challenged, Thompson's accomplishment at the Banff Springs has never been surpassed among mountain courses. Many consider it the crowning achievement of a life's work that included such Canadian classics as St. George's in Toronto, Capilano in West Vancouver and Highlands Links in Cape Breton. Never does Thompson's layout at the Banff Springs impose itself on the perfection of the natural setting. Rather, he created with the subtle strokes of a painter, bringing the artistic elements of balance, harmony and proportion to his work. In Banff and elsewhere, Thompson pushed the frontiers of the designer's craft.

My arrival in the mountains fell at a time when the Banff Springs was finally back at full operation following a $4.5-million two-year restoration that was receiving raves from the golfing press.

Like the *Mona Lisa* or Sistine Chapel in need of a touch-up, the course's lustre had dimmed with age. A long succession of groundskeepers softened and otherwise distorted many of the finely etched details of Thompson's design. The original mainline of the 1920s irrigation system deteriorated, and ice and snow mould damaged fairways and greens beyond repair. Worst of all, improvements to golf clubs and balls made what had once been a championship course play far too short for today's low-handicap golfers. Much of the challenge in Thompson's masterwork had been lost.

The restoration, which included almost every aspect of the Banff Springs operation, had three primary goals: to lengthen and otherwise toughen-up the course in adapting it to the modern game; to make it more environmentally friendly in keeping with the course's prominence in beleaguered Banff National Park, by far the most altered by man's hand of all our national parklands; and to return it with as much historical accuracy as humanly possible to Stanley Thompson's original vision.

"If we've done our work properly, the golfer should almost feel as if he has travelled back in time to 1929 when the course opened," Doug Wood, the Banff Springs director of golf, earnestly told me when we first met. "This is a golf course known and loved around the world, and everyone involved in the project took it as a kind of sacred trust."

In getting to know Doug Wood and the two other leaders of the restoration team—Canmore designer Les Furber and course superintendant Kevin Pattison—I quickly became infected by their enthusiasm for the project. Together they gave me a crash course in who does what at a major golf club, particularly during the hard slog of a restoration. But even more important, my time among them at the Banff Springs provided my first close-up look at the genius of Stanley Thompson, arguably the single most influential figure in the history of Canadian golf.

BEFORE GOLF ARRIVED IN the Rocky Mountains, first came the Canadian Pacific Railway, which built a railway siding near the future townsite of Banff while completing Canada's first transcontinental line in 1885.

CPR, convinced that tourists would flock to the site for the scenery, fresh air and the invigorating effects of the nearby hot-water springs, constructed the first Banff Springs Hotel (the world's largest hostelry at the time, with 250 rooms) on the cliffs overlooking the Bow River in 1888. Then began an intensive pro-motion campaign that quickly sent word of the hotel's opening around the world.

By the early years of the new century, enthusiasm for golf had spread like a fever across Canada, with dozens of clubs flourish-ing from St. John's to Victoria. At the Banff Springs, hotel guests pursued the game on a makeshift course with sand put-ting surfaces. That lasted until 1911, when a challenging new nine-hole track (including one par five measuring over 650 yards) opened in the valley below the hotel. The designer was William E. Thomson, a young golf professional imported from Scotland by CPR.

Demand for the game at what was billed "The Course on the Roof of the World" continued to grow so rapidly that in 1918 the decision was made to expand to a full 18 holes, the work directed this time by Donald Ross of Pinehurst, North Carolina, who was considered North America's leading course architect. Work dragged on until 1924, but when the results were finally unveiled, the prestige of having a Donald Ross–designed course instantly elevated the Banff Springs into the ranks of the world's élite golf clubs.

Soon, though, Ross's nine was revealed to have a fatal flaw: not enough money had been invested in adding quality topsoil to the thin rocky earth of the Bow River Valley.

Almost overnight the health of the course's turf deteriorated alarmingly. To make matters worse, in 1926 a mountain course so stunningly beautiful that it threatened to eclipse the Banff Springs fame was opened in Jasper National Park by CPR's arch rival, Canadian National Railways. Built as a twin attraction to Jasper Park Lodge, a rustic retreat set in the wilds just outside the town of Jasper, the course was designed by a 32-year-old Torontonian named Stanley Thompson.

At Jasper Park, Thompson cleared gaps through the forest of fir and spruce to point the golfer toward greens aligned with distant mountains, then whimsically patterned his bunkers after the snow formations on their peaks. In choosing a circular course path that flowed with the natural contours of the land, Thompson made the most of lovely Lac Beauvert by setting three holes against its shores. And in a major philosophical break from the "penal" tradition of North American course design, which demanded the golfer hit the shot dictated by the architect or find himself sorely punished, Thompson always offered players a safer, albeit usually longer, alternative route to the green.

As Thompson would write, "The most successful course is one that will test the skill of the most advanced player, without discouraging the 'duffer,' while adding to the enjoyment of both."

Acclaimed an instant classic, Jasper provided a template for Canada's mountain courses that is followed to this day.

Naturally, officials at CPR headquarters in Montreal viewed the overnight ascendance of the Jasper course with alarm. Ever since the company's tracks first opened the West, CPR had considered local tourism its private preserve.

Edward Beatty, CPR's president, decreed that no cost be spared in returning the Banff Springs to its rightful place at the summit of Rocky Mountain courses.

AFTER STANLEY THOMPSON'S DISPLAY of genius at Jasper, there was little doubt about who would undertake the makeover of the Banff Springs. Could anyone else reasonably be expected to improve on his own model?

Often during my time at the Banff Springs, I imagined Thompson, the man now regarded as the father of Canadian golf course architecture, walking the same ground more than seven decades before, making his final plans for the 18 holes that would seal his reputation. With the passing years, it has increasingly become clear that Thompson ranks alongside A.W. Tillinghast, Alister Mackenzie and Donald Ross as one of the premier designers of the 1920s and '30s, the so-called golden age of golf.

Several of my rounds were played in the company of a group of 10 visiting American golf writers, some of whom were only vaguely aware of Thompson's achievements. That's largely because most of the architect's work was done in Canada, far beyond the radar of the self-absorbed American sporting press.

The writers had already played Jasper Park and come away astonished by Thompson's work there. "That's one of the most beautiful courses I've ever seen," a jovial writer from San Francisco, a freelancer for several national magazines, told me. "I can't believe I've never heard of this Thompson guy."

A bluff, hard-living and fun-loving man who enjoyed good cigars and old Scotch, Stanley Thompson was born in Toronto in 1893, the fourth of five brothers—Nicol, Mathew, Bill, Stanley and Frank—who collectively became known in Canadian golfing circles as the Amazing Thompsons. Frank captured the Canadian

Amateur title in 1921 and again in 1924, while William took the same crown in 1923. Mathew and Nicol both prospered as club professionals, the latter serving for 47 years as head pro at the Hamilton Golf and Country Club. Stanley, no mean golfer himself, led the qualifying round of the 1923 Canadian Amateur while playing with a set of borrowed clubs.

The brothers started as caddies at the Toronto Golf Club under club professional and freelance course architect George Cumming, a former Canadian Open champion. Stanley, who displayed an early interest in Cumming's design work, studied landscape gardening at the Ontario Agricultural College in Guelph before serving as an artillery officer in France during World War I.

Upon his return from the trenches, Stanley joined with his brother Nicol and Cumming in 1920 to form the design firm of Thompson, Cumming and Thompson. Business was so good that within a year Stanley felt confident enough to go out on his own, opening up shop as Stanley Thompson & Company at 24 King Street West in downtown Toronto.

The commission in Jasper that made his reputation came just three years later. Then, in almost immediately turning his attention to the Banff Springs, Thompson faced a far different and in some ways even more daunting challenge. In Jasper he had enjoyed the luxury of working with virgin land, but in Banff there was already an 18-hole golf course. Thompson's task was not to merely remodel the existing layout; he had to somehow make it uniquely his own.

So Thompson did what he always did when starting a new project. Cane and sketch pad in hand and a flask of alcoholic refreshment stashed in his jacket pocket, he tramped every inch of the valley floor for more than three weeks searching for the inspiration for his designs.

In such a setting, it wasn't long in coming. On land almost directly below the hotel near the confluence of the Spray and Bow Rivers, he envisioned a sensational opening hole (today's 15th) where golfers would hit across the Spray from a set of men's tees set beside the outdoor patio of a new Tudor-style clubhouse. A set of championship tees (for use during tournaments and other special occasions) would be sited another 100 yards or so farther up the slope toward the hotel.

That the land in question was at present occupied by a campground troubled Thompson not in the least. CPR, who had told him to spend whatever he needed, would simply have to find a way to acquire rights to the parcel from the parks department.

Thompson was not a man who hesitated to spend other people's money—or his own. A notoriously poor financial manager, he made and spent fortunes during his lifetime. One associate recalled that during the Great Depression Thompson routinely tipped railway porters $5, at the time a full day's wages for many working men.

Sometimes, though, Thompson's best ideas came to him on the cheap. The possibly tall tale is often told of the inspiration behind Banff's Devil's Cauldron, the photogenic par three where players hit from an elevated tee over a glacial lake filled with huge boulders to a small sloping green set in the shadow of Mount Rundle.

Thompson, the story goes, was sitting on a rock, enjoying a wee nip from his flask, when suddenly a rockslide came crashing down from the cliffs above. After the dust cleared, Thompson saw that the slide had dammed the watercourse and in the process transformed the small valley into a natural amphitheatre of breathtaking beauty. The shaken architect, recognizing the divine hand of a design talent even greater than his own, immediately decided to build a golf hole on the spot.

Devil's Cauldron is the most famous example of Thompson's widely admired expertise in the shaping of par threes. He had two typical styles: shorter holes of perhaps no more than 120 yards, but so heavily trapped that a misplayed tee shot might easily result in a double bogey, and the less common and generally more straightforward colossus of 220 yards or more. Whenever the landscape permitted, Thompson preferred par threes with elevated tees to enable golfers to better admire the scenery.

His completed plans for the Banff Springs called for four completely new holes as well as extensive changes to the old ones absorbed into his new design. In the spring of 1927, work got underway on what, despite Thompson's firmly held conviction that the best design always follows nature's own model, would prove to be a massive undertaking. Many thousands of tons of rock would have to be dynamited and laboriously removed, rivers and streams bridged and acres of trees felled to create a golf course that in full maturity would for all appearances be at one with God's plan.

Meanwhile, at clifftop, the Banff Springs Hotel was itself in the final stages of a refurbishment begun in 1911 that saw the old mostly wooden structure blossom into the rock-faced and green-roofed palace still seen, with a few additions, today.

Initially, work concentrated on the golf course's four new holes to allow the existing layout to remain open. A crew of 200 joined in the blasting and clearing and in the unloading of long lines of railway cars filled with topsoil and manure hauled in from the prairies. Thompson, whose company had been hired to design the course as well as supervise construction, was not about to repeat Donald Ross's mistake. In some places, the new soil bed would be as much as two feet deeper than the former base.

The architect contoured his fairways to follow the shapes of the mountain ranges beyond, bordering many of them with sloped mounds to help bring errant drives back into play. Fairways were also made extra wide to accommodate his philosophy of providing two distinct routes to each hole.

Thompson, a mischievous man with an earthy sense of humour, who liked to tell jokes and talk and drink with cronies long into the night, always had his best fun when designing his distinctively bold and cunningly shaped bunkers. At Jasper, he had patterned them to create the outline of a rose, a painter's palette, the footprint of a giant and, on the par-three ninth hole known as Cleopatra, the outrageously voluptuous form of a woman. Unamused by this last gag, CNR officials ordered Thompson to go back and disguise the ancient queen's charms.

Often Thompson built his bunkers into the sides of hills and his fairway mounds, sweeping sand up the slopes to create flashed faces, thereby increasing their visibility from the tee. Yet they were not always as they at first appeared. Depending on the angle of approach or the sun's position, the bunkers mysteriously seemed to change in shape and size before the golfer's startled eyes.

Finally, Thompson rebuilt and retrapped the Banff Springs greens. He contoured the surfaces into distinct levels, and then added hollows, runoffs and bumps for additional character. Though tricky, Thompson's greens were unfailingly fair.

The overall result of Stanley Thompson's meticulous planning was a golf course on which every hole was unique — another of his trademarks. Just as at all Thompson's best courses, Banff's holes stick in the memory because each one, like a living thing, has an appearance and personality entirely its own.

Work on the new clubhouse and a few holes had yet to be completed when, on August 1, 1928, a small crowd gathered at the first tee to cheer on grizzled Tom Wilson, a legendary CPR trail guide and Banff's most famous citizen, who awkwardly stroked the ceremonial first ball for the opening nine. The remaining work would be completed in time for the start of the next season and an official opening attended by the Prince of Wales, whose appearance CPR considered a major coup. Clearly a crown prince outranked the mere military man, World War I hero Field Marshal Haig, whom rival CNR had imported to open its Jasper course.

MY NEW AMERICAN FRIENDS proved to be engaging companions, warmly welcoming "the token Canadian" writer into their midst.

Often I was partnered with Bob, a portly, ponytailed California publisher in his late forties and the only member of our troupe with a game even rougher than my own.

Bob enthused over the Alberta scenery and thought all the golf courses he had played on the trip wonderful. But what really caught his attention was our lip-smacking selection of chocolate bars. During breaks in our rounds together, I introduced him to Sweet Marie, then Coffee Crisp and Caramilk, all unavailable in the candy-bar deprived United States of America. A grateful Bob would depart the country hauling bags full of chocolatey treats.

It was while playing with Bob one day that I suffered my most embarrassing moments of a trip filled with muffs and hooks and Spray River splashdowns. On my second shot at Banff's par-four sixth hole, my 7-iron broke off at the hosel, the club-face hurtling about 20 yards forward while I stood there dumbstruck, gripping a suddenly featherweight shaft.

That was bad enough. Then, on the very next hole, my 6-iron

broke apart in exactly the same fashion. Two clubs in a set bought just weeks before wrecked on consecutive holes! What were the odds?

"How much did you pay for those clubs, anyway?" asked Bob, unwrapping a Coffee Crisp and slowly shaking his head in wonder. "That just shouldn't happen. You'll get your money back for sure."

"You think?"

That night at a cocktail party in their honour, the Americans ribbed me unmercifully about my cheap exploding golf clubs. Everyone was in high spirits following a gorgeous, sunny day spent on a course for which they had only praise. The one thing they couldn't agree on was which Stanley Thompson creation they liked better, Jasper or Banff.

Doug Wood and I stood in a corner discussing the history of the golf course, a topic that by now had firmly gripped my imagination.

I told him frankly that I envied him. "You're the top dog at one of the most beautiful courses in the world," I said. "How much better does life get than that?"

Wood, a lean and youthful-looking 39-year-old with short brown hair and horn-rimmed spectacles, eagerly nodded his agreement. "I feel blessed to be here," he said. "When I was a kid growing up in Calgary, I dreamed of one day having this job. If I'd been able to choose from any course in the world, this is the one I would have picked."

Considerable prestige and not a few other advantages come to the top man at the Banff Springs. The most glamorous perquisite of the job is greeting and sometimes playing rounds with the many celebrities who make pilgrimages to the course. A few years before, a frail Bob Hope had played six holes before heavy winds chased him into the clubhouse. At a dinner party that evening, Hope insisted that Doug sit by his side. The two happily talked golf for the next three hours.

"He told me about all the joy he'd gotten from the game during his lifetime," Wood recalled. "Hope's old friend Bing Crosby had told him that Banff was one of the courses he had to play before he died."

Then there was his round a few years back with Byron Nelson, the golfing immortal known as Lord Byron, who racked up 11 consecutive tour victories in 1945. In his early eighties when he visited Banff, Nelson still possessed a stylish stroke and a soft touch on the greens. "He was a real gentleman," Doug said admiringly, "the type of man you aspire to become one day."

Though he didn't get to play with him, Wood also acted as host to Clint Eastwood, another passionate golfer. One visitor who impressed him was Japanese home-run king Sadaharu Oh, who Doug, himself one of the longest hitters in the mountains, appreciatively watched boom drives incredible distances in the thin mountain air.

Wood served his apprenticeship at several Calgary courses before moving on to the position of head pro at the Canmore Golf Club. In 1988, at the age of 28, he became just the third head professional in the history of the Banff Springs. The first pro, Bill Thomson, the Scotsman imported by CPR to design the original course in 1910, stayed on until 1949, leaving only after he had shepherded the club through the dark days of the Great Depression and World War II.

As luck would have it, the official opening of Stanley Thompson's masterwork came in the year of the stock-market collapse that sent the global economy reeling. CPR, desperate to keep the tourists coming, tried an endless variety of promotional gimmicks at the Banff Springs, including the unfortunate idea of having tribe members from the nearby Stoney Indian reserve dress in traditional garb and serve as caddies. Hotel advertisements of the day show natives in feathered headdresses and with braided hair—men whose grandfathers had roamed the mountains as hunters and warriors—humbly toting the bags of affluent white golfers.

The practice was finally stopped, not due to worries about political incorrectness but only after the citizens of Banff complained that the Stoneys were taking work away from local lads.

Doug, a walking encyclopaedia of course lore, told me of the exhibition match in 1936 that left Gene Sarazen shame-faced after he had disregarded his caddy's advice before an approach shot to a green with a mountain backdrop. The winner of seven majors chose a club with a high loft only to watch his well-stroked ball barely make it halfway to the pin.

The great Sarazen, Doug informed me professorially, had fallen victim to the common mountain phenomenon of optical foreshortening. The clear air combined with the distraction of the peaks often causes golfers to underestimate shot distances, just as hikers in high elevations frequently misjudge the distance to their destination.

The hard times of the Depression were just ending when the world plunged into war in 1939. Rationing of gasoline and restrictions on civilian train travel forced the hotel to close down for the duration in 1943. The golf course, however, stayed open, CPR officials believing it their patriotic duty to provide a source of recreation for soldiers and airmen on furlough from prairie training bases.

Prosperity returned to the Rocky Mountains after the war, and the Banff Springs Golf Course finally welcomed the steadily growing numbers of golfers foreseen ever since Stanley Thompson first tramped the valley floor almost 20 years before.

Malcolm Tapp, a Vancouver golfer still in his early twenties, replaced old Bill Thomson as head pro. A natural charmer, with thick wavy hair and a dazzling smile, Tapp would enjoy the enviable task of teaching Marilyn Monroe the basics of the game when she stayed in town during the making of *The River of No Return* in 1953. Some might envy him almost as much for the rounds he played with Monroe's fiancé, Joe DiMaggio, when the actress was busy filming. And it was Tapp who partnered Bing Crosby, the lifelong golf fanatic who tipped off Bob Hope about the Banff Springs.

The good times continued largely unabated until 1986, when the Alberta government opened a splashy new resort in nearby Kananaskis Country, complete with two 18-hole golf courses by the acclaimed American designer Robert Trent Jones, who for a time in the 1930s had been Stanley Thompson's junior partner. CPR, determined to maintain the prominence of its Banff Springs property, first embarked on a major upgrade of its hotel facilities and then, in 1989, opened an additional nine-hole course designed in the style of Stanley Thompson by another of his former assistants, Geoffrey Cornish, and his partner Bill Robinson.

The opening of the new nine, called the Tunnel Nine, necessitated the reconfiguration of the original Thompson 18 into what became known as the Rundle Nine and the Sulphur Nine. Also unveiled was a new $3-million clubhouse constructed to emulate an Indian teepee, with 360-degree views of the surrounding mountains.

Just in time for all the excitement, Doug Wood arrived in October of 1988. His immediate predecessor, Malcolm Tapp, had enjoyed a 40-year run in Banff. Before him, Bill Thomson had lasted 39 years.

"I remember thinking, God, I'm only the third golf professional in eight decades of golf," Wood reflected at the cocktail party for the American golf writers. "I thought, What an honour that is."

CPR, or CP as the modern company prefers, imagined even bigger things for the Banff Springs course. The master plan included another nine-hole addition to complete two full 18-hole tracks, an attraction certain to draw even more golfers to the Rocky Mountains.

Except this time the expansion announcement by CP was greeted by an outcry from environmentalists convinced that golf course development, especially in a national park, ranks with the razing of rain forests as an ecologically hostile activity.

Once considered environmental havens, golf courses have come under increasing attack ever since the introduction of chemical fertilizers following World War II and an explosion in the game's popularity that has seen new courses open at an unprecedented rate. Even the most benign of golf course designs cause massive disruptions of the natural landscape and can destroy wetlands and other wildlife habitats, while pesticide use by groundskeepers has been blamed for everything from breast cancer among women golfers to reproductive and central nervous system disorders. As well, pesticides and fertilizers have been known to leach into groundwater supplies and pollute lakes, rivers and streams.

The protests over CP's intentions came at a time of growing concern for the health of Banff National Park. Penetrated by two major transportation corridors, the Trans-Canada Highway and the railway, Banff is particularly vulnerable to ecological damage. More than four million people — and 10 million vehicles — a year visit what is by far the most developed national park in North

America. Wildlife counts reveal that grizzly bears and wolves are dying more rapidly than they can reproduce in the congested environment. Attempting to halt the slide, the federal government has declared the park environmentally degraded and placed severe limits on future development.

Finally admitting defeat to the environmentalists, CP abandoned its plans for a new nine over the winter of 1995–96. At any rate, come that spring, Doug Wood and his crew realized they had far more immediate concerns.

A killer ice storm the previous autumn had irretrievably damaged the turf on Stanley Thompson's 18. "But it was more than that," Doug told me. "The old course was just plain worn out. The soil beds beneath the greens had shifted. The main line of the irrigation system was shot. And many of the sharp edges of the original design, the Thompson touches that made the course famous in the first place, had been softened or lost over the years."

Hundreds of thousands of golfers had trod the celebrated fairways and greens since the official opening in 1929. What contributed even more to the decline was the damage done almost every day in recent years by the hooves of elk that freely roam the golf course.

A six-mile-long fence kept elk off the course from the 1930s until 1986. That year, in return for allowing CP to build the Tunnel Nine, Parks Canada demanded the fence's removal so the herd could return to its historic grazing and breeding grounds on the grasslands of the valley floor. Elk have since become such a common hazard on the golf course that club rules permit a golfer who hits one to replay the shot without penalty.

The Banff Springs dropped from number seven on *Score* magazine's 1994 ranking of Canada's top courses to number 22 just two years later.

Not that golfers had stopped coming. "That was the funny thing," Doug Wood remembered. "We were setting attendance records at a course CP and the staff here had come to feel a little embarrassed about. The truth is, there are golfers who love the Banff Springs so much they'll come back year after year, no matter what."

They may well have kept coming indefinitely. But CP, whose name had been synonymous with the Banff Springs since 1888, considered the course too much a reflection of its own prestige to permit it to rest on past laurels. The decision was made to restore Stanley Thompson's entire 18 to its former glory.

AFTER COCKTAILS, WE ALL trooped down to the Waldhaus Restaurant, located in the old Tudor clubhouse built in Thompson's day. Sitting across from Doug Wood and me during dinner was Les Furber, the Canmore architect recruited to do the restoration.

While awaiting the arrival of our fondue, the house specialty, I regaled my companions with the story of my encounter with a silver-haired woman from New York earlier that week in the Banff Springs coffee shop. After we had struck up a conversation, I told her about my project, which immediately launched her into an anti-golf harangue.

"What is it with you middle-aged golfers, anyway?" she angrily demanded. "You discover golf and suddenly that becomes the most important thing in your life—more important than your kids and even your wife. You're all a bunch of obsessed, silly asses!"

"Sounds like you hit a nerve," Les Furber said dryly.

"What the hell is my ex-wife doing here?" yelped one of the writers at our table to loud guffaws.

Over dinner Furber, a powerful-looking man in his early fifties, with a shock of grey hair and the build of a wrestler, explained how he, Doug Wood and Kevin Pattison, the course superintendent, had proceeded once plans for the restoration had been announced.

"Everyone was encouraged to speak their minds without worrying about anyone else taking it too personally," Furber said. "We didn't want to hear months later that someone thought all along that, say, the irrigation system should have been installed in a different way. We all had to be absolutely comfortable with every decision."

At first a representative from Parks Canada attended the weekly restoration meetings to ensure that the team respected park values and environmental standards.

"Yeah, but that lasted only until the second or third time we met," Doug Wood put in. "Les, Kevin and I were sitting there talking for hours about how this or that old tree absolutely had to be brought back into play, and about how we really should plant more trees around this one because, you know, 200 years from now it might be gone, or a windstorm could take it out tomorrow. Then we got into a long conversation about ribboning off our grass areas so that nothing could disturb them during construction, and about how, no matter what, we had to preserve the naturalness of our riverbanks."

After that, the man from Parks made himself scarce. "I guess he figured things were in pretty good hands," Furber noted with satisfaction.

The restoration team pored over old blueprints and photographs for glimpses of the golf course that once was. Much of the material was drawn from the Canadian Pacific Archives in Montreal and the collections of the Whyte Museum of the Canadian

Rockies. Nothing was overlooked. Even yellowed advertising posters might reveal the original contours of a bunker or green. As word of the restoration spread, past guests of the hotel responded by mailing in postcards and snapshots from family vacations.

Maybe the most difficult challenge was determining how much to lengthen the course to counter improvements to golf clubs and balls over the past 20 years or more. Better players were hitting driver-wedge into many of the par fours, making a joke of Thompson's original design. The par fives weren't playing much tougher.

Dutifully, Les Furber, Doug Wood and Kevin Pattison took up their clubs and played the course day after day, experimenting with hundreds of shots to decide where to place the new tee boxes in order to restore the degree of risk and reward Thompson had intended. A scratchy film from the 1930s of two low-handicappers enjoying a round at the Banff Springs revealed how the course had played in its heyday. From all this, the team concluded that some holes would have to be stretched as much as 100 yards from the back tees. Overall, the course has been extended 457 yards.

All three men, but especially Les Furber, the architect, constantly fought the human impulse to leave his own mark, like footprints in cement, on Thompson's handiwork. This, in every sense, was to be a restoration of a classic golf course to its original character, with only a few accommodations to the demands of the modern game.

Furber and his partners were determined to roll back the clock in Banff to a time before the advent of what has become known as the Augusta National Syndrome, which has seen courses across North America emulate the exacting grooming standards of the Georgia shrine. Augusta's fairways are walk-mowed and then cropped to 0.39 inches, making them play about as fast as the average putting green of 20 years ago. Even Augusta's ponds are dyed with aquatic colourant to turn them a deep, television-friendly turquoise.

Golfers watching the Masters at home naturally wonder why they can't enjoy the same conditions at their own course. "Too much is being done solely for aesthetics," Les Furber said disdainfully. "You see courses cut in precise straight lines, diamonds and criss-crosses, all so club members can have the satisfaction of saying, 'Boy, doesn't that look great.' But what these people don't realize is that the closer you cut the grass, the more stressed out and unhealthy it becomes. Then you have to use even more water, chemicals and fertilizer."

While claiming to endorse environmental awareness and responsibility, the golf industry has at the same time become infatuated with beauty for beauty's sake alone.

"I think golf course design has strayed too far away from minimalism and naturalism, especially here in North America," Furber went on. "Many courses have introduced types of vegetation foreign to their areas. With heavy irrigation, you can grow almost anything. What I most admire about the famous old links-style courses of the British Isles, where the game was born, is that God built them. Architect unknown. It's only in the past few years that designers on this side of the Atlantic have finally started to consider a more humble approach."

At about the same time work on the course began, the Banff Springs joined the Audubon Cooperative Sanctuary System, an international program begun in 1990 designed to encourage landowners to preserve and enhance the environmental quality of their properties.

"I've been coming to the mountains all my life," Doug Wood

told me. "Kevin lives in a house right here on the golf course. Les lives just down the road in Canmore. It's important to all of us that golfers get the most out of their round in a national park. We see it all here—from bears to elk to foxes and field mice. Being in a national park, we've always had more restrictions than other courses anyway. We're all convinced that most of these restrictions are constructive things."

In the restoration, among many other environmentally friendly initiatives, 32 acres of previously groomed fairways were returned to the natural, free-growing golden montane seen in Thompson's day. These knee-high grassy patches extend from the forward tees to about 50 yards out into the fairway, snaring the balls of duffers like me prone to the occasional squibber. The native grasses, also seen dancing in the breeze at the backs of numerous bunkers, create corridors for mice and other small animals to travel through, protected from birds of prey.

I studied Les Furber from across the sizzling fondue pot. Through the countless details of the restoration, he had walked in Stanley Thompson's footsteps for almost three years by the time we talked. After all that time for reflection, I wondered if his opinion of the famous architect had changed since he first accepted the assignment.

"Absolutely not," he answered emphatically. "I went into this thinking that Stanley Thompson was a genius and I still feel the same way. His work at Jasper and Banff has been copied ever since he built the courses. Both had great natural sites, but I still find myself wondering how he created such beautiful golf courses with the primitive equipment he had to work with at the time.

"Thompson rates right up there in the pantheon," Furber continued. "Certainly among the top five to 10 architects in the history of golf course design."

Earlier Doug Wood had told me that one important reason Les Furber had been chosen to conduct the restoration was because of the humility with which he approached the project. He wasn't looking to make this a Les Furber–Stanley Thompson co-creation. In truth, as he told me, he didn't care if he got any credit at all.

"This property is a symbol of Canada," Furber said. "Wherever I travel around the world, people have heard of the Banff Springs. I'd be foolish to think that golfers are ever going to associate anyone but Stanley Thompson's name with it. All I want is for people to come here and rave about what great shape the course is in."

There are only about a dozen full-time course designers in Canada. Alongside Graham Cooke of Montreal and Tom McBroom and Doug Carrick, both of Toronto, Furber stands in the front rank. He has built more than 50 courses (including such applauded Canadian layouts as Predator Ridge and SilverTip), restored 50 more and had projects worldwide—from the Czech Republic, Switzerland and Germany to the United States and Cuba.

Growing up on a farm in Tisdale, Saskatchewan, Furber imagined a life spent tilling the land, not moulding it into golf courses. In 1966, after graduating from high school, he and two friends travelled to California on vacation. When Furber's money ran out, he found work on a golf course project in Santa Barbara, designed by Robert Trent Jones Jr.

Already adept at driving heavy machinery from life on the farm, Furber demonstrated such a flair for the moving and shaping of earth that he soon caught the attention of Trent Jones Sr., the legendary architect who was Stanley Thompson's junior partner in the design firm of Thompson, Jones & Company during the 1930s. For the next two years, Furber worked illegally in the United States for both Joneses, Jr. and Sr., never applying for the work visa that would have made him eligible for the military draft during the height of the Vietnam War.

Deported to Canada in 1969, Furber then embarked on an international career as a field supervisor and project director for Jones Sr. Furber handled on-site construction for courses in Europe and Africa that included Spain's Valderrama, a 45-hole resort track for the king of Morocco, and 18 holes on a Sardinian island commissioned by the Aga Khan. Meanwhile, since there are no schools for golf course architects, Furber took courses on turf drainage and management and read journals to keep abreast of the latest trends.

Furber's last project for Trent Jones Sr. was the 36-hole Kananaskis Country Golf Course, the resort facility one hour west of Calgary whose emergence in the mid-1980s sparked the expansion of the course at the Banff Springs.

In 1980, Furber formed his own company, Golf Design Services, in partnership with his brother-in-law Jim Eremko, another Saskatchewan native and a former project manager for the Jones organization. Though the two are equal partners, it's Furber's reputation that draws the clients. Eremko, a quiet and shy man by nature, handles the administrative side of things.

After almost 35 years in the business, Furber didn't hesitate when I asked him to list the qualities he considers essential to superior golf course design.

"I always strive for what we call 'artistic eye appeal,'" he said. "A course should look beautiful or else why would a player want to be there? A round of golf should appeal to all the senses, making you feel more alive, like you're really a part of the natural world."

Furber, like Stanley Thompson, has a special fondness for

elevated tees that offer golfers panoramic views of the surrounding countryside and of the particular hole awaiting their
pleasure. He eschews deceptive routing and hidden hazards. A
superior golf course is always a fair golf course.

An eight-handicapper when he has the time to play regularly,
Furber expressed particular disdain for uphill, blind par threes,
where the golfer is unable to see the hole from the teeing area.
"Imagine sinking a hole-in-one and not even being able to see the
ball drop into the cup," he said indignantly. "You'd be missing out
on one of the game's greatest thrills."

In many ways, designing a course from scratch is far easier than
undertaking a restoration, especially of a Stanley Thompson
course. Any restorer must approach a Thompson project with the
reverence of a pilgrim at Jerusalem's gate.

Would Stanley Thompson recognize his own course after it
had been reworked? More to the point, would the great man
approve of what has been done? Furber and his partners in the
Banff restoration asked themselves these questions over and
over again.

Equipment improvements had turned many of the 150 bunkers
in the original design into mere decorations. Faithful to Thompson's vision, fairway bunkers were shifted to bring the architect's
intended hazards back into play. Bunkers that had been filled in
over the years were similarly restored, while clusters of two or
more traps that had been joined together to simplify maintenance
were again separated and given their original shapes.

Restoring the greens to Thompson's original specifications
presented one of the unique challenges of the restoration.
Tests revealed that over the years mercury levels exceeding
accepted standards had built up in the soil from treatments
for snow mould and other ailments. Indeed, the soil was so

poisoned that if excavated it would have had to go straight into a toxic waste dump. Furber's solution was to cap the greens and build on top, then shape the surrounding areas to reintroduce the correct slopes.

"The new greens are 16 inches higher than in Thompson's day," Furber said. "But in every other way, they're identical to the originals."

Naturally, particular care was taken with the par-three Devil's Cauldron, the Banff Springs signature hole. Tee boxes were widened and their tiers altered so that players hitting from the back tee could fully admire the glacial lake below, a view slightly obscured in the past. The burying of an old septic tank close by the teeing ground helped return the area to picture-postcard condition.

As well, the restoration saw the resodding of fairways, the rerouting of cart paths, the tearing-down of unsightly fences and the installation of a sophisticated new irrigation system linked to a computerized weather station that tells the sprinklers when to turn off and on.

Modern innovations such as the weather station have all been carefully kept out of sight. More than anything, the goal of the restoration was to take the Banff Springs course back to simpler days. Greenskeepers once again use hand mowers to cut the greens, and staff shape the edges of bunkers with shovels, painstakingly restoring the fingers and toes with which Stanley Thompson created illusions against the mountain backdrop.

Even the scorecards, ball washers, flagsticks and tee markers have subtle, old-fashioned designs that together help create the impression that golfers have stepped several decades back in time.

ONE DAY I ASKED A UNIVERSITY student working at the Banff Springs practice range how he was enjoying his summer.

"Well, sir," the clean-cut youngster replied, "I sure do miss my girlfriend. I'm thinking of quitting and going back home to Ottawa."

I could scarcely believe my ears. By this point every member of our mostly middle-aged writers' troupe would have traded his soul to turn back the clock 30 years and spend a summer at the mountain resort. Each spring at the conclusion of the school year thousands of kids from across Canada descend on Banff to find employment in the tourist trade. No less an authority than *Rolling Stone* magazine has called it one of the swingingest party towns in North America. We were getting whiplash ogling all the beautiful girls.

"How old are you, son?" I asked sternly.

"Nineteen, sir."

"Well, let me give you some advice," I began, before stopping myself, suddenly remembering how little use I once had for the opinion of adults.

"No. The last thing you want is to hear an old guy like me spout off."

"That's not true, sir," he answered, a quavering note of desperation in his voice. "Tell me."

"Then my advice is to forget the girl back home, at least until the fall. You're too young to get tied down. Live every moment, chase lots of girls and at the end of the summer be sure to do one thing, dammit!"

"What's that, sir?"

"Beg them to let you come back again next year!"

One of the benefits of growing older is that we're more likely to appreciate where we are in life and what we've got. Doug Wood told me there are only two or three jobs in the golf world that would even tempt him to leave the Banff Springs, and even then he'd most likely stay put. Les Furber travelled the globe in the employ of Robert Trent Jones, but when it came time to settle down he returned home to Canada and the Alberta Rockies, setting up shop just a few miles from Banff.

Of all the people I met at the Banff Springs, I don't think anyone appreciated his situation more than Kevin Pattison, the course superintendent.

An energetic, compact man in his late thirties, Kevin has a blissed-out enthusiasm and an impish sparkle in his eyes that reminded me of a Disney cartoon character happily ensconced in an enchanted forest. Kevin, his wife and their three young children share the picturesque cottage between today's 13th and 17th tees built as the original 1911 clubhouse. Every morning he awakes with the dawn, kisses his family goodbye and bounds happily off to the work he loves. Rain or shine, the message on his office answering machine begins, "It's another beautiful day here at the Banff Springs . . ."

"My whole goal in life was to work at a golf course that has environmental issues, someplace I could clean up and put back on the map," Kevin told me over morning coffee in the clubhouse. "I don't think there's another property in Canada that could offer the opportunity I have here to make a difference."

Pattison is one of the new breed of superintendents who are forcing golf courses to become more environmentally friendly by adopting what he likes to think of as a "holistic" maintenance philosophy. In particular, they're determined to sharply curtail the use of harmful chemicals once spread so unthinkingly over fairways and greens. Many course workers, ignorant of the potential dangers, actually used to mix chemicals by hand in open containers.

In responding to studies that found unusually high cancer rates among groundskeeping staff, pesticide manufacturers developed products that, if used properly, are far less dangerous to humans and wildlife than those formerly on the market. These new products even go easier on the insects they're designed to target, interfering with reproductive and growth cycles rather than killing the pests outright.

Kevin's duties at the Banff Springs include supervising the golf course's participation in the Audubon Cooperative Sanctuary System. Agendas detailing ACSS goals are available for golf courses, schools and businesses, individual property owners and corporate properties such as parks, factory lots and cemeteries. The Banff Springs signed on in 1997 and received its full certification in the spring of 1999.

To become Audubon certified, a golf course must first develop an environmental plan and then meet dozens of targets in a variety of areas—including wildlife and habitat management, integrated pest management, water conservation and quality management, and outreach and education.

More than 250 golf courses across Canada have come aboard. Creative initiatives never imagined a decade ago have now become commonplace. At Chateau Whistler, another CP mountain retreat, a fish ladder was built in the water that cuts across the 18th hole in order to help the rainbow fry on their journey to the pond at the second hole. George Knudson's first Toronto home, the Oakdale Golf and Country Club, has dug a 13-foot-deep snake pit and painstakingly furnished it with rotten logs and gravel to make the reptiles feel right at home.

In returning 32 acres of previously groomed golf course back to natural montane, the Banff Springs jumped on a trend that has seen many courses cut back on their maintained areas to incorporate native grass roughs. Similarly, sensitive habitats such as wetlands and sand dunes are now often placed off limits to golfers searching for lost balls. And when planning new courses, top architects frequently opt for links-style designs that offer the wild appearance of traditional Scottish tracks.

Kevin proudly ran down the long list of Audubon initiatives undertaken at the Banff Springs during his watch. Frequent soil testing helps determine the nutrients already in the soil, as well as those that need to be added to maintain the health of the vegetation. Slopes and water escapes are never fertilized, and fairways receive only light dustings. To provide homes for coyotes, rabbits, pine martens, weasels and mice, brush from the trees is gathered into piles throughout the golf course. Turf cuttings are composted and spread back onto the fairways. Kevin and his staff are also assisting naturalists in their surveys of the types and quantities of birds that make the golf course their home.

The Audubon program encourages environmental education to bring the general public onto the golf course. Kevin enthusiastically told me of a tour of the property he'd conducted the previous fall for a group of local public-school kids.

"We found an old elk carcass, just bones on the ground, and we showed the kids how the backbone of an elk works," Kevin began. "Then I had the kids hug trees and smell them, telling them to try to feel the tree's energy, its life force. After that, the kids planted a few trees so they can come back years from now and see what they helped create. We ended with a ride in a hay wagon, followed by hot chocolate served by one of our chefs."

Watching the animation with which Kevin told his story, I couldn't imagine that any of the children on the field trip enjoyed themselves more than their host.

"My wife often says to me, 'You don't even work, do you?'"
Kevin said with a contented sigh. "And she's right. I live my job."

Born in Calgary, Kevin knew even as a boy that he wanted to
spend his life in the outdoors. He graduated with a degree in turf
management from the University of Massachusetts and worked in
the United States before returning home with his Class A superintendent's ranking and a job at the Woodside club in Airdrie, just
outside of Calgary. From there he moved on to nearby Priddis
Greens and then, in 1996, to the Banff Springs.

All of it was solid preparation, though nothing can adequately
prepare a groundskeeper for the unique reality of plying his trade
in a national park. Few courses in the world are as open to animal
life as the Banff Springs. Golfers are given a welcome speech at
the first hole that includes a warning about the large and potentially ferocious animals they're likely to encounter.

The summer of my visit, three black bears and two grizzlies
made their way onto the course within a single week, forcing the
closing of several holes. Bears, though, are of only passing concern to Kevin. They rarely linger and don't usually cause damage
to the property.

It's the 75 to 250 elk on the course every day of the golf season
that drive him to distraction. Almost every morning Kevin discovers
at least one green that has suffered extensive damage from the
hooves of elk during the night. His crew of 37 groundskeepers
spends 48 work hours a day repairing the damage caused by elk
activity—fixing greens, removing dung, re-raking bunkers and
removing flagsticks every evening to prevent elk from gathering to
lick them for the salt left by human hands.

Kevin grimaced when he recalled the damage done one summer evening when two rutting bulls locked horns on the ninth

green in full view of the clubhouse dining room. So ferocious was the battle that diners rushed to the window for a better view.

"Afterwards, the green looked as raw as a piece of tenderized meat," Kevin said. "We had to pick up pieces of antler, blood and hair. It was really gross!"

Another time Kevin and his crew were slowly moving 90 or more elk who had gathered by the 10th green. Elk will usually disperse without incident if they're approached slowly and unthreateningly. Suddenly, one of them got spooked, sending the entire herd trampling back toward the clubhouse area, where they mauled the practice greens and driving range as if in wilful retribution for having been disturbed.

"It's these types of things that make me lose my hair," Kevin joked, doffing his golf cap to display an already high and fast-receding hairline.

Almost hunted into extinction by the end of the nineteenth century, elk, larger than deer but smaller than moose, have made a remarkable local comeback since 1917 when 250 of the animals were imported from Yellowstone National Park to restock the area. Since then their numbers have increased so dramatically it often seems as if they've taken over the town of Banff. Elk nonchalantly stop traffic on the main street, doze on people's front porches or anywhere else they choose and frequently, especially when the males are in rut from late August to mid-October, charge anyone too dumb to keep his distance.

Even Parks Canada has come to believe there are too many elk in the Banff townsite, and that they are interacting with humans in an unhealthy way. At the time of my visit, a plan was afoot to reintroduce the elks' most feared natural predator, wolves, back into the area to help cull the herd. And the decision had already been made to relocate as many as 150 of the 450 elk living in the townsite elsewhere in Banff National Park.

Talk was even going around that an elk fence might once again be constructed around the golf course, this time with the blessing of Parks Canada, who back in 1986 had insisted the old fence come down in return for allowing the building of the new nine.

Though he would welcome the elk fence's return, Kevin, typically, chose to look only on the bright side of the presence of elk, grizzlies and other often troublesome beasts on his golf course. "I think people who golf in a national park arrive with different expectations," he said. "The animals add to the thrill of playing so close to nature."

There's another advantage Kevin had noticed.

"Whenever a bear is on site," he added with a smile, "the pace of play picks up amazingly."

HAVING SCORED HIS BACK-to-back aces at Jasper Park and the Banff Springs, Stanley Thompson stood as arguably the world's number-one golf course architect. Still to come were such celebrated courses as Capilano in British Columbia, Westmount and St. George's in Ontario, Highlands Links and the Pines in Nova Scotia, and Green Gables in Prince Edward Island. During a career that spanned more than three decades, Thompson designed or remodelled some 145 courses in Canada, the United States, the Caribbean and South America.

Thompson also trained a number of assistants who enjoyed illustrious careers in their own right, including Robert Trent Jones, C.E. Robinson, Norman Woods, Howard Watson, Kenneth Welton, Robert Moote and Geoffrey Cornish, co-designer of Banff's Tunnel Nine but best known as the co-author of *The*

Architects of Golf, considered the definitive tome on golf course architecture. The Winnipeg-born Cornish, who apprenticed with Thompson for several years in the 1930s and '40s, recalled that one of his tasks as a junior designer was to make certain his hard-drinking boss's flask was kept filled with a potent mix of tea laced with whisky.

Trent Jones, Les Furber's former employer, went on to become perhaps the most influential course designer in history after he left Thompson, famous for his oft-quoted philosophy that every golf hole should be a hard par but an easy bogey. Colleagues remembered that Thompson and the equally headstrong Jones often had heated battles when planning their projects together, and that the American frequently had his way. If Jones's idea succeeded, Thompson would slyly try to take the credit. If it failed, he left his junior partner to suffer the blame.

In 1948, together with Trent Jones and Donald Ross, Stanley Thompson founded the American Society of Golf Course Architects, serving as its president the next year. Yet despite his prominence, Thompson's profligate spending and heavy drinking kept him constantly in and out of debt. He was apparently bankrupt, though still busy working, when he died of a stroke in Toronto on January 4, 1953, at the age of 59.

"Stanley Thompson has left a mark on the Canadian landscape from coast to coast," the *Ottawa Citizen* wrote in eulogy. "No man could ask for a more handsome set of memorials."

"I THINK STANLEY WOULD have loved how it turned out," Doug Wood said confidently of the Banff Springs restoration.

It was my last day in the mountains. The American writers had all left, and I would catch my own plane home from Calgary the next morning. I told Doug how eager I was to revisit the 15th tee one last time.

He nodded thoughtfully. "I know what you mean. People are in heaven up there. They feel like they're touching the Big Guy himself."

During the restoration, Doug and Les Furber had been determined to bring the hole's elevated back tee with its spectacular views of the Bow River Valley into everyday play. Though Thompson had set a "championship" tee on the site, it had only been used during tournaments and on other special occasions. Before the coming of electric carts, when this was the opening hole, the walk up and then back down the hill would have hopelessly stalled traffic on the course.

Early that evening, standing once again at the 15th's white tee, I gazed in renewed admiration at the beauty of the valley below. The sky beyond the mountains was the bluest blue I had ever seen. The Spray River surged forward. Magpies sang and elk grazed contentedly.

Setting up slowly, imagining in my mind's eye a shot as lovely and true as the one I had hit the last time, I swung through.

A moment later my frantic cry of "Fore!" pierced the valley's tranquility. Tourists strolling on the cart path to the left of the fairway scattered for their lives as my ball landed on the path and rebounded deep into the woods.

The magic in my swing was gone. Yet as I put my club away and got in my cart, I found that the mountain air smelled just as sweet. In such a setting, on such a course, no golfer had the right to feel anything but blessed.

Stanley Thompson himself could not have hoped for more.

CHAPTER 6

DOME ON THE RANGE

JACK SASSEVILLE PACED THE LOWER deck of the Oakville golf dome's driving range in frustration, every fibre of his being aching to dispense his years of hard-won teaching knowledge — if only someone would ask.

"Most people here haven't got a clue about what they're doing," the veteran pro said, casting his gaze dismissively over the two dozen or so golfers scattered about the dome on this late-winter weekday afternoon. "They're working on the latest thing they saw on the Golf Channel or read in *Golf Digest*. Or maybe it's something a friend who's a 40 handicap told them worked for him."

Sasseville was about to go on, then stopped himself. Slowly, his face broke into a sheepish grin.

"But you know what?" he said. "In the end, we're all alike. Every one of us is in some stage of addiction. Like the rest of these people, I can hardly wait to get here every day and hit golf balls."

From bubble domes to an entirely new breed of driving range, a variety of options are available to Canadians to keep them close to the game without having to leave the country during our long winters. The latest craze is luxuriously appointed ranges where golfers hit balls into distant outdoor nets or onto frosty fields from covered and heated platforms. At the most extravagant of these facilities, which usually include a table and four plush chairs at each hitting station to encourage socializing, attentive serving staff deliver drinks and food, while pros stroll like major-domos among the patrons, dispensing advice for a fee.

One of these newcomers, Launch, has given the old game an additional twist. The Toronto range simulates a round of golf by challenging players to keep score while they hit to different areas of a field divided into numbered grids. Just as in conventional golf, the goal is to shoot the lowest possible score. Though critics have dismissed Launch as "bowling alley golf," the game undeniably provides a solid workout. Except for a putter, every club in the bag sees action.

Then there are electronic golf simulator screens, where golfers smack balls into giant photographic backdrops and wait anxiously while the simulator decides whether their shot has, depending on the program, plunged into the surf alongside Pebble Beach's 18th or landed as gently as a butterfly on the third green at Firestone. These marvels, which first appeared about a decade ago, are found in better arcades and at golf travel and merchandise shows across the land.

I tried them all. But ultimately my search for a winter home led me to the Oakville golf dome, officially known as the Air Athletics Sports Centre. The two attached, softly triangular inflated bubbles beside Southern Ontario's busy Queen Elizabeth Way, not far from famous Glen Abbey Golf Club, have been a landmark for local golfers ever since the oxygen was first pumped in back in 1990.

The driving range found inside the larger of the two domes (the smaller dome is used almost exclusively for soccer) was exactly the retreat I was looking for now that the first season of my golfing journey had come to an end. A place free of gimmicks, where I could work on my game with single-minded purpose. At last I'd have the time to get comfortable with the new set of clubs I'd bought after the debacle in Banff of watching my clubs disintegrate before the disbelieving eyes of my American friends. And though I'd been scoring reasonably well—usually in the low to mid-90s, occasionally the high 80s—here I would rid myself, or so I vowed, of a wicked slice that had hampered my progress in the waning days of autumn. But most of all, I looked forward to a winter of talking and living and breathing golf with a whole domeful of fellow addicts.

We were a wildly varied lot, no question. Mornings at the dome seemed to attract older converts, among them recently retired couples searching for a common interest to enrich their Golden Years. Oh, the skulls and shanks and other mis-hits we saw fly off their mats. Watching the old-timers' painful struggles, the rest of us squirmed with uneasy visions of getting stuck in the group behind them during a Sunday afternoon round from hell.

Naturally, just as at every urban golf facility across the country, there were large numbers of Asian Canadians, many of them recently arrived from Hong Kong, mainland China, Vietnam and Korea. Golf is such an élitist and expensive pastime throughout Asia that the opportunity to give it a try in their new home must seem heaven-sent. More than one told me they rarely took their games outside onto an actual course. The trance-like calm achieved by methodically hitting balls hour after hour at the dome provided everything they wanted from the game.

Of particular fascination to us all were the frequent visits by disabled golfers. One remarkable fellow in a wheelchair routinely hit drives that outside the confines of the dome would easily have travelled 200 yards on the fly. A one-armed golfer drove them even longer, though maybe not as straight.

But the best fun came from observing the true eccentrics among us, the golfers who had somewhere lost their way and whose games were now permanently mired in the tangled fescue of their minds.

Foremost among these was a middle-aged man known as the Stork, who for better than an hour every visit would stand on one leg hitting golf balls. Even between shots the Stork was loath to let his other foot touch the floor, hopping comically about while he set himself to hit again. Clearly, he was convinced that this one drill would magically transform his game. Yet none of us ever saw the slightest evidence of progress. The Stork remained a lousy golfer.

"I know I could fix him up," Jack Sasseville said of the Stork. "But if I walk up to him and most of the people at this range, they'd think, He's just trying to make money, or He's going to mess me up."

Most golfers are self-help junkies who prefer to get their tips from the pages of golf magazines and by watching instructors on the Golf Channel rather than pay hard cash to real live professionals. It's easier that way and, besides, lessons might undo whatever limited success they've already managed to achieve. Teaching pros have a nasty habit of forcing duffers to start all over again from scratch.

In Jack's experience, golfers trust pros about as much as they trust used-car salesmen. Sasseville spent much of his time roaming the dome trying to overcome this prejudice by getting to know potential customers on a first-name basis. When asked, he would offer one or two free pearls of wisdom in the hope that the golfer might eventually pay for more.

A trim man in his middle years with an open, boyish smile of considerable charm, Sasseville is the director of instruction for ClubLink, the Ontario-based firm that over the past decade has rapidly become Canada's largest operator and developer of golf facilities. ClubLink briefly owned the Oakville dome before first leasing and then selling to the current owners, Air Athletics of Toronto. Under the terms of the deal, ClubLink agreed to continue providing golf instruction at the dome.

During the summer months, Jack hangs his shingle at ClubLink's prestigious Lake Joseph Club in the Muskoka tourist region north of Toronto. He'd spent this winter and the last at the Oakville dome giving individual and group lessons and watching with mounting disgruntlement all the hopeless hacks who persisted in turning a blind eye whenever he approached.

Sasseville has spent most of his adult life teaching—not just golf but cross-country skiing, the biathalon and mountain biking. From 1979 to 1992, he participated in four Olympics while serving as a coach with Canada's national cross-country ski team. He has since provided commentary for CBC's Olympic cross-country coverage. Sasseville, better than almost anyone, understands how important it is for a golfer or any other athlete to have a solid grounding in the fundamentals of his sport.

Most people are intimidated by instructors, Jack was convinced, because they've never met one who truly grasps the extent of their frustration.

"Almost all golf teachers learned to play when they were young, so they have no understanding of how hard it is to do well when you get started as an adult," Sasseville said. "Since few people have much time to put into their golf games, they're filled with insecurities. The biggest worry is that they're going to go out onto the course and really embarrass themselves."

As a teacher, Jack had struggled to overcome the disadvantage of his own start in the game at the age of five back in his home-town of Saskatoon. After turning pro at 19, he played on the old Peter Jackson Tour for two summers without notable success. Of his final year as a playing pro, he wryly recalled, "I never missed a cut and never made a cheque."

Some are born for glory, others to teach. Just four days after taking up cross-country skiing in 1972, he was offered a job as an instructor. In 1977, Sasseville was hired to coach the Manitoba cross-country team. Two years after that he joined the coaching staff of Canada's national team.

For the next decade, Jack was so consumed by his duties with the national team that he gave up golf completely. It wasn't until the summer of 1987, while working with the squad at its Can-more training base, that he dug his clubs out of the closet and began playing the local mountain courses as a way of relieving the stress of preparing for the upcoming Calgary Olympics.

Sasseville quit the national cross-country team in 1992, worn down by a gruelling schedule that saw him on the road 260 days a year in Europe and North America. He kept busy by teaching cross-country, biathalon and mountain biking and by getting the remaining rust off his golf game. In 1998, two years after joining ClubLink, he was named the growing chain's director of instruction.

"Everyone here is actually hurting their ability to play better golf," Jack said of the crowd at the Oakville dome. "If you don't start with the right knowledge, practice only makes permanent all your misconceptions. Really, they'd be better off staying home."

Sasseville gestured toward a tall sweaty fellow smacking iron shots like a rhythmless automaton a few mats away. Even before his previous ball had landed, he was already midway through his next swing, grimly determined not to get shortchanged by the dome's general admission policy of charging by the length of the visit rather than by the number of balls hit. Range memberships offering unlimited mat time are available, but not many golfers make the purchase.

"We call guys like him AK-47s," Sasseville said of our neighbour. "They're like machine guns, hitting as many as six or seven balls a minute. But to see real progress you have to slow it right down, do drills so that the correct swing becomes a repeating process. And then you have to listen to your body for feedback, allowing yourself to *feel* if you did right or wrong. If you're hitting more than about one ball a minute, you're going too quickly."

Though maddening at times, the upside of being constantly surrounded by so many godawful golfers is that Jack could only see business getting better. Despite the game's booming popularity, only an estimated 3 per cent of golfers regularly take lessons. That leaves a lot of room for growth. If pros like Sasseville can make even a small breakthrough in their ground-level public-relations efforts, professional golf instruction could become one of the fastest-growing market niches in all of sport.

So Jack kept smiling and working the dome, knowing everything at stake. Even when the very honour of his profession was questioned, he turned the other cheek.

One day a woman tentatively approached, saying she needed to talk to him. Then in an instant her attitude stiffened, and suddenly she was ripping a divot off his hide.

"I've talked to a lot of golf professionals and I've disagreed with every one," she said. "I think you're all full of shit!"

Rather than being insulted, Jack recognized her anger as a cry for help. "The whole thing was like 'I need help, I want help, but I don't trust you,'" he recalled. "'So you're going to have to prove to me that you know what you're doing before I'll even begin to listen to you.'"

Like a car salesman, Sasseville not only had to gain their trust, he had to do it fast before they walked off the lot. He knew that with diehard sceptics he had maybe 10 minutes to close the deal. Most people were looking for Band-Aid solutions. "Just fix my slice," they'd say. If Sasseville's advice produced instant results, there was a good chance they'd sign up for a lesson or two. But even then the tension remained. "A golf pro gets about $200 worth of trust," he said.

At least, that's the way it starts with golf lessons. As the lessons progress, the student's handicap begins to drop, and suddenly golf offers a whole new level of enjoyment and personal satisfaction. Two lessons become five, then 10, and before long the sessions with instructors like Jack Sasseville are as essential to life's routine as morning coffee.

As Sasseville said with a salesman's Cheshire-cat grin, "The hook gets in their mouth, and that's that."

CAM STUART, AIR ATHLETICS' vice-president of business development and the on-site manager of the Oakville dome, jokingly told me that the most frustrating aspect of his life inside an inflatable playpen was the encounters with golfers who showed up at the dome before heading south on a winter vacation.

"I'm going down to Arizona next week. I'm just here to get the rust off my game."

"Oh yeah . . . well, piss off!" Cam would give right back at them.

A wiry, balding 41-year-old with a jailhouse pallor and a dry wit, Stuart had himself found the time to hit no more than a dozen buckets of balls during 14 months of 70-hour weeks at the dome. A lifelong golfer, he once boasted a three-handicap. He didn't care to think what it might be now.

The Oakville dome had been Cam Stuart's personal baby ever since he'd signed on with Air Athletics the year before. Previously, he'd spent 15 years in sales and marketing with Bell Canada. Though Air Athletics already owned and operated several tennis domes throughout Southern Ontario, the Oakville bubble was the first in what the two-year-old company intended to be a succession of multiple-sports facilities. Cam's assignment was to get the flagship operation up and running smoothly before moving permanently to a desk job in the Toronto head office.

Stuart's years with Ma Bell did little to prepare him for his new challenge. "I didn't know the first thing about operating a dome," he admitted with a good-natured shrug. "I've had to learn everything by the seat of my pants."

Complicating the learning curve was the unique nature of the Oakville dome, a one-off creation designed and built in France. Soon after its delivery, engineers had to be called in to strengthen the crests of both domes, which though different in scale are identical in shape. The French designers, it seemed, hadn't reckoned on the volume of snow and ice build-up during a typical Canadian winter.

In fact, the French made a botch of almost the entire production. Unlike North American manufacturers who weld together the polyurethane rubber panels of their domes, the French preferred stitching. Yet every stitch hole represents a potential leak. Air that escapes has to be replaced. Operating costs at the Oakville dome are approximately 25 per cent greater than at North American–made domes of comparable size.

Otherwise, Cam was faced with all the problems that apply to the operation of any other bubble dome: making certain the temperature remains comfortable in a facility that can rapidly become a sauna on a warm day; most of all, maintaining a constant interior air pressure to avoid the cost and embarrassment of a structural collapse.

"I thought I'd be lying awake at night worrying, What if this baby blows?" Cam said with a chuckle. "I relaxed after finding out that a dome takes at least three hours to completely deflate."

One considerable strength of the Oakville dome's design is its unusual triangular shape. Built specifically for golf, the dome, though not necessarily greater in overall size than many rectangular bubbles, is wider than most at its widest end, where an impressive 72 hitting stations are found on two curved decks aimed toward nets 100 yards down the narrowing triangle. An artificial turf putting green is located in the extra space to the rear of the deck. Another advantage is the dome's generous 85-foot height, which allows golfers to practise even with their pitching wedges.

Still, the Oakville dome's flaws outweigh its advantages. Air Athletics intends to eventually replace it with a conventional,

North American–built model. Ambitious plans have also been made to add an attached tennis bubble, as well as a combination ball hockey, roller hockey and basketball dome. The expansion will also creep onto the property outdoors, with beach volleyball courts and possibly even an open-air driving range joining a mix that already includes a nine-hole mini-putt course and a nine-hole pitch-and-putt. Air Athletics' goal is to tranform the site into a major year-round sports destination.

Regular visitors pausing to look at an architectural sketch of the master plan displayed outside the pro shop couldn't help worrying that the feeling of intimacy, the sense that everyone at the dome was a valued member of an extended, golf-crazed family, might get trampled in the march of progress.

Like all hands-on managers, the genial Cam Stuart set the tone for the entire operation. Golfers made a point of stopping by his office to shoot the breeze, and often planned their practice sessions so they could join him on his coffee break in the lounge. Though Cam was eager to move on to head office, to cut back his hours and maybe get a little sun on his face, he knew he'd miss the close-knit gang at the dome when it finally came time to leave.

He'd miss the camaraderie and one other thing. Cam's greatest thrill at the dome was driving the screened tractor used to gather the golf balls scattered over the range floor.

Whenever he hopped in, every golfer on the range gleefully took aim, trying to rattle his cage. Soon a hail of balls would be thudding off the screen all around him, while inside Cam could be seen grinning like a maniac. No one, he told me seriously, would ever invent a better way to relieve the stress of 70-hour work weeks.

EVERY WEEKEND DOZENS of kids noisily destroyed the serenity so appreciated by dome regulars the rest of the week. By far the most disruptive arrivals were birthday celebrations that had booked time on the mats. Some kids came only reluctantly, left to run amok while their parents practised. But there were still others, not a few of them, who arrived as full of purpose as any adult in the place.

I watched a young girl with a blond ponytail hanging out the back of her Nike cap hit balls through an entire Saturday afternoon under the stern supervision of a father unmistakably intent on creating Canada's next Lorie Kane.

A husky 13-year-old boy spent an hour every Saturday morning at the dome with his coach. They had two more sessions together after school during the week. The boy confidently told me he intended to earn a golf scholarship to an American university. After that he planned to play professionally.

One afternoon I met Brian McCann, a 25-year-old playing pro who had been coming to the Oakville dome ever since his teenage days. He even used to bring his dates there, stopping by after a Friday night movie to share a Coke and fries over a bucket of balls.

His future had also once seemed full of promise. But now a gnawing sense of uncertainty accompanied his workouts. The summer before, Brian had suffered the indignity of missing 14 cuts in the 14 tournaments he entered on the Canadian Tour during his rookie season.

"I went through one of those incredibly bad spells that golfers can go through," Brian recounted, a look of gloom settling over his clean-cut, boyish face. "I knew I was capable of a hell of a lot better. It was the most frustrating summer of my life."

Until then, McCann had enjoyed an almost uninterrupted

run of success, starting when he won the Canadian Juvenile Championship at the age of 16 in 1991. From 1995 to 1997, McCann, who by then attended Arkansas State University on a golf scholarship, was Ontario's top-ranked amateur. And twice, in 1995 and 1996, he qualified for the United States Amateur Championship.

First as a junior and later at the U.S. Amateur, McCann saw first-hand the genius of Tiger Woods and came away dazzled but undaunted. "The first time I ever played against him I was 16 and Tiger was a year younger," he remembered. "Like everyone else, I couldn't believe the things he did on a golf course. He was tall and really skinny, but even then he was hammering the ball better than 300 yards."

Tiger won both U.S. Amateurs in which McCann competed. Yet for a single day, at least, Brian had been better, beating Tiger by four strokes during one of the qualifying rounds. This was the keepsake he took home.

McCann's professional career even started auspiciously. He earned his playing card by finishing a strong seventh at the Canadian Tour's fall qualifying school. Then, from out of nowhere, came the troubles of the past summer. "I developed some faults in my swing that I'd never seen before," he said, sounding as mystified as a weekend hack. "Suddenly I didn't know where the ball was going, and I had no idea how to fix it."

Brian failed to requalify at Q-school that autumn. Now, out of grim necessity, all his efforts were pointed toward the spring qualifier in Kamloops the second week of May, toward resurrecting the dream of a playing career he'd been nurturing ever since he entered his first tournament at the age of 10.

For the past four months he had been seen at the dome every weekday, faithfully doing the drills prescribed for him by a coach in Florida. The goal was to quiet his swing, making it more consistent by eliminating all unnecessary movement. Brian meant to find out if Ben Hogan had it right when he said, "Outwork everyone and you become the best."

Like most professionals, who are rarely asked to pay for a round of golf or practice time at a range, Brian came and went at the dome for free. Cam Stuart knew his history and respected what he was trying to achieve. In the greater scheme of things, what was the cost of a few hundred hours' worth of mat time to Air Athletics compared to the satisfaction of helping launch—or rather, relaunch—a Canadian golfing career?

FROM THE MOMENT I FIRST stepped into the dome, everyone I met—from Cam Stuart and Jack Sasseville to the part-time teenage help pushing brooms—insisted that I absolutely had to get to know Shelley Cook, the unanimous choice as the golf bubble's most unforgettable character.

For all who entered, the dome offered refuge from a cold and temporarily golfless landscape. But for Shelley, one of Canada's leading stuntwomen, it meant much more. For several precious weeks late every winter, the Oakville dome was where Shelley pursued an obsession with the game that had at times threatened to overwhelm her life.

Though fighting the lingering effects of the flu, Shelley arrived so early the morning of our first meeting that she took it upon herself to open the restaurant-lounge. She flicked on the light, brewed herself a pot of coffee and then sat down at a table to enjoy the quiet before hitting the mats. A while later Cam joined her for breakfast, and other employees and regulars came over to say hello as they arrived.

Shelley was in a nostalgic mood when we talked a few hours later. "I started coming to the dome four years ago this month," she said with the clarity of a woman recalling her wedding anniversary. "For my money, this place is the best thing that ever happened to the QEW."

Blue-eyed and fine-featured, with a curly mop of shoulder-length blond hair, Shelley, a trim five foot seven, appeared entirely too delicate for someone who for the better part of 20 years had made her living crashing cars and taking fiery freefalls out of windows. In television productions and on the sets of big- and small-budget feature films, the 36-year-old had put her life on the line hundreds of times.

Shelley told me she had worked 300 days out of the past year, which is enough for anyone, but far too much in her line of work. Now, as usually happened in late winter, she was enjoying a relatively peaceful time before the production units arrived back in Toronto (or Hollywood North, as local boosters like to call it) for the start of the spring shoots.

"Every spare minute I have, I'm here," Shelley said of the dome. As many as 20 days in February. Eight or nine days already to this point in mid-March. And when she counted days, she meant full days. Her visits often lasted eight hours or more. Shelley, who is single, usually came alone. But sometimes she invited along her golfing friends in the stunt profession. She had also brought the nephews and nieces she dotes on, her mother, her grandmother and even her standard poodle, Blackjack.

"When you start bringing your grandmother and your dog, I guess you know a place has become home," Shelley said, laughing.

She always arrived with a firm plan of her day's activities. That morning Shelley had spent half her time hitting balls with one hand. She felt the drill helped teach her to keep her head down, and that enduring its tedium improved her ability to concentrate.

Even the hardest-working touring professionals, who hit between 200 and 300 balls a day to stay sharp, come off as slackers compared to Shelley. George Knudson himself, who practised till his hands bled, would have been awed by her single-minded determination.

"I've already hit 600 balls today," Shelley said matter-of-factly. "The only reason I haven't hit more is that I've got the flu. Most days I hit around 1,500 and some days I go as high as 3,000."

The really fun part of her days at the dome are the hours she sets aside to play simulated rounds of golf off the mat. In her mind's eye, she might be at Royal Woodbine, Lionhead, Angus Glen or any of a handful of other Southern Ontario courses she plays as often as she can during the summer. "I have a memory for golf like you would not believe," boasted Shelley, who in both her real and imagined rounds shoots in the high 70s. "I play shot by shot, club by club, hole by hole, one through 18. Everything except for putting."

Always a tomboy, Shelley has been obsessed with sports from her earliest memories of growing up in her hometown of St. Catharines, about 70 miles west along the QEW from Toronto. For years her first love was baseball. Shelley played softball, fastball and slow pitch at the highest levels. She represented Ontario and Canada at dozens of international tournaments and was offered baseball scholarships by several American universities.

Shelley didn't pick up a golf club until she was 20. But within weeks she found herself so enthralled with the game that she left behind her family and friends and a budding career as a stunt-woman to move to Florida for the winter and devote herself to golf full-time.

"I found a place to live with other golfers and started hanging around a range near the Tampa airport," Shelley remembered. "I'd start hitting balls at 6:30 in the morning and still be out there at 8:30 at night. I couldn't think of anything but golf. I went from a 36-handicap to a six in a matter of months."

Moderation is not a concept with which Shelley is familiar. When she tries something new, it's not enough that she be good at it, she has to be great—or as near to great as her natural ability combined with superhuman effort will allow.

"I'm a real individual and I like to do things the way I like to do them," Shelley said. "Ever since I was a kid, I've tended to pick the hard road."

Like the combustible John Daly, with whom she identifies, Shelley wears her emotions on her sleeve. "I am so tough on myself, an absolute perfectionist," she confided. "I'm getting better now, but in the past I cried on the course in frustration dozens of times. If the shot wasn't perfect, I'd pick up a club and . . . I mean, that club would be a hundred yards out of here."

The reason Shelley cares so much is that like others who see the game's complexities as a metaphor for life, she's convinced that somehow, someday, golf will give her a new sense of perspective and calm. "I have this feeling that the discipline I put into my game will help me survive both the good and the bad of whatever lies ahead."

During those early days in Florida, golf's rigid dress code and other rules of etiquette helped smooth the rough edges of a young woman whose standard wardrobe when she started playing was short-shorts, a tube top and sneakers. Naturally, Shelley attracted attention wherever she went.

The Tampa driving range she frequented happened to back onto the spring training complex of baseball's Cincinnati Reds. During breaks from her training routine, Shelley often stood by the range's back fence, watching the big-leaguers work out. One day she struck up a conversation with a tall man of about 50 wearing a Reds' uniform.

"You play golf?" Shelley asked.

"Well, I try," he said.

"Tell you what. I'll teach you to play golf if you throw me a few balls in the batting cage."

Thus began Shelley's friendship with Reds' pitching coach Jim Kaat, a former all-star who won 283 games during 25 seasons in the big leagues.

"It was great. Golf and baseball, my two favourite things in the world," she recalled. "I'd teach Jim what I was learning from the golf pro I was working with and in return he'd throw batting practice to me and let me shag flys for the team."

Through Kaat, Shelley also met Johnny Bench and baseball bad boy Pete Rose, both former Cincinnati greats, who invited her to play with them in a pro-am.

Shelley, more one of the guys than just another pretty girl, fell effortlessly into these friendships, which were based on a shared love of sports. One day at the range she met Theo Bell, a star wide receiver with the NFL's Tampa Bay Buccaneers. In exchange for Shelley's teaching him how to hit his driver, Bell indulged his new pal by throwing long spirals to her from the 50-yard line at the local football stadium.

Working to the point of exhaustion at the range, Shelley exulted in her rapidly improving golf game until one day she slammed into a wall even her iron will couldn't budge. "Suddenly I just stopped getting better," Shelley remembered of her date with a destiny inevitably faced by every golfer. "My biggest weakness was my putting. I hit the ball like a two-handicap and putted like a 15."

Not having taken up the game until the age of 20, Shelley was never foolish enough to believe she had a future as a playing pro. Rather, her goal in going to Florida had been purely to test the extreme limits of her golfing ability.

After two winters in Tampa, Shelley returned home badly burnt out. Though she was still an avid golfer, the game quickly became more of a torment than she cared to bear. One day, while playing with her father, Shelley snapped a 7-iron over her back in frustration. Her father, shaking his head sadly, suggested that such a reaction was neither normal nor healthy.

"You know what? You're right," Shelley answered, seeing things clearly for maybe the first time in two years. "I hate this game."

She didn't pick up her clubs again for another seven years. In the meantime, she concentrated her energy on a flourishing career as a stuntwoman, which had begun with a fluke encounter with the actor Ed Asner during a trip to Los Angeles when she was 16. Intent on seeing all the sights, Shelley and her boyfriend, who together had hitchhiked all the way from St. Catharines, met Asner when they were apprehended by security guards after trying to scale the gates of Universal Studios, which was shut down by a production strike.

The guards were about to call the police when Asner, who was the head of the screen guild picketing Universal, happened along and intervened on their behalf.

"Aw, they're just kids," the man famous as Lou Grant growled to the guards. "Give them a break."

The actor figured Shelley for just another starry-eyed girl dreaming of becoming a movie star. But no, Shelley told Asner after he'd secured their release, she craved a life of action. If anything, she'd like to become a stunt double.

Asner gave Shelley the number of Dwayne Mclean, one of Canada's leading stuntmen, with whom Asner had worked during a Toronto shoot. Befriended and guided by Mclean, Shelley quickly became one of the country's busiest stunt performers.

Shelley crashed and rolled cars, buses and trucks, flung herself out of windows from as high as 90 feet and had been set ablaze hundreds of times. Even after all that, the self-confessed adrenaline junkie still loved her work. "The best is being set on fire," Shelley said, her blue eyes turning dreamy. "It's such a rush! The first time they lit me up I was so pumped I actually heard a ringing in my ears."

Colleagues call her the Chameleon for her uncanny ability to look like the famous actresses for whom she stands in. She has worked with such disparate physical types as Carol Burnett, Kathy Bates, Olympia Dukakis and Mira Sorvino. "I mean, Mira Sorvino is five foot ten, with long, straight brown hair and a bust out to here," Shelley said, describing that particular metamorphosis. "But I put my lifts on and my fake boobs and my nice wig and Mira looked at me and said, 'I cannot believe how much we look alike!'"

To vent her pent-up energy after quitting golf, Shelley began playing baseball again with the same group of women she had started out with as a teenager.

"When you gals become old fat chicks who can't run and won't slide, I'm not playing any more," Shelley informed her mostly older teammates upon her return. By her cold reckoning, that day finally arrived during the summer of 1994. Shelley quit the team and soon after pulled out her golf clubs, having at last accepted the inevitable.

The truth is, no other sport could offer anything close to what Shelley got from golf—the opportunity to challenge her fiercest opponent, herself, for as long and as hard and, thanks to a wintertime haven like the Oakville dome, as often as her perfectionist soul demanded.

First to arrive in the morning, she is also sometimes the last to leave the dome at night, even helping the staff to tidy up before making her way home. One night Shelley, who is fiercely protective of her domain, shooed away a group of rowdy young soccer players who had snuck over from the smaller dome. "The kids began hacking balls at the side of the bubble, where there isn't any netting to protect the seams," she remembered. "I said, 'Hey, guys, this is *my* dome. Knock it off!'"

Shelley enjoys playing up the natural rivalry between the dome's golf and soccer factions. On nights when the range is closed early and transformed into a soccer field for adult players, she always leads the chorus of good-natured booing when they come onto the field.

By now it was late in the afternoon and Shelley and I had talked for better than two hours. She had been at the dome since shortly after dawn. When I noticed her start to fidget, I thought she might finally be ready to go home, have a bowl of soup and nurse her flu.

"Go home?" Shelley said, surprised by the question. "What would I do at home except go crazy from boredom?"

Instead, she was heading for her favourite mat, number 19, smack in the middle of the range's lower level, where she planned to simulate a full 18 holes at Royal Woodbine, one of her favourite courses.

A while later, passing her on my way out, I caught her eye as she was reloading and asked her where she was in her round.

"On the sixth," Shelley said happily. "I just hit a great drive. It's a beautiful sunny day and so far I'm having one of my best rounds of the season."

CHAPTER 7

EUROPE AT PAR

EVERY MIDDLE-AGED GOLFER who ever dreamed of autumn years of fairway glory has played alongside Bill Hardwick and Doug Robb, two Canadians who found their bliss on the European Senior Tour.

During the final round of the 1998 Ryder Senior Classic in England's Stratford-upon-Avon, Hardwick, a 57-year-old former Toronto businessman, produced the five-hole burst of a lifetime—birdie, eagle, birdie, birdie, birdie—on the first five holes and went on to shoot a course-record 63 in clinching his first tour victory.

"What made it all the more incredible was that the win came on Father's Day, and I'd recently become a grandfather for the first time," remembered Hardwick, who outplayed a star-studded field that included Britain's Tony Jacklin and Spain's Jose Maria Canizares. "No matter what happens now, I've done it. I'm so grateful that it finally happened for me."

For Doug Robb of Abbotsford, British Columbia, the full realization that he had turned his own mid-life fantasy into reality sank in while he explored the sights of Paris with his wife, Adeline, after having tied for first place at the European Senior Tour's Q-school on the Calais coast. To celebrate, the Robbs immediately hopped on a train for the French capital, a city neither of them had ever seen.

Almost the moment they arrived, the rain clouds that had followed them since their arrival on the continent parted, and the City of Light sparkled like a jewel while they took in the Louvre and Luxembourg Gardens and dined in quaint outdoor cafés. "It was magic," recalled Robb, a 53-year-old who rebuilt his game after having actually quit playing golf for several years in the 1980s. "At first I was numbed by what had happened. But by the time we got to Paris we were both high with excitement. Everything we'd hoped for was about to come true. It was as if we had the licence to be kids again."

Bill Hardwick and Doug Robb have found a home on a tour that has grown in importance with every year since its formation in 1992. The European Senior Tour (organized by the European PGA Tour) averages 18 to 20 events a season, with prize money ranging from approximately $245,000 to $367,000. Internationally famous golfers like Gary Player and Bob Charles make appearances, and most tournament fields include 15 or more former Ryder Cup players, each hoping to carve out a lucrative late career on a circuit that includes some of Europe's best watering holes.

Ageing golf fans have gratefully embraced both the European Senior Tour and North America's Senior PGA Tour for allowing them to continue following the idols of their youth. But best of all, the senior tours give all middle-aged golfers—especially the fortunate few blessed with actual talent—permission to dream of one day finally making the big time themselves.

Other golfers have come from out of nowhere to do it, so why not them?

Just a few years ago, Bill Hardwick, now one of the stars of the European Senior Tour, manufactured windows for a living, while at the same time Doug Robb was a partner in a golf equipment distributorship. Several previously unheralded players—including Walter Hall, who used to sell appliances in North Carolina, and former club pros Jim Albus and Tom Wargo—emerged from obscurity to make millions on the Senior PGA Tour.

Of the two tours, the Senior PGA is both the richest and deepest in talent, having exploded in growth from a mere two-card event in 1980 to today's 44-tournament behemoth offering purses totalling more than U.S.$53 million.

But Hardwick and Robb have found that the European Senior Tour more than makes up in life experiences what it lacks in prize money.

While roaring around Europe in his BMW, which he parks at his flat in a posh London neighbourhood, Bill Hardwick has been known to take a leisurely detour through the Bordeaux wine country, or to dash off on a whim to explore a historic château or castle. The palaces and fortresses of Europe have become a particular fascination of his. Bill has also expanded his palate considerably, evolving from a basic meat-and-potatoes man to a point that he now doesn't actually wince at the sight of herring for breakfast when the tour stops in Sweden.

After four years on the tour, Hardwick, a tall man with a red-cheeked face who exudes good health, had even picked up a faint British accent, and peppered his speech with expressions such as "Isn't that lovely?" and "Brilliant."

"I've tried not to get an accent, but it just sort of happened," Bill told me sheepishly. "My wife, Pat, and our two boys are always kidding me about it."

In recent years the tour's itinerary, which changes annually, has featured stops in Britain, Ireland, Scotland, Norway, Sweden, France, Holland, Switzerland, Germany, Spain, Monaco, Italy, Greece and Turkey. Everywhere the players are pampered and fed like sporting royalty. Sumptuous breakfast and lunch buffets are almost always offered, and sometimes a dinner banquet as well. Many tournaments, especially on the Continent, are held at luxury resorts, where players and their wives enjoy free run of the property. Some events provide courtesy cars.

Then there are all the fascinating people one meets. At the 1999 Monte Carlo Invitational, Doug and Adeline Robb partied through a long Riviera night with Prince Albert and actors Kevin Costner and Robert Wagner, all of whom played in the pro-am that preceded the tournament. Doug partnered Costner for a hole, and Wagner, known as R.J. to his friends, insisted on buying him a drink.

"Adeline and I would look at each other as if to say, What's going on here?" Doug recalled, the wonder of it still in the voice of the robustly handsome and gracefully balding grandfather. "Believe me, this was not a lifestyle we were used to."

SOMETIMES, AS HE TUCKS into another fabulous smorgasbord or explores a castle in an enchanted setting, Bill Hardwick can't help reflecting on the twisting path that led him from the Toronto suburbs to the better fairways of Europe.

Hardwick grew up just west of Toronto in the town of Port Credit. At the age of eight, he and a buddy, hoping to earn enough money for the movies and popcorn, started caddying at the nearby Mississauga Golf and Country Club. Instantly bitten by the golf bug, Hardwick eagerly shagged balls for the lessons conducted by head pro Gordon Brydson, who rewarded the boy by giving him pointers.

I was struck by how Hardwick's start in the game was almost identical to Marlene Stewart Streit's beginnings with her coach Gord McInnis in the Ontario town of Fonthill.

Hardwick nodded his agreement. "If you did a survey, you'd probably find that's how most golfers over a certain age got started—first caddying, then being taken under the wing of the club professional."

There's another connection between Hardwick and Streit. "I caddied for her back in the fifties," Bill remembered with a smile. "I was the only caddy she knew willing to cut school to go to tournaments. Marlene was so grateful she'd even pick me up at my house."

After finishing high school, Bill worked as an assistant pro at two Toronto-area clubs, Lakeview and York Downs. By the time he turned 25, he stood ready, at least in his own mind, to assume the position of head pro. The problem was Hardwick still looked about 14. "I was one of those guys cursed, I guess you could say, with looking very, very young," he said wryly, pointedly running his fingers through a now-sparse crop of blond hair. "No one wanted to hire me, and I was stuck as an assistant, a job that in those days paid starvation wages."

Eager to marry and start a family with Pat, a petite and vivacious blonde he met roller skating, Bill decided to leave golf and find a "real" job, but with the intention of one day getting back into the game he loved.

Hardwick joined a company that manufactured windows, learning the business from the ground up. Then he and a partner started their own company, Hardwick & Florian Windows, which flourished for more than a dozen years. Bill and Pat lived in a big house in the suburbs, joined a private golf club, enjoyed vacations at their mobile home in Florida and eventually sent their sons to prestigious universities in the United States.

The best thing about life as a businessman was that Hardwick found he played considerably more golf than he ever did as an assistant pro, when he spent most of his days in the pro shop. His game grew sharper with every passing summer. After a wait of seven and a half years to regain his amateur status, Bill racked up a string of successes in the amateur ranks, including victory in the Ontario Champion of Champions, a competition for club champions.

Bill and Pat still talked of his going back to golf full-time, though no longer as a club professional, a job that paid a fraction of what he pulled in from the window company. Now the plan was for him to one day sell the business and try to make it onto the rich Senior PGA Tour in the United States.

The Hardwicks' two boys, Stephen and Greg, as fanatical about the game as their old man, also encouraged Bill to give the senior tour a try. "It was a dream we talked about regularly at the dinner table, something we shared as a family," Bill said. Today, both sons make their living in the golf industry. Stephen is a course superintendent and Greg a club pro.

When the recession of the early 1990s hit the window business, Bill thought about selling out and taking up his golf clubs full-time. But after all the years of planning and dreaming, Hardwick hesitated. The nest egg he and Pat had carefully built up to finance his golf career had shrunk alarmingly with the business's decline. They also took a big hit when they sold their house at what proved to be the worst possible time in the market. If Bill did manage to qualify for the senior tour, he'd have to make money almost from the start, or else find another way to earn a living. Maybe it would be smarter to try to build the business back up first.

Then, as good wives sometimes do, Pat gave her husband a solid kick in the behind.

"Bill, we've always talked about this," she sternly reminded him. "Now's the time. If it doesn't work out, you've at least tried."

"I couldn't have done it without Pat," Bill acknowledged gratefully. "To be married to an athlete who's away for weeks and maybe months at a time was going to be a big adjustment for her. Unless a couple is working toward this together, it just won't happen."

In 1993 and again the next year, Hardwick joined about 1,200 other senior golfers attempting to qualify for the handful of spots open on the Senior PGA Tour. Both times he fell short.

"It's such a crap shoot," Hardwick said of the tour's Q-school. "Most of the spots on the tour automatically go to players who have graduated from the regular PGA Tour. That leaves many of the world's best senior golfers all trying for about eight full exemptions. If you're just slightly off your game, there go your chances."

It's a selection process that still offended Hardwick's sense of fair play. "The top players on the European Senior Tour—Jerry

Bruner, Alan Tapie, Neil Coles, Eddie Polland—would all kill on the American tour," he insisted. "But they can't get on. It's almost a closed shop."

From 1993 to 1995, Bill played on the second tier Senior Series, a brutally competitive circuit for golfers who, like him, couldn't quite perform the miracle demanded to make it onto the top tour.

When Hardwick finished seventh in his first Senior Series event, he wondered why on earth he had sold windows for so long. He kept on improving, always earning more than enough to pay his way and to keep the dream of even bigger paydays alive.

Hardwick's toughest adjustment was learning to maintain his focus even on a bad day. "As an amateur you just sort of wash it off and say tomorrow's going to be better," Bill said. "But as a pro, the challenge is to salvage what you can out of every round, because the putt you miss Friday morning is going to cost you money come Sunday afternoon."

Soon it became apparent that the Senior Series, which eventually went bankrupt, was a career dead end. After Hardwick kept hearing good things about the fledgling European Senior Tour, he fired off his application. The tour, which hadn't yet organized qualifying schools, answered back that Hardwick was welcome, but he would have to pre-qualify for each event until he earned a sufficiently high standing on its Order of Merit to gain his exemptions.

Once more Bill hesitated to take the fateful step. He had never even been to Europe before. He didn't speak a foreign language. The costs of travelling and living abroad would be prohibitive unless he enjoyed the same immediate success he had on the Senior Series.

It was Pat who again stepped up and gave her husband the

final push he needed to get on the plane and go. "Europe was just too exciting an opportunity to let slip away," she told me. "Bill felt certain he had the game to succeed and I believed in him. He had to go."

LIKE HIS PARTNER ON THE European Senior Tour, Doug Robb would ultimately need a not-so-gentle nudge from his wife before making his own leap across the great water hazard. If anything, Robb's decision was even more difficult than Hardwick's. He had been away from competitive golf for so long.

Born and raised in Vancouver, Doug began playing golf at the age of seven, urged on by his father's passion for the game. Stan Leonard, the greatest of all West Coast golfers, who won three times on the PGA Tour and twice finished in the top four at the Masters, coached him as a boy. In 1966, when Robb was 16, he took top honours in one of North America's most prestigious junior tournaments, the Pacific North-West. Two years later he became the assistant pro at Vancouver's Langara Golf Club.

Alongside such Canadian golfing legends as Moe Norman, Wilf Homenuik, Bob Panasik and a young Dave Barr, Robb was a regular on the old Peter Jackson Tour during the early 1970s. Occasionally, George Knudson would stray from the bright lights of the big circuit in the United States to make an appearance on his home turf.

Like everyone who played with him, Robb is awed by the memory of Knudson's ability to routinely make what appeared to be impossible shots.

"I saw him make one on the par-three eighth hole at the Quilchena Golf Club in Richmond, B.C., that I still can't believe," Doug recalled. "George started by hitting an absolutely terrible tee shot—a 2-iron that hooked way left over some small trees and landed in a deep ditch, about 40 yards from the pin. I mean, this ditch was deep with a really steep slope. In front of the ditch, nothing but deep rough stretched all the way to a green-side bunker. I couldn't see that George even had a shot. But he grinned that little grin of his and pulled out his putter. Setting up left-handed, he took a huge swipe at the ball. The ball ran up the bank, over the rough, bounced over the trap and stopped about four feet from the cup.

"You know, people always say that George couldn't putt," Doug added. "But all the other elements of his game were so great, he didn't need to putt that well to win."

Then there was the enigmatic man-child Moe Norman, another shot-making genius, whom the galleries he astonished christened "Pipeline Moe" for the unfailing consistency of his drives. Norman played faster than any man alive, setting up in his stiff-legged, bolt-upright stance, sneaking a quick look down the fairway, then swinging through with a long reach that ended with arms aimed straight as a rifle at his target. Before the ball had even dropped to earth, Norman was off in hot pursuit, eagerly antici-pating the undiminished pleasure of doing it all again.

So widespread is Moe Norman's fame as the purest of ball strikers that when Doug Robb joined the European Senior Tour in the spring of 1999, the first thing former Ryder Cup captain Bernard Gallacher asked him was, "Do you know Moe Norman? Are all the stories true about how well he hits the ball?"

Indeed they are, replied Doug, who regaled Gallacher with the tale of the practice round he once shared with Norman before a tournament in Calgary. "The 12th hole, a par five, had a power line running across the fairway about 160 yards out from the tee," Doug began. "Moe took out his driver and winged his ball off the power line. Then he teed up and did it again. Then he hit the power line a third time."

It goes without saying that Robb was dumbstruck by what he had seen. "It wasn't even as if Moe was trying to hit the power line," he said. "It was just that his swing was so perfectly grooved that each ball took off on exactly the same trajectory. After the third ball, Moe put the driver back in his bag and took out a 3-wood. This time the ball missed the power line. Moe turned to me and said, 'Well, I guess this is a 3-wood shot.'"

Though he never earned more than $12,000 in any of his years on the Peter Jackson Tour, Doug counts his experiences with Norman, Knudson and the rest as priceless. For most of two summers he joined Wilf Homenuik as a passenger in Moe Norman's Cadillac while they criss-crossed Canada from one tournament to the next. Norman, a notoriously bad driver, had the unique habit of getting into the left lane and stubbornly staying there, his high beams switched on.

"'Left Lane Moe,' I called him," Robb said, chuckling at the youthful folly of driving with a crazy man. "Moe didn't care who flashed at him with their lights or who cursed him or how many people slammed on their brakes. He refused to budge from the left lane. Moe thought he owned it."

During a break from the tour to build up his bank balance in a job with a Vancouver brokerage house, Doug met Adeline, a stunning brunette employed as a telephone operator. After a brief courtship, they married and Doug rejoined the tour, this time travelling the country with Adeline and his brother Dan, who squeezed into their Volkswagon bug as the designated caddy.

Robb thought about trying his luck at the PGA Tour's Q-school, but then the first of four daughters arrived and the idea faded as he tried to figure out how to best provide for his family.

Anyway, given his limited success on the Canadian circuit, Doug wasn't at all convinced he could go much further as a player.

In 1975, Robb quit the Peter Jackson Tour to become the head pro at the Ledgeview Golf and Country Club in Abbotsford. Four years later, he left to join his brother-in-law in the construction of an executive par-three course and driving range in nearby Langley. Doug designed the course and ran the operation until he sold out in 1985 to enter into a sales partnership with Mitsushiba, a Japanese line of golf equipment then virtually unheard of in Canada.

Over the next nine years, while helping to build up the Mitsushiba brand, Robb rarely touched a golf club outside of a sales room, a bum shoulder having drained his enthusiasm for playing the game.

The catalyst for Doug's return as a player was a pro-am at his old club, Ledgeview, which he felt obligated to attend. Embarrassed by his performance, Robb resolved not to let the game defeat him. He began whacking balls at the local driving range and soon saw real progress. Most encouraging of all, the time off had largely healed his shoulder.

In 1994, when Robb sold his partnership in the Mitsushiba distributorship, he got down to serious work on his swing. Before long, Doug was playing so well that he began to think he might have a future as a senior golfer. A top 10 finish in his first Senior Championship of Canada further boosted his confidence. If things kept progressing, maybe he'd try his luck at the Senior PGA Tour's qualifying school.

Then, like Bill Hardwick before him, Robb began to hear wonderful things about the glamorous new European Senior Tour. For years Adeline had been after him to take a trip to Europe, but Doug, a confirmed homebody, had always resisted.

Now Adeline pleaded with her husband to give the tour's Q-school a try. The kids were grown up, there was money in the bank, and if they weren't prepared to go off on an adventure like this now, Adeline demanded to know, when would they ever be?

Talking it over, Doug and his wife agreed that whatever he did in golf from that point on had to be fun for both of them. If he didn't succeed in Europe, what the heck, at least they'd have seen some of the sights together.

Early that spring of 1998, Robb sent off his application form to tour headquarters. For the next six months he haunted the driving range of the Redwoods Golf Club in Langley. "I must have hit at least 30,000 balls trying to get ready," Doug estimated. "One day I ran into one of the owners of the club and complimented him on the quality of the facility. 'You know,' he said, 'we have a golf course here, too. You should think about trying it sometime.'"

Robb's jitters grew as he counted down the days to their departure. "At first, I tried to treat the whole thing as a kind of lark," he said. "But the more I worked at my game and thought about it, the more I wanted to succeed. When we got on the plane to go, I honestly had no idea if I even had a chance."

NOT SINCE HIS WEDDING DAY had Bill Hardwick been so nervous as when he stepped off the airplane at London's Heathrow Airport upon his arrival in Europe in the spring of 1996. Having never been outside of North America, he faced entirely uncharted territory.

"I was standing in the airport thinking, Now what am I supposed to do? I had to rent a car, and then drive it on the wrong side of the road to my first tournament, all the while trying not to kill myself or somebody else."

Pat, who would have loved to be there with him, remained behind in Toronto, where she worked as the manager of a nursing home. Though the job paid extremely well, within a year Pat would give it up to take a seasonal position in the office of the Seaton Golf Club, not far from their home. That way she and Bill could at least spend winters together at their mobile home in Florida, where he annually retreats to continue working on his game.

"That's the type of thing that separates good marriages from bad," Bill said appreciatively of the sacrifices made by his wife. "Like I said before, I couldn't have done any of this without her."

Hardwick soon made friends and got comfortable in his new surroundings. Some foreign players on the PGA tours in the United States, including Australian Greg Norman, have complained that they at first found American players aloof, treating them as interlopers come to steal their money. That definitely wasn't Hardwick's experience in Europe, where he was instantly accepted as an equal on a tour that prides itself on its multiculturalism.

Bill thrilled to the challenge of testing his skill on the links courses of Scotland and Ireland, and on the layouts of wildly varying quality at the tour stops in England and across the Continent. In Greece and Turkey, where golf was only just starting to catch on, the greens were often barely more than bumpy patches of brown. None of the courses he visited anywhere in Europe had adopted the North American mania for walk-mowing fairways, trimming back rough and scalping greens until they play so fast that golfers can almost skate on them.

European golf was designed for hardier souls. In the British Isles especially, Bill often found himself playing in unrelenting downpours driven by gale-force winds off the icy Atlantic, conditions that undoubtedly would have seen the round cancelled back home.

When friends in Canada heard that Bill had carded a round in the mid-70s, they shook their heads sadly and said his game must be slipping. "What they couldn't see were the conditions the tournament was played in," Bill said impatiently. "On a tough day, with heavy rain and high winds, you might come off the course with a 74, but that would probably be the equivalent of shooting 67 in good conditions."

Despite the weather, course conditions and all the other changes he faced, Hardwick enjoyed a wholly satisfying rookie season on the European Senior Tour. He finished 30th on the Order of Merit after playing in only seven of that year's schedule of 12 tournaments. Hardwick missed just one cut in the eight pre-qualifying rounds he played.

The next year Bill continued to improve, moving up a notch to 29th spot on the Order of Merit. Newspapers and golf magazines back home began to note his achievements, one writer calling Hardwick the "best-kept secret in Canadian golf."

DOUG AND ADELINE ROBB SPENT a few days vacationing in London before boarding the ferry for France and the tour's qualifying school in the Calais town of Hardelot, which is not, as a wag suggested, the birthplace of Viagra. Taking a train through the Chunnel would have been the easier way to go, but Adeline, who wanted to see all the sights, insisted on a ferry from Dover.

Alas, the weather was dreadful all the way. "Bam, slam . . . twenty-foot waves were hitting the boat so hard you could hear them crashing against the hull," Robb grimly recounted. "Poor Adeline spent the entire time in the loo.

"We saw the sights, all right. Four walls and the porcelain bowl."

The downpour followed them to Hardelot, then rarely let up

throughout the four rounds of Q-school. Each day the winds blew in at more than 50 miles per hour. By the final round, groundskeepers removed water from the greens with squeegees.

While other golfers huddled under their umbrellas and cursed the late-autumn skies, Doug felt certain the miserable conditions actually gave him an advantage. "Who knows how to play in the rain better than someone from Vancouver?" he asked logically. "The weather also helped me in another way. For the first two days, just when the pressure should have been the worst, I was so busy trying to stay warm and dry that I didn't have time to be nervous."

His confidence had already received a boost when he arrived in Hardelot and read the list of 177 players trying for their cards. Though there were golfers from more than a dozen countries, some from as far away as South Africa and Malaysia, except for American Alan Tapie, who had once played on the PGA Tour, Robb hadn't heard of a single one.

"I already knew the European Senior Tour had a lot of outstanding golfers, guys like Tommy Horton and Brian Barnes and other big stars," Doug told me. "So I certainly wasn't underestimating the difficulty of the tour. But I have to confess that when I went down the lineup at Q-school, I thought, Hey, this shouldn't be too difficult."

By the end of his first round, Robb saw how wrong he had been. The no-names he dismissed turned out to include some of the most talented players he had ever competed against. Not that it much mattered. Doug played so unbelievably well that week he might have prevailed over a field that included Jack Nicklaus, Lee Trevino, Tom Watson and a host of the world's other top senior golfers. He was that hot.

"Hardelot was probably the only golf tournament I've ever

played where I didn't have a single negative thought while standing over the ball," Doug said, still marvelling. "It was like Moe Norman once said to me, 'To be successful you have to play golf as if you're wearing blinkers.' In other words, you have to block out everything except the shot at hand. That whole week I had the blinkers on."

Robb was in the hunt for the top spot right from the start, carding an opening round score of 75, which he reckoned would have been the equivalent of a 66 in better weather. The next day, when the elements angrily conspired to limit play to 15 holes for all competitors, he shot an "even par" 61. Final rounds of 73 and 74 in the unrelenting downpour earned Robb a tie for first place with Gordon MacDonald, a building contractor from Scotland.

Adeline, too nervous to watch Doug play, paced the floor of their hotel room the entire tournament. So many of their hopes for the future depended on his success. When Doug entered the final round just one stroke off the lead, she felt as jumpy as a cat. All day Adeline constantly watched the clock on the wall, trying to guess where her husband might be in his round.

By late afternoon Adeline knew it had to all be over, yet Doug still hadn't returned to the hotel or even telephoned. After a while, no longer able to stand the suspense, Adeline called the golf course. The girl who answered in the pro shop couldn't speak English, nor could Adeline speak French. With painful deliberateness, Adeline tried to make her request clear. "Doug Robb. . . . Qualifying school. . . . How did he do?"

Finally, the girl understood. "Doug Robb? Oh, he win," she said. With the news, Adeline let out a whoop and both she and the French girl started laughing and clapping over the phone.

"The tension is always worse for the people who aren't playing," mused Doug, who had been detained at the club by officials and reporters and other players offering their congratulations. "I had a way to get rid of my stress. For Adeline, it all had to stay locked inside."

Though Doug caught hell from his wife for not calling, he had long since been forgiven by the time they went out that evening for a celebratory dinner. The $5,000 cheque he received as his share of the first-place prize would just about pay the expenses for their entire European trip. After a couple of glasses of wine, the Robbs spontaneously decided to take the celebration on to Paris, where they couldn't help but view the sudden sunshine that greeted them as yet another sign of their incredible good fortune.

AS IT DOES TO ALL THOUGHTFUL travellers, Europe changed Bill Hardwick into a better, more interesting person. He developed an appreciation for fine wine and food, and he became fascinated by the architecture that constantly changed with the landscape.

The splendour of Europe was a far cry from anything Hardwick had seen during his apprenticeship on the old Senior Series in the United States. "America is so much the same," he said, shuddering at the memory of those uncivilized days. "The motels and hotels all look the same. The stores are all the same. The food is all the same. It seemed that even the names of cities we played in always ended the same—Nashville, Evansville. Sometimes I had to walk outside my motel and look at a signpost to figure out where I was."

Hardwick's most difficult adjustment was learning to live without Pat by his side for months at a time. "The golf and the competition is wonderful and I love it and I live off it, but it's a lonely life after you leave the golf course," he complained. "Being by yourself can really eat at you, especially if you're not playing well and have too much time to brood about your troubles."

In 1998, Bill's third summer on the tour, he finished 18th on the Order of Merit, a standing that translated into earnings of approximately $105,000. Appearances in pro-ams further boosted his income.

That year Hardwick enjoyed the victory he had been striving toward ever since he chucked his window business for the uncertain life of a tour pro. He'd had his chances to win before, but always fell just short.

Standing four shots back at the start of the third and final round of the Ryder Senior Classic, Bill still wasn't completely convinced that his time was at hand. Then came his phenomenal six-under-par burst over the Welcombe Golf Club's first five holes, and suddenly the Canadian stood in front of the pack at seven under.

"Now that was quite amazing," Bill recalled. "Starting off with a birdie gave me a big boost, but the eagle three that followed really got me going. The 4-iron second shot I hit on that hole from the back of a bunker to within three feet of the pin has to be the best shot I've ever made in my life. I've never had a series of holes like I had that day. It was really a beautiful feeling."

Hardwick's final-round score of 63 set a new course record and sealed a two-stroke victory over his nearest challengers, Englishman David Creamer and Italian Renato Compagnoli.

"Success begets success," Hardwick was convinced. "The near misses I'd had before were all part of the learning process. It's like baseball. Once you get up to bat a few times, sooner or later you're bound to get a hit."

A FOG OF HAPPINESS ENVELOPED Doug and Adeline during their return from Paris to Abbotsford. Then the full realization of what Doug's accomplishment would mean to both their lives hit home.

"It was like Holy cow! We've just qualified for the European Senior Tour," Doug remembered. "Then we panicked a little. We had to figure out what to take. What to leave. Think through our itinerary. Before we left for Q-school, we really hadn't considered everything involved if I actually did make it."

The Robbs' first thought was to relive the untamed days of their newly wedded youth on the old Peter Jackson Tour by renting a camper and driving to the various tournaments. That idea lasted only until a friend asked Doug and Adeline if they'd be interested in switching houses for the summer with an English couple he knew in Stratford-upon-Avon who were anxious to spend time with a daughter living in Vancouver. A home base in the heart of Shakespeare country, gateway to the legendary beauty of the Cotswolds, was an opportunity too good to refuse. At any rate, Doug wasn't at all certain his middle-aged back could withstand a bumpy summer on the road nearly so well as it had a quarter century before.

In his first weeks on the tour, Robb displayed the same focus and form that had swept him to victory in Hardelot. He finished well up in the standings in his first two tournaments, and had a shot at winning the third entering the final round at England's Millride Golf Club. Then, when he was still in sight of a second or third place finish as he teed it up on the 18th hole, Doug's game suddenly fell apart. A nightmarish triple bogey dropped him all the way down to 11th spot.

The memory of that one wretched hole haunted Doug for weeks. "I couldn't seem to get it out of my head," he said ruefully.

"I'd play well for most of a round and then have one bad hole. I really let the pressure get to me. Instead of just going out and enjoying the game, I'd get all wound up thinking about my score and where I stood in the standings."

A dawning realization of who he was up against each week on tour also contributed to Robb's insecurities. "Everywhere I looked I saw another former Ryder Cup player," he said, the cockiness of his first day at Q-school by then a distant memory. "Pretty soon I began to see those guys in my dreams."

Yet even during the worst of his slump, Robb never regretted for a moment his decision to join the European tour. Like Bill Hardwick, he felt grateful for the opportunity to play such wonderful courses as Britain's Wentworth and Northern Ireland's Royal Portrush, even in weather that might include rain and wind and cold and sunshine, sometimes all in the same round.

Every stop on the tour offered unforgettable new experiences. Doug and Adeline happily recalled the unrestrained opulence of their oceanfront hotel in the French resort town of Biarritz, where the dirty old men of the tour drooled shamelessly over the topless sunbathers. Also never to be forgotten was the exotic romance of the black-tie evening cruise down the Bosphorus laid on in Turkey for the players and their wives.

One of the Robbs' favourite memories was of the moonlit night they strolled hand in hand along the seafront in Monte Carlo to the gala dinner attended by Prince Albert, Robert Wagner, Kevin Costner and other celebrities.

Costner held court at the table next to theirs. "All the gorgeous young things were trying desperately to get his attention," Adeline told me, her heart still aflutter. "Oh, my God! I thought, staring at him. He really is cute. It's not just the camera. He has the cutest dimples."

Sometimes their new life seemed almost too incredible to be true. "How can I prove to the kids that this really happened," Adeline found herself thinking time and again. "I felt like bottling the moment and taking it home so we could share it with everyone."

But after a while, to their surprise, all the glitz started to strike Doug and Adeline as maybe too much of a good thing. They took a pass on the closing soirée in Monte Carlo to enjoy a quiet evening entirely on their own. "We finally said, 'Enough is enough,'" Doug remembered. "The whole experience started to seem slightly decadent." By now the Robbs didn't care if they ever again tasted caviar or foie gras or met another crown prince or movie star.

Doug realized that at heart he was really a very simple man. "All that stuff is great to a point," he said of the tour's glamorous side. "But my idea of a perfect day is to play a great course like Royal Portrush and afterwards go talk golf with the caddies."

APART FROM THE OCCASIONAL overdose of superficiality and the worry of packing on a few too many pounds at the buffet table, Bill Hardwick and Doug Robb agreed there is very little downside to life on the European Senior Tour.

Hardwick did confess to feelings of guilt over visiting places on his own he knew Pat had always wanted to see. Being a good husband, he did what he could. "When the tour visited Athens, I stayed in my room rather than go sightseeing," he said, proud of his sacrifice. "I wanted to save it for when Pat could be there to enjoy it with me."

"I think that's pretty sweet," Pat said adoringly of her husband. "Imagine saving the Parthenon just for me."

Pat usually joins Bill in Europe for two weeks in the summer, meeting at the small flat he rents in London. They hook up again in autumn after the tour ends and then extend Bill's season by travelling together to an even more exotic golfing destination. When I first met them, the Hardwicks had just returned from South Africa, where Bill played in four senior events. The year before, they had journeyed to Japan, where he competed in the Japanese Senior PGA championship.

Hardwick regarded these late-season trips as working vacations. "It's a way to let Pat share in the fun and for us to see new things together," he said. "I'm happy as long as I make my expenses, and in both Japan and South Africa I made more than enough to pay our way."

From the beginning, Doug and Adeline Robb viewed their European adventure as an opportunity to bring Doug's career in golf full cycle by finishing up almost the way they started out on the Peter Jackson Tour. Like a couple of moonstruck kids, they were together again on the open road—except this time they had signed aboard a tour offering slightly more fascinating stops than Dauphin, Manitoba, and Grande Prairie, Alberta.

If anything, Doug was kicking himself for not having had even more fun during his rookie campaign. The prolonged slump he suffered through after that blown opportunity at Millride not only eroded his confidence but took some of the shine off the trip. He put so much pressure on himself that going to the golf course started to seem like work. And unused to the weekly grind of tour life, Doug felt worn out long before the campaign's end.

Robb planned to conserve his strength and play no more than 12 tournaments in 2000, four fewer than the year before. Though this might cut into his winnings, money was never Doug's primary motivation for joining the tour. With official winnings of approximately $26,000 (placing him 61st on the Order of Merit), in addition to the $21,000 or so he pocketed in various pro-ams, Doug more than paid his expenses his first season. If things continued to go as well, he might play the tour another three or four years.

Any way he looked at it, Doug figured, he and Adeline had made out like bandits during their first season abroad. An Abbotsford travel agent estimated that if they had been over there strictly as tourists and paid for everything themselves — rent on the house in Stratford-upon-Avon, greens fees, air fares, car rentals, the gourmet meals and all the rest — the whole trip might have cost $250,000 or more.

Bill Hardwick, like his junior compatriot on the tour, hoped to play another three or more years in Europe. But with his 60th birthday looming at the conclusion of the 2000 season, Bill knew only too well that his time as a competitive golfer was running out.

"Golf is a funny game that way," he said grimly. "The difference in your game between the age of 25 and 40 isn't that big a deal. After that, though, the decline constantly accelerates. Now I'm playing against guys who are close to 50 and there's a big difference in how we play."

Hardwick's official earnings dropped to about $60,000 in 1999, placing him 41st on the Order of Merit. The best news was that unlike many senior golfers whose decline is marked by a significant loss of power, Bill was still hitting it long and straight off the tee, averaging drives of between 260 and 265 yards. He felt optimistic about coming back strongly. "One advantage I have is that with the years I've become a smarter golfer," he said. "I may still have another championship in me."

Hardwick found it hard to imagine one day having to give up

the London flat, the BMW and all the other familiar pleasures of the life he had built.

"I don't know how many middle-aged golfers dream of doing what I'm doing," Bill told me in parting. "All I can say is if it isn't their dream, they're missing out on a good one."

CHAPTER 8
GOLF LIKE AN EGYPTIAN

JUST AS ALEXANDER THE GREAT and Julius Caesar came, conquered and left their marks, Chris Miranda, a 25-year-old golf pro from Stoney Creek, Ontario, made his own not insignificant contribution to the rich tapestry of Egyptian life. For eight unforgettable months, Miranda served as the first head pro of the lavish new Royal Valley Golf Club in Luxor, helping to establish the kingdom of golf in the ancient land.

Luxor, which in antiquity was known as Thebes, is located 400 miles south of Cairo in the heart of the legendary Valley of the Kings.

Entombed here are scores of royalty, including Amenhotep, Ramses III, Queen Nefertiti and Tutankhamen, the last best remembered as the boy ruler King Tut. In their time, just as today, the mighty Nile River divides the living city on one side from the world's most elaborate necropolis on the other. Chris drank in the history every day on the way to work, asking his driver to slow down as first the obelisk and columns of Luxor temple came into view, and again when he spotted the even more imposing temple of Karnak, which was once the focus of power in all Egypt.

Then Miranda would shake the past from his thoughts and concentrate his energy on the maddeningly frustrating job of bringing golf to the Egyptian desert. Some days went so badly that he thought of buying a plane ticket back home. But every morning when Chris passed through the gates of the golf course and saw the beauty of what he was helping to create, he resolved to stay on.

Designed by American architect Arthur L. Davis and built at a cost of U.S.$12 million, the course — the first in Luxor and one of only a handful in the entire country — is a palm-tree-studded oasis stretching 6,735 yards from the tips. Miraculously, considering the sun-baked harshness of the surroundings, water ponds (fed by 11 deep wells) are featured on 10 holes. One huge pond runs from tee to green between the 10th and 18th holes, which are parallel-running par fives.

"My jaw just dropped when I first saw the golf course," recalled Chris, a sturdily built young man with a goatee and brown buzz-cut. "It's such a beautiful layout that I wouldn't be surprised to see it one day host a European Tour event."

Tulip Investments, the Egyptian financial group that developed the course, expects golf to take off in Luxor in a big way.

Local tourism is steadily building again in the aftermath of the 1997 massacre of 60 tourists by Islamic extremists at the temple of Queen Hatshepsut. And Egypt is fast becoming an especially popular destination among Asians, a vast market that includes many of the world's most rabid golfers. Located about 10 minutes from the airport and 25 minutes from the city centre, the Royal Valley Golf Club property will one day include a hotel complex.

Another selling point for local tourism is the absolute dependability of the weather. When Chris Miranda first arrived in October of 1998, Luxor hadn't seen a drop of rain in more than two years.

He'd read the ad for the Luxor posting in the Ontario PGA's in-house publication. Chris, who at the time was an assistant pro at the Glendale Golf and Country Club in Hamilton, recognized it as an opportunity not only to see the world, but to put his career on the fast track. It might be years before he got a chance to become a head pro locally.

The money wasn't hard to take either — about the equivalent of what a head pro with 10 years on the job might make over here. And the Egyptian who interviewed Chris over the telephone from Cairo assured him he would be paid in American dollars, which of course made the package even more attractive.

His interviewer painted a glowing picture of what awaited Miranda at the other end. Everything at the golf course was up and running, he assured him. The place couldn't possibly be in better shape. All they needed was the right man to steer the entire operation, from running the pro shop to overseeing food and beverage service in the clubhouse.

In the end, Chris beat out dozens of applicants from around the world. Though never quite certain why they chose him, he thought it might be that he was clearly so willing to make a new life in a foreign land. Chris held a romantic notion of himself as a born adventurer. His new employers told him they planned to build golf courses in South Africa and probably Dubai in the United Arab Emirates. They stressed that if things went well in Luxor, he could have his choice of their properties — or even possibly oversee the operations of them all.

Miranda took it as a sign of their faith in his abilities that they left the hiring of a course superintendent entirely to him. Chris, delighted to be able to take along someone he already knew and with whom he felt comfortable, gave the job to Ronan Goollily, who had been the assistant groundskeeper at Glendale.

A young man chasing his destiny, Miranda was still riding an emotional high during the long flight to Cairo, which was his first trip overseas. By the end of the short hop to Luxor he could barely contain his excitement. The first thing he did when he landed was to head straight for the golf course. And, sure enough, at first glance the Royal Valley Golf Club appeared every bit the desert miracle promised by his employers.

Emerald fairways cut a swath around and between palm trees and shimmering ponds, slicing the sand like a genie's carpet to the horizon. Miranda stood silently awestruck for several minutes, savouring it all.

But then, slowly, he realized that things were not quite as they were supposed to be. The clubhouse, which had been described to him as an extravagant affair in the style of an Egyptian temple, was as yet no more than a few cement foundation blocks in the sand. Chris's employers had assured him that the clubhouse was both built and fully operational.

Walking around his domain, Miranda also saw that though the course might *look* ready to play, in fact it was nowhere close to an opening date. "The tees, greens, bunkers and fairways were all done, that much was true," Chris remembered. "But there were no tee markers, flags, ball washers, rental clubs, driving range balls and a hundred other things that a golf course has to have to function."

Chris angrily confronted the management team of three Cairo-based businessmen to whom he reported and demanded to know why he had been so completely misled.

Sheephishly, his employers admitted to stretching the truth about the readiness of the clubhouse in their eagerness to get him to come. Their only excuse was that they believed him to be so right for the job they didn't want to risk losing him. But Miranda's other complaints genuinely puzzled them. Tee markers? Ball washers? Flagsticks? Why were such things necessary?

"I realized they had no concept about how the game is played," Chris said. "When I tried to explain why we needed flagsticks, they answered, 'Why can't golfers just aim for the green?'"

Already tempted to buy that ticket home, Chris next discovered that the golf course's 70 employees stood on the brink of open rebellion over long overdue back pay. Most were labourers earning less than U.S.$2.50 a day. Talking to them, Chris suddenly remembered that there was also a cheque due to him upon his arrival, and he hadn't seen that yet either. Back to the Cairo management team he went on both counts.

THOUGH STILL BITTER THAT he had been deceived, Miranda chose to believe in the good intentions of his employers once he and his staff got their money. At any rate, he had nothing to lose by sticking the job out and seeing what the next few months might bring. Chris had hungered for new experiences, and on that score at least he wasn't being disappointed.

He had a notion that the Luxor posting might be even more of an opportunity than he first imagined. "I was the one with all the knowledge about the game," Miranda said. "Because my bosses knew so little, I'd be able to get involved in almost every aspect of the golf course's operation—from designing a scorecard to creating a marketing plan to helping build a website. Not many pros back home get to put their stamp on a course as completely as I did."

Chris could already see that there were certain aspects of the Luxor lifestyle he was definitely going to enjoy. His employers arranged for him to live in a luxurious three-bedroom suite at the local Sheraton Hotel, complete with a large sundeck overlooking the tennis courts. He was also assigned a car and a personal driver, an affable and soon indispensable fellow named Nashat, whose duties ranged from acting as a translator to dashing into town for emergency takeout orders of McDonald's fries and Big Macs.

Miranda plunged in and worked feverishly toward a revised opening date now pegged for sometime early in the new year. For the first months he served more like a technical adviser than a traditional head pro. While workers made slow progress on the clubhouse, Miranda commanded operations from behind a desk in a large portable office trucked onto the site.

Entirely on his own, he designed the course's first scorecard, a handsome, full-colour production featuring a heraldic crest with crossed golf clubs that Chris nostalgically patterned after the National Hockey League's official insignia.

Next he turned his attention to tee markers, although his bosses still weren't clear on the concept. "They didn't understand why golfers couldn't tee off from the same spot every time," recounted Chris. "I had to explain over and over that like a carpet, the grass would soon wear out unless the markers were regularly moved."

Three meetings and several faxed pleas from Chris later, his bosses, who had lavished millions on building the course, only reluctantly approved a U.S.$300 invoice for the tee markers.

With the exception of Miranda's scorecard homage to his hockey roots, most often what he purchased or helped design reflected the golf course's Egyptian setting. Chris had given himself a crash reading course in Egyptian history. Now the knowledge he'd absorbed was witnessed by the small marble statues of King Tut, Ramses III, the Sphinx and Queen Nefertiti he employed as tee markers. "I saw them at a local craft market," Chris told me proudly of his find. "King Tut was one of the most powerful kings, so I had those statues painted black and placed on the championship tee decks. Ramses III was also mighty, so those were painted blue and used on the next deck. I chose the Sphinx because it's such a famous symbol of Egypt. Those were painted white. And for the ladies' tees, I picked the legendary Queen Nefertiti, whose statues were painted red.

"I wanted people to never forget, even on the golf course, that they were in this exotic and unique place," Chris explained. "That was important because I knew many of them might never get back to Egypt again."

Miranda continued the historical theme in the golf course's signage. The hole signs placed at every tee, for instance, included representations of the gates of Luxor and Karnak temples.

Once the course opened, dozens of people would compliment Chris on these thoughtful flourishes. But not his Cairo bosses. Seeing the tee markers finally in place, they became stubbornly convinced that the golf balls of players using the back tees would routinely smack into Queen Nefertiti or the other markers up front.

Chris responded by grabbing a club and a bucket of range balls and saying, "I'll stand here all day and never hit one of them!"

"But you're the pro!" they angrily retorted.

Already Chris could see that his middle-aged Egyptian employers didn't appreciate being contradicted by a younger man, especially someone they regarded as their social inferior. He never quite figured out how to bridge that cultural abyss. A young Englishwoman he hired to help him in the office was treated even more disdainfully by the management team. "Why does she work? Can't she get a man?" they sneered to Chris.

Miranda ruffled feathers just a month into his tenure when he insisted on the dismissal of the Egyptian manager who had hired him over the telephone.

"I found out he was the reason the workers at the course hadn't been getting paid," Chris remembered bitterly. "He skimmed half their money for himself. I don't know how deep the corruption went with the others. But I'm sure they didn't appreciate me sticking my nose in."

Chris could see no other way than to keep pushing hard for changes. The brass in Cairo hadn't given the slightest thought about how to market the course, assuming that if they built it, golfers would come. So Miranda involved himself in creating a comprehensive marketing plan, suddenly thankful for the two years he had studied business at a community college before becoming a golf pro.

He helped to hire a marketing specialist, then sent him off to drum up business in Europe and the Far East. Chris also assisted the new hire in developing the golf club's website.

The young head pro even put on his designer's cap and tinkered with the course's layout. "As beautiful as it was, I didn't feel that it was playing like a true desert course," Chris told me. "The desert sands rarely came into play because the fairways were so wide—almost 40 yards, with another 15 yards or so of rough on either side. You could hit a terrible drive and still be safely on the grass."

He ordered Ronan Goollily and his groundskeeping crew to shave the fairways down to 30 yards in width, retaining just five yards of rough on both sides. "We took out so much sod that we went through three sod-cutters," Chris noted with satisfaction.

Miranda also discovered that the playability of the course could change with a sudden shift in the desert winds. On a calm day, he frequently hit driver-wedge on the 380-yard opening hole. But should the wind sweep across the desert, Miranda might require as much as a 4-iron for his second shot.

Then there were the feared windstorms called *khamseens*, which occur about five or six times a year. No golfer could even think of playing once they blew in. The scorching, gusty storms carry the force of giant sandblasting machines, blotting out sun and sky.

EVERY DAY, EVERY HOUR, Miranda grew more confident in himself and his abilities. Remembering his struggles with high-school French, Chris shocked himself by quickly picking up Arabic words and whole phrases, which he always carefully noted at the back of his office diary for future reference. His linguistic skill helped him forge an even closer bond with a staff who already loved him for having delivered their back pay. To them he was always "Mr. Chris," a sign of respect and devotion he tried hard to reciprocate.

Chris dispatched his driver to buy dozens of pastries for a staff blowout before the start of the strict 28-day dawn-to-dusk fast of the Muslim holiday Ramadan. Friday afternoons, the entire crew would eagerly gather around him at the driving range for their weekly golf lesson. Many stayed to practise at the range or to play a few holes on the course. Although his employers forbade it, Chris never hesitated to let these humble peasants, known as *fellaheen*, use the golf course they had built.

"What the hell," Chris said with a shrug. "My bosses were up in Cairo."

From the start, Miranda was fascinated by the exotic mix of the timeless and the modern in everyday Egyptian life, by the sight of farmers tilling the soil with oxen, camels laden with produce for market and water buffaloes turning water-wheels, all within minutes of the high-rises, video stores and fast-food outlets of Luxor, a city of 150,000.

He sampled the restaurants and the local nightlife, and new friends led him through the colourful swirl of festivals that accompanied Ramadan. The sightseeing intensified when his girlfriend, Lisa, arrived from Stoney Creek in time for a Christmas vacation. Christmas morning Chris surprised Lisa by taking her up in a hot-air balloon for a three-hour ride over the Valley of the Kings, down the Nile River and back over the golf course. Afterwards, they played nine holes of golf and lounged around the Sheraton's pool, feeling sorry for the folks back home.

ONE UNEXPECTED DELAY followed another, but by early April the golf course finally stood ready for its grand opening. Miranda organized an extravagant weekend-long bash that attracted 100 people, many of them golf-loving American, Canadian and British expatriates who flew down from Cairo. The package included a golf tournament, dinner outdoors at an ancient temple, a Nile boat cruise and entertainment by musicians and belly dancers.

What soon became apparent was that even though Luxor's was the only golf course for at least 100 miles around, business would take time to grow. The busiest day during Chris's time there saw no more than 30 golfers go through. To help promote goodwill and encourage repeat business, the Cairo bosses asked Chris to play with as many of the guests — especially visiting VIPs — as he could. Soon his game was in better shape than ever.

Miranda partnered such dignitaries as the crown prince of Denmark, the South Korean ambassador to Egypt and the Middle East CEOs of both McDonald's and Coca-Cola.

One day, in an agitated state of awe mingled with abject terror, he gave a lesson to Egyptian president Hosni Mubarak, who dropped in unexpectedly while on a visit to Luxor. "I'm standing out at the practice range when a fleet of limousines pulls up," Chris recalled. "Suddenly a couple dozen or more really scary-looking security guys surround me, each one of them armed with a machine gun. Mubarak, who's in a business suit, gets out and watches me hit a few, then asks for a lesson."

For the next half-hour Chris demonstrated to Mubarak, who was a rank beginner, the proper grip and the fundamentals of the swing. But he noticed that every time he made even the slightest move toward his pupil the guards tensed up and their trigger fingers twitched. Or it could be he just imagined that.

"I was kind of freaking," he remembered with a laugh. "What if I forgot myself and touched the president's back or shoulder while teaching him something? I seriously thought these guys might take me out."

Apart from a healthy fear of Egyptian security forces and the occasional squabble with his employers, Chris didn't know how his life could get much better right then. Every day he marvelled at the loveliness of this golf course that had sprung like a miracle from the desert sand. Often at sunset, when the light was just right, he thought it was the most beautiful place he had ever seen.

Miranda had even adjusted, as well as could be expected, to the unrelenting and at times unbelievable desert heat. Temperatures routinely hit 49 to 54 degrees Celsius, and one day the thermometer at the home of his English assistant showed a reading of 68. That afternoon when Chris took a dip in his hotel pool, he was dry even before he got back to his lounge chair.

It was so hot that Chris, who wore shorts and sandals to work every day, kept his office air conditioner turned on full blast not more than two feet behind his desk chair. Most days he genuinely feared to go out in the midday sun, and planned to refuse to allow golfers to tee off between 11 a.m. and 1 p.m. once the even fiercer heat of summer arrived.

One blistering morning, accompanied by Ronan, the course superintendent, Miranda played a round of Egyptian golf he'll never forget.

"Ronan got into some trouble in the desert sand on the fourth hole, scraping one shot after another while I waited in the cart," Chris recounted. "By the time he finally picked up, I'd been sitting there for about 10 minutes, not moving. Then, when I went to get out, my feet wouldn't move. I looked down and saw that my soft spikes had melted into the cart's floor."

It's difficult for most Canadians to imagine why anyone would even want to play golf in that type of heat. "You'd think that, wouldn't you," Chris said musingly. "But the fact that it's a dry heat definitely makes it more bearable. And the difference between, say, 41 and 49 is barely noticeable. By that point it's just hot. Damn hot!"

THOUGH HE MISSED LISA and his family, and daily fought a craving for the pizza at a place called the Attic in Stoney Creek, Miranda might have stayed on in Luxor indefinitely if only he and his Egyptian employers could have learned to get along.

"From the start, we had been butting heads," Chris said sadly. "They resented it more every time I corrected them about one of their misconceptions about the game. But, you know, the truth was that in many ways I admired them. They had the vision to build this beautiful thing in the desert and then the determination to see it through."

A bitter dispute over a phone bill provided the first clear sign that the end was near. Using a cellphone his managers had given him, Chris began making dozens of calls to suppliers everywhere from South Africa and Asia to the United States and Canada, ordering flagsticks, range balls, golf clubs and other essentials in time for the official opening. He would have bought locally, but there were no local suppliers.

This went on until one day his bosses presented Miranda with a stack of telephone bills and told him they were deducting the total from his pay. Curiously, the amount was the exact figure of one of Chris's monthly pay cheques.

"But those were business calls," Chris angrily protested. "I had to make those calls to get product in here!"

"Your phone. You pay," the Cairo managers answered with a smirk. No amount of protesting by Chris could get them to change their minds. He thought of quitting on the spot, but realized he wasn't yet ready for such a drastic step.

"I knew these guys were just ripping me off," Miranda told me. "They were doing to me what they had tried to do with the back pay of the labourers at the golf course. But I still hoped that somehow we could work it out."

By this point the Cairo office was aggressively questioning every decision Chris made. They even began raising all the old issues he thought had been put to rest: Why did they need marketing? Why build a website? "It was getting pretty heated between us," Chris said. "They were constantly in my face."

The straw that broke the camel's back, so to speak, came when Miranda returned to Luxor following a two-week vacation back home. Originally, his employers had agreed that this was to be part of his paid vacation package. But now he found his pay had been docked.

"We changed our minds," they said.

The strangest thing was that Chris knew they didn't want him to quit. Not one of them ever suggested he wasn't up to the job. Rather, he thought they simply hoped to put him in his place, to teach their young golf pro the proper respect.

Miranda, though, had finally had enough and planned his escape. Maybe he had seen too many films like *Casablanca* and *Midnight Express* about travellers trapped in foreign lands. But Chris's imagination began to run wild with the fear that his employers might somehow prevent him from leaving the country if he told them he was through. He knew them to be powerful men with friends in high places. And what might the penalty be for a foreigner trying to skip out on a contract in an Arab land?

So he left secretively, under cover of night, informing only Ronan Goollily that he would never be back.

A YEAR LATER, WHEN WE met, Chris told me that his time in Luxor sometimes seemed like an incredible dream. "Despite everything, I'm glad I went," he said. "What an unbelievable experience. I learned more in Luxor in just a few months than I might have here in 10 years."

Less than a week after his return, Miranda was offered the position of head pro at Cuba's first 18-hole golf course, Las Americas, designed by Canadian Les Furber and built on the site of the abandoned DuPont family estate at Veradero Beach.

"You're just the type of pro we're looking for," the fellow on the phone told him. "You already know what it's like to run a club in a third-world country."

Chris declined with thanks. Instead, he took a job that summer as an assistant pro at Glen Abbey Golf Club in Oakville, about a half-hour's drive from Stoney Creek. In the spring of 2000, he moved to another ClubLink course, Rattlesnake Point in Milton, which is even closer to home.

"It's so good to be back in Canada," said Chris, who told me he and Lisa planned to marry the next spring. "I guess I'm not the born adventurer I thought I was. Home is looking pretty good right now."

I asked him if he'd heard anything about what went on in Luxor after he left.

"Yeah," Chris answered, trying hard not to smirk. "About two months later they hired an Australian pro. He quit after just three weeks and said the guy before him must have been nuts for staying as long as he did."

CHAPTER 9

CLIFFHANGER

LIKE THE LIGHTNING FLASH OF inspiration that led Stanley Thompson to imagine Banff's famous Devil's Cauldron, Doug Carrick instantly recognized the gift he had been given at Greywolf Golf Course.

The Toronto course architect recalled the bitterly cold day in January 1996 when, on the back of a snowmobile, he anxiously explored for the first time the spectacular British Columbia setting of his first mountain commission.

"I'd already studied the topography maps of the site, so I had an idea we might have something pretty special," said Carrick, who had never designed a course west of Ontario. "But I knew from experience that maps don't nearly do justice to the real thing. Suddenly I drove out onto a small open area perched on the edge of vertical rock cliffs. Mountains towered all around, and in one direction you could see for miles down an incredibly beautiful river valley."

About 180 yards across the sheer drop of Hopeful Canyon, Carrick spotted a wooded outcrop, slightly higher than where he stood, that would make a perfect teeing area. "I'd never seen a more dramatic setting for a par three," Carrick told me with a smile. "By the time I got back on my snowmobile, I had the entire hole set in my mind."

What the architect didn't know, but might already have hoped, was that Cliffhanger, as it's aptly known, was destined to become the signature hole of an artfully designed layout *Golf Digest* would name Canada's best new course of 1999. Seen in its glory on the front cover of this book, Greywolf's sixth hole has come to rival Devil's Cauldron as the most photographed and talked about par three in the land.

Greywolf, which is tucked in the Purcell mountain range about a 90-minute drive from Banff near the British Columbia–Alberta border, is part of the popular Panorama Mountain Village ski and golf resort owned by Vancouver's Intrawest Corporation. Intrawest also owns resorts at B.C.'s Whistler-Blackcomb and Quebec's Mont Tremblant.

Joining a growing legion of Canadian golfers, I had been irresistably lured to Greywolf by magazine photographs and advertisements featuring its signature hole. Such images are a kind of golfer's erotica, transmitting the same siren's call and the same warning signals. Though you want desperately to believe such earthly perfection exists, you also can't help but suspect at least a little airbrush trickery.

And yet Cliffhanger proved even more spectacular than I dared hope. Recalling the Aussie golfer in Yellowknife who told me flying over the northern bush was exactly as he'd always imagined Canada to be, Cliffhanger seemed to me symbolic of the very best golf in this country has to offer. Rugged peaks towering in every direction; evergreens straining toward the blue sky; clean, crisp, pine-scented mountain air. The only thing missing from this iconic setting was a Mountie standing on guard at the tees.

BACK IN TORONTO, I SAT down with Doug Carrick at his suburban office. I was curious to learn about the designer who has frequently been called the spiritual heir to Stanley Thompson, the godfather of Canadian golf course architecture. Carrick is in the vanguard of architects who are adopting a more traditional approach to course design. They're examining the qualities of the older courses, their shot values, routings and other features, and trying to incorporate the best of those elements into their own work.

Carrick, a gracious, soft-spoken man of 44 with thinning blond hair, told me how excited he had been to finally get his chance at designing a mountain course. "Greywolf was probably the most beautiful site I'd ever worked with, and the most humbling," Doug said. "When you're in the mountains you can't help feeling more insignificant. But at the same time I felt inspired to be there."

His course at Panorama stretches 7,140 yards from the tips, bent grass all the way, with tree-lined fairways, mountain views on every hole and almost 500 feet of elevation change. At the par-four fourth hole, the drop from the elevated tee to the green is a dizzying 200 feet. Adding an extra dash of drama to the scenery are the rapids of Hopeful Creek, which slash the fairway on the par-five fifth.

Observant golfers have noted the similarities between Greywolf and Stanley Thompson's mountain courses. Carrick's uneven fairways, subtle greens and fondness for elevated tees are all in keeping with Thompson's design philosophy. So is Greywolf's "risk and reward" routing. Like Thompson, Carrick has provided golfers with alternative routes to the green, with the shortest inevitably being the most difficult. The result is a course that challenges the scratch golfer without unduly frustrating a duffer like me.

What, I wondered, was Doug Carrick's reaction to so often having his name mentioned in the same breath as Stanley Thompson's, one of the giants of his field? If he were a painter, it would be like being compared to Rubens or Rembrandt.

Carrick practically blushed at the audacity of the comparison. "Well, of course I'm flattered," he said quietly. "Who wouldn't be? I've always been a huge fan of his work. To me, Stanley Thompson ranks among the top designers who ever lived. He was as good as anyone."

And maybe better than one legend whose name is spoken with even greater reverence, at least in the United States. "I'm a member of the American Society of Golf Course Architects, the organization Thompson helped found, and whenever I attend meetings people are always going on about Donald Ross, putting him on a pedestal," Doug told me with feeling. "I admire Ross, too, but do I think he's better than Thompson? No. But because most of Thompson's work was done in Canada, Americans don't appreciate him the way they should."

Like scores of pilgrims before him, Doug first recognized the scope of Thompson's genius when he played his courses in Jasper and Banff. Carrick came away dazzled by Thompson's famously innovative bunkering, and most of all by his knack for making each hole, one through 18, stand out in the golfer's memory. He couldn't think of another designer, Donald Ross included, who so consistently had that ability.

It would be wrong to suggest that Carrick is a strict traditionalist in his approach to golf course design. Rather, as all successful designers must, he varies his style from project to project, depending on the site and the client's wishes. Doug's influences range from the innovative work of such acclaimed contemporary designers as Tom Fazio and Pete Dye to the classic links courses of Scotland and Ireland.

Still, there's no doubt that his heart is firmly rooted in golf's past. "I am influenced more by the old classic courses," Carrick was quoted as saying in *Maclean's* a few years ago. "That is not meant to slight modern design—there is a lot of good work out there. But I grew up playing on old courses, and I think those designs have a lot to offer."

Once asked by the *Vancouver Sun* to name his five favourite Canadian courses, Doug's first four picks were Stanley Thompson designs: Capilano (Vancouver), St. George's (Toronto), Cataraqui (Kingston) and Westmount (Kitchener). For his final selection he chose the Toronto Golf Club, which was designed by Harry Colt, another towering figure from golf's golden age.

As a boy growing up in Toronto, Carrick played his golf at Uplands Golf and Country Club, just one of several Stanley Thompson courses in the metropolitan area. Doug had the opportunity to admire and learn from most of the others while visiting them for junior tournaments. During a distinguished amateur career, Doug participated in several provincial and national championships, including three Canadian Amateurs.

Not quite gifted enough to consider playing golf for a living, Carrick instead enrolled in the University of Toronto's School of Landscape Architecture, graduating in 1981. For a time he worked with another talented young Canadian landscape architect, Tom McBroom, who went on to design such championship courses as Cape Breton's Bell Bay and Prince Edward Island's Crowbush Cove. In 1987, Doug joined forces with the venerable C.E. "Robbie" Robinson, establishing the firm of Robinson and Carrick.

For many years after Stanley Thompson's death in 1953, the two top names in Canadian golf architecture were the friendly rivals Robbie Robinson and Howard Watson, who like so many other designers got their start as apprentices to Thompson. In fact, both Robinson and Watson began working for Thompson on the same day in 1929.

Whether they were in the office or working together at a site, Robbie Robinson, who was well into his seventies by then, loved to regale Doug with tales of his younger days at the side of the charming Thompson, who dominated the Canadian golf landscape for better than 30 years.

"I was like a sponge," Carrick remembered. "Robbie told his Stanley Thompson stories so well, I almost felt like I was there."

One of his favourites is Robinson's account of the day in the mid-1930s when a police officer confronted Thompson at the construction site of the Capilano Golf and Country Club in West Vancouver. Complaints had been made that the architect was cutting old-growth trees not actually on golf course property.

"You'll have to come downtown with me, Mr. Thompson," the officer insisted. "This is a very serious charge."

"Certainly," Thompson replied. "But before you take me away, I'd like you to at least have a look at what we're doing."

So Thompson took the policeman to the spot where the clubhouse stands today. Then, grandly sweeping his arm toward a wide gap in the forest through which was a breathtaking view of the city far below, the architect said, "Now isn't that the most magnificent sight you've ever seen?"

Just as at Banff and Jasper, where Thompson had artistically cut through the forest to point golfers toward greens aligned with far-off mountain peaks, he had worked his sculptor's magic at Capilano.

Silently, the policeman took a long look at the designer's handiwork.

"Very well, Mr. Thompson," he said finally. "Carry on. But mind now, no more cutting of trees off the property or we'll both have to answer for it!"

Robbie Robinson also recalled for Carrick how together he and Thompson had first walked the forested site of the future Westmount Golf and Country Club in Kitchener. From sunrise to sundown they had stumbled and hacked their way through the bush and bramble.

"Robbie told me that he had assumed they were lost, and that Thompson had no more clue where they were going than he did," Carrick recounted. "But back at the hotel that night, Stanley pulled out an aerial photograph of the site and started to route the golf course. 'Do you remember that little swale, Robbie?' he asked. 'We'll take the fairway across right there. . . . '

"Robbie could hardly believe his ears. Thompson had memorized the map! He'd known exactly where they were every step of the way."

AFTER ROBINSON'S DEATH in 1989, Carrick quickly made his own mark. His firm, Carrick Design, produced a string of lauded Canadian courses, including King Valley, Greystone, Osprey Valley and Angus Glen, which *Golf Digest* named the best new Canadian course of 1995. Doug also busied himself with remodelling and restoration jobs that included more than a dozen Stanley Thompson courses. Capilano, St. George's and Cataraqui were among the gems restored under his direction.

Though Robinson has gone, his influence— and through him, that of Stanley Thompson—can still be seen in Carrick's work. "Robbie drilled certain principles into my head when I was young and first learning, things he had learned from Thompson," Doug said. "Mostly, he taught me the importance of designing a course that's playable for golfers of every level. Young architects too often think the way to make their reputation is by building really difficult golf courses."

Carrick remembered how Robbie once looked over one of his hole designs and asked, "How's the average golfer going to hit his ball onto the green here with the bunkers right across the front? He's not going to hit a wedge in like you are. Why not angle your green and bunker to one side, but leave the front open?"

This democratic design approach is built into Greywolf, where golfers can pull out their drivers and swing away without hesitation on the tee of every par four and par five. "Fairly generous fairways make the course fun for everyone to play," Doug said. "Most of the classic courses are designed that way."

Where Carrick injects strategy and creates challenge is in the grading of the fairways, in the way the routing sets up angles to the greens and in his bunkering. As well, Carrick likes to provide chipping areas around the greens that are cut to fairway height. That way, a better golfer can choose any one of several shots with different clubs, while a less skilled player has the option of putting from off the green.

Robbie Robinson had suggested something I also wondered about. Does the fact that Carrick is himself an excellent golfer affect the design of his courses? Indeed, it seems that most top architects are accomplished players with an innate understanding of the game's strategies. Graham Cooke, Tom McBroom and Les Furber, Canada's other leading designers, are all or were once low-handicappers. And, of course, in his day Stanley Thompson was one of the country's best amateurs.

After a thoughtful pause, Doug answered, "I think it probably does affect the way I look at things. When I was younger and played a lot, I drove the ball well, almost always putting my drive somewhere on the fairway. That might be one reason why I like holes that set up nicely from the tee, where you can hit your driver and not have to lay up."

Similarly, Carrick's preference for lengthy par fours that usually require a golfer to pull out a long iron for his second shot has its roots in his own game. "As a player, I've always felt that if you can't hit a long iron, then there's something fundamentally wrong with your swing. So I prefer courses that force better golfers to hit those types of shots."

ARMED WITH A HATCHET, A cane and a flask, Stanley Thompson liked to explore a site for as long as three or four weeks before finally putting pencil to paper. Then, bursting with inspiration, he would return to his office and furiously produce sketches for as many as 100 holes.

Doug Carrick, too, begins his creative process with a close tour of the golf course property, whether on foot or, as at Greywolf, on the back of a snowmobile. The most dramatic holes, such as Cliffhanger, often emerge almost of their own accord, as if they were simply meant to be. But at first Doug is more concerned with getting an overall feel for the site, trying to imagine how everything will fit and flow together in the end.

Though a summertime visit is preferable, a first look in winter isn't necessarily the drawback one might imagine. "Of course, what you can't judge is the quality of the soil," Carrick said. "But with a little imagination you can see past the snowdrifts and visualize what the scenery will be like in summer. The main thing is the topography, and that doesn't change."

Even after a single visit, Doug is often ready to start sketching holes. Most of his work is still done the old-fashioned way, with a pencil and a pad. A computer technician then builds a 3-D model of the proposed course that is so lifelike Carrick can do a virtual fly-over of the site and even change the colours of the sunset. The imaging helps clients understand exactly what Carrick is proposing.

Adopted as gospel not just by Carrick but by most modern architects is Stanley Thompson's firmly held belief that a golf course must be at one with the natural landscape.

"Without even realizing why, golfers will play a Thompson course like Capilano or Jasper and think, This course looks right. It belongs here," Doug said. "Unless you're working with a relatively featureless piece of property, it's almost always better to let the land dictate the course's final character. Who am I to think I can improve on Mother Nature?"

For a mountain course, Greywolf needed surprisingly little rock blasted. Most of the work was at Cliffhanger, where the face of the green site sloped from front to back and had to be reduced by about six feet to make it more receptive. Blasting was completed in a day and cost between $10,000 and $15,000, which is a pittance as such projects go.

Cliffhanger's total cost came in at around $150,000. That's about average for a par three, but less than half what it typically costs to build a par four or a par five. Any way you look at it, Greywolf's owners got themselves a bargain. Their course's signature hole turned out to be one of the cheapest on the property.

Doug told me that even during construction Cliffhanger was already such a popular attraction that a temporary tee box covered with synthetic turf had to be built for workers and visitors determined to try their luck over Hopeful Canyon. It was also during this time that a Greywolf tradition of howling like a wolf after a particularly good shot, especially at the signature hole, first started.

Fittingly, Greywolf's architect was there at the tradition's birth. As Doug recalled, "Whenever I was on site, a few of us would go out in the dirt and hit balls as a way to pass the time at the end of the day. The howling began as a play on the course's name. When someone hit a good shot, we'd howl like a wolf, 'Owwwooo!'"

"And after a bad shot," Doug added with a laugh, "we'd break into a pitiful low whimper, like a whipped dog."

A two-ball rule applies at Cliffhanger, which stretches from 200 yards at the back tees to 142 at the reds. If neither of the golfer's first two shots carry the canyon, then the third has to be played from the drop area adjacent to the green. Club selection must take into account the constantly swirling winds through dramatic Toby Creek Valley. And even if the ball successfully carries the vertical rock cliffs guarding the left and front sides of the green, an overly aggressive shot might end with a plunge off the severe drop at the back.

The best I managed from the 155-yard white markers during

my two visits to Cliffhanger was a decently stroked 7-iron that caught the fringe just to the right of the green. A lovely chip and a tap-in got me down in par, which I reckoned was good for if not a full-blooded wolf howl, at least a long, self-satisfied growl.

Carrick told me that whenever possible he reserves a site's most dramatic features for his par threes. "Waterfalls, river rapids, the canyon at Cliffhanger . . . natural theatre like that is ideally suited for short holes," Doug explained. "I think it's a real treat for a golfer when he can stand at the tee and take in that kind of spectacular scenery at a glance."

Another consideration is that an obstacle such as Hopeful Canyon might too heavily intrude on a course's playability if routed into a par four or par five. For instance, a second-shot carry over the chasm for a better player could in turn mean a second-shot layup for a golfer who is shorter off the tee.

I asked Doug if back on that wintry day in 1996, when he first envisioned Cliffhanger, he imagined it had the makings of a Canadian golfing landmark that might one day compare in stature to Stanley Thompson's Devil's Cauldron.

"Actually, I did," Doug answered with only a moment's hesitation. "I thought right away it had that potential. But that type of popularity is a phenomenon you can never count on. I just knew the scenery was there for it to happen."

Doug then confided that though he is proud of Cliffhanger, it's not even his favourite hole at Greywolf. If he had to pick the one dearest to his heart, he'd choose the 527-yard 14th, a twisting uphill par five.

Like the rearing of a difficult but beloved child, the 14th was a hole that gave Carrick fits during construction. The fairway required a deep and troublesome cut, and tons of dirt had to be hauled in to raise the tee area. Though Doug knew the hole had a lot of potential, he wasn't sure how it would turn out until all the work was finally done. Then it proved to be one of the strongest holes at Greywolf.

"When you get on the green, you look to your right and see this full, beautiful mountain range unfold," Doug said enthusiastically. "And that's a sight you don't have a clue about until you're actually standing there. I love that element of surprise."

Maybe, I suggested, when compared to the hard labour that went into the 14th, Cliffhanger had come too easily to him to inspire the same level of emotion.

"That might be right," Carrick acknowledged with a grin. "Mother Nature gets most of the credit on that one."

CHAPTER 10

CHIP OFF THE BLOCK

WHILE I TOOK A FEW LAST warm-up swings before the start of our lesson at the Woodbine Golf Range, Paul Knudson, middle son of George, reminisced about how he had never truly grasped his father's stature in the game until he accompanied him to a tournament in Japan.

It was in Japan that Georrge Knudson captured the individual title at the 1966 World Cup, a triumph—perhaps the greatest of his career—his hosts had never forgotten.

"Even though this was 1983, well past my father's heyday as a player, the Japanese made a fuss wherever we went, calling out to him, 'Georgie Knoodo-son, Georgie Knoodo-son,'" remembered a laughing Paul, who was 18 at the time. "The little cottage he had stayed at during the World Cup even had a commemorative plaque over the door with his name on it. What shocked me was discovering that these people put my father in the same league as Jack Nicklaus and Arnold Palmer. I had never thought of him that way. He was just my dad."

Paul, the only one of George Knudson's three sons to follow him into the game, was teaching full-time after four years as the head pro of the Richmond Hill Golf Club, where administrative duties had chained him to a desk. When we met, the 35-year-old fairly bubbled with enthusiasm for his new freelance life in the great outdoors of the range, a few miles north of Toronto. "I feel reinspired about golf," he told me happily. "I never realized how much I missed teaching."

A short, slight man with a goatee and his father's dark colouring, Paul intently studied my swing from behind yellow-tinted sunglasses, his sensitive eyes another inheritance from his dad.

I had arrived with the hope that a little of the Knudson magic might be just the thing to cure the slice that had plagued me for the past several months. But after only a few minutes of observation, Paul had the look of a doctor about to deliver news of a terminal illness.

"You say you've taken lessons before?" he asked, shaking his head sadly when I nodded.

"Well, somewhere along the line your swing has gotten out of sync. The slice could be a result of any number of things—or all of them. But the biggest problem is you're not getting enough of a turn. Remember, the swing is a full-body motion in which everything works together, just like my father stressed in his book. Right now you're working the swing too much with just your arms."

Was there anything he liked?

"Sure," he said, grateful for the chance to say something, *anything*, positive. "Your tempo's not bad. That's a good start. Natural rhythm is something you can't teach."

STILL TRYING TO BUCK UP my spirits after we had taken our conversation from the range to a table at the greasy spoon across the street, Paul talked about how difficult he had always found the game. "I've watched many of the best players in the world up close ever since I was a kid," he said. "Imagine how frustrating that can be. My dad and the other guys on the tour made shots I still can't believe. In golf, there are those few great players and then the rest of us."

Paul's earliest childhood memories are of summers spent travelling across America with the entire family—his dad, mom, brothers Kevin and Dean, and two dogs—from one PGA tourney to the next. In the evenings he and the other tour kids, most memorably the Nicklaus boys and Charles Coody's son, would splash in the pool or hold putting tournaments in the hotel hallways, using ashtrays for holes. Paul's most prized possession was an old putter his father had cut down to his size.

Often the family joined his father's gallery at the golf course. But George would never acknowledge their presence. "Dad was always very tense when he played," Paul recalled. "He was so focused I think he barely realized the gallery was there. Sometimes he'd even walk by himself, apart from the other players, trying to stay in his own thoughts."

Those were wonderful years for the Knudson clan. Looking back, Paul regretted only that he wasn't a few years older during the height of his father's playing career so he could better remember the celebrated golf courses they visited and all the other experiences the family shared.

As a young boy Paul scarcely realized that his father was one of Canada's leading athletes. To him and the children of the other tour players their lives seemed perfectly normal. It was Paul's friends and especially their parents back home in Toronto who gradually made him aware that his dad was no ordinary man.

"I remember being at a buddy's house when my father won the Kaiser in 1972," Paul said. "I really hadn't thought that much about it. But my friend's mother was so hyped about his win that she couldn't talk about anything else. That was one of my first clues about how much my father meant to his generation of Canadians."

Growing up, Paul emulated his father and the other pros he watched every summer by tirelessly playing an eccentric 18-hole chip-and-putt course he created on his front lawn. The route went through and over hedges and flower beds, while the street and driveway were treated as water hazards.

Paul once tried to cajole his father into a match. But George Knudson was far too practical in his approach to golf even to indulge his son. "He took one look at the first hole, which called for a wedge shot over a 10-foot tall hedge, and lost all interest," Paul remembered with a smile. "Dad said, 'You know what? I'm never going to be anywhere that I need this shot, so I'm not playing.'"

It wasn't until he was 12 that Paul started taking his game onto real golf courses. By that point back problems had curtailed his father's playing career and the family was spending most of the summer at home.

Surprisingly, considering the elder Knudson's perfectionist nature, he chose to take a hands-off approach with his son. "I think maybe he was shying away from the Hockey Parent Syndrome," Paul reflected. "He wanted me to have fun with golf and not feel I was being pushed into the game. I also think he felt certain that I'd eventually get around to asking for his advice."

At any rate, Paul had already enjoyed the advantage of studying the swings of the world's premier golfers. And like most kids, he was a gifted mimic. Paul struck the ball solidly almost from the start.

The swing wasn't bad. But one thing that drove his purist father to distraction whenever he looked on was Paul's habit of putting left-handed, even though he played every other club in his bag from the right side. Paul had been doing it that way ever since those putting contests against the Nicklaus brothers a few years back.

"For God's sake," his father said, only half joking, "wherever you go, don't tell them your last name."

Though reluctant to interfere, George Knudson also clearly disapproved of Paul's lackadaisical approach to practising. "I've always hated practising," Paul told me. "I still do. But of course that's exactly the opposite of my father's outlook. He would rather practise than play, and I know my attitude drove him nuts. I remember him saying to me, 'If I could only put my head on your young body, I'd beat the world.'"

YET DESPITE THEIR DIFFERENCES, golf brought Paul, who alone among the Knudson boys had a real passion for the game, and his father closer together. George thrilled his son by asking him to be his caddy in the Canadian Open at Glen Abbey.

"I was 16 and you can imagine how huge this was for me," Paul said. "But my dad made it clear that this wasn't exactly going to be a partnership. 'Don't say anything,' he warned me. 'Just hand me the club and stay off the green.'"

Canada's most popular golfer was paired with Arnold Palmer the first two rounds, a combination organizers knew would bring out the crowds. "Though both my dad and Palmer were past their prime, there were people everywhere," Paul recalled. "What really impressed me was what a regular guy Palmer was. Knowing I was Knudson's son, he made a point of coming over to talk to me and make me feel comfortable."

Another memory that stayed with Paul was how, after they had driven back home from Glen Abbey at the end of a round, his father tried to teach him that golf wasn't all fun and glamour.

"I was dying to go out and see my buddies, who were all waiting for a first-hand report," Paul remembered, laughing.

"But my dad said, 'No, take my clubs down to the basement and give them a good cleaning. And don't forget the grips,' he called after me. 'Give them a good scrubbing, too.'"

A solid rather than a gifted player, Paul didn't seriously consider a career in golf until he was casting about for something to do after having earned a diploma in outdoor recreation from a community college. Golf, a recreation played in the outdoors, fitted the description, so he went to work at his father's golf school. Though he did a bit of everything, Paul's days were mostly spent helping run the driving-range side of the family business.

His father had always told him, "When you're really interested in learning, you'll come to me."

That summer, for the first time, George began teaching his son the finer points of the game. "He helped give me a better understanding of what was going on in the golf swing," Paul said. "But more than that, he tried to get me to understand the head space a golfer has to get into to play the game well. How to work your way around a golf course.

"We were always two completely different creatures in the rounds of golf we'd played together before that," Paul continued. "He was so rock solid, while I'd be all over the map—birdie, birdie, eight! My dad would stand there shaking his head."

"Golf is like chess," George Knudson kept repeating to his son that summer. "Always think at least two moves ahead."

By this point Paul fully appreciated that his father numbered among the most gifted ball strikers in the history of the game. Almost daily at the range admiring fans or pros who dropped by told him stories about incredible shots they had seen him make. Some tales were like fish stories, embellished with every telling. Already the Knudson legend was beginning to grow.

Paul loved every moment he spent by his father's side. Their time together became even more precious when George was diagnosed with lung cancer. But even that seemed but a passing shadow. A few months later, after intensive chemotherapy and radiation treatment, doctors announced that the cancer had gone into remission.

By then Paul and a partner had taken out a small business loan and leased a driving range at the Thunderbird Golf Course in Whitby, Ontario, for the next season. Paul's brief apprenticeship with his father had convinced him to make a career in golf. They ran the range for two more years before Paul ended the partnership by taking a position as an assistant pro at Thunderbird.

From the start, Paul made it a point of pride not to cash in on the Knudson name, a practice that somehow seemed even more important to him after his father's relapse and death in early 1989. "I wanted people to respect me for who I was, not for being the son of somebody famous," he said. "I always used just Paul when introducing myself to people. Some students knew me for months before they found out my last name."

After six seasons at Thunderbird, Paul moved on to the Richmond Hill Golf Club, where he started as an assistant before becoming the head pro in 1995. He spent most of his days at the busy public course planning corporate events and managing a staff of 35. Only rarely did he find the time to teach, something he had always loved.

On March 6, 1999, a day seared into his memory, Paul received his pink slip. That very morning he had finished all his buying for the coming season. Everything was set. Then they lowered the boom.

"Talk about a lesson learned," Paul told me. "The Canadian PGA is right. Everyone who works in this business should have a written contract. I only had a letter of agreement for the first couple of years. After that I didn't think I needed one."

The timing couldn't have been worse. Paul and his wife had recently separated, a traumatic situation that struck him as bitterly ironic, since a major cause of the breakup had been the long hours Paul put in at the golf course.

"I was enraged. I was heartbroken. Only my sense of humour got me through," he said ruefully of that difficult time. "I thought, Gee, I'm ageing quickly here."

Living on his severance package, Paul paused to reclaim his life and contemplate his future. His outlook brightened considerably when he met Janice, a federal government employee who transferred from Ottawa to be with him. What Paul called their "spiritual marriage" took place in the spring of 2000 on a sailboat off the coast of Lombok, an Indonesian island. The legal ceremony followed a few days later in his mother Shirley's Toronto condominium.

By now Paul had decided to start afresh as a freelance instructor rather than look for another club job. Though not the most secure living, it did seem the ideal solution. Freelancing would allow for more time with Janice and let him spend his working days doing exactly what he liked best.

Paul told me his long-term goal is to one day own a driving range of his own. It could be located almost anywhere in Canada or as far away as the Caribbean. An on-site restaurant is also in the plan. Both he and Janice love to cook.

Meanwhile, Paul was busy building his current practice. But for someone just getting started, he seemed unusually fussy about the type of clients he was willing to take on. "As a teacher, I've always found most frustrating the people who pencil me in between their analyst and their tennis lesson," he said. "People who are so casual about the game that they would never dream of practising. But what's the point for either of us? In order to keep improving as an instructor, I need constructive feedback from serious students.

"My father felt the same way, although he eventually learned to be a little more patient than I am," Paul continued. "Ideally, I'd like 50 to 100 students who are really eager to learn."

Another surprise was the discovery that Paul is not a strict Knudsonian in his own approach to teaching. Certainly, like so many others, he admires the crystalline purity of what his father preached. "Dad believed that the swing motion should be directed in perfect balance toward the target," Paul said, breaking it down for me. "The golf ball merely gets in the way. Swing at the target, not the ball. Take the motion through it."

It's a swing theory Paul believes works especially well for beginners. "The real beauty of it is there's not an overload of information. It's a very simple, basic approach. A golfer can become proficient at it very quickly."

But Paul is also convinced of the validity of other teaching philosophies. "People all have different learning cues," he explained. "Some are better visually or verbally or learn better through trial and error. It's crazy to throw all your eggs in one basket, saying this is the one and only way to teach."

What's more, Paul felt confident his father would have eventually come to agree with this approach. "Remember, my dad was really just getting started with his teaching. I think he would have realized that there are a lot of theories out there that are all intertwined."

OTHER SONS MIGHT FEEL intimidated at having inherited the legacy of the Knudson name. But Paul has always embraced it with good humour, often poking fun at himself and the fact that on a golf course, he is barely recognizable as his father's boy.

He told me with a thin Knudson grin of competing in the Canadian Masters at Southern Ontario's Heron Point Golf Links a few years back. Paul, who was given a sponsor's exemption to the Canadian Tour event, shot 77 in the first round and found himself so overmatched by the likes of Scott Dunlap and Mike Weir that he remembered thinking, Thank God I don't play this game for a living!

Even more nerve-racking was the silence that followed the announcement of his name over the public-address system when he stood on the first tee. "It was almost like they expected my father's ghost to be standing there," Paul remembered. "People were just stunned to hear the name Knudson again. Meanwhile, I'm praying to myself, Oh, Lord, airborne please. Just don't let me cold-top it."

Invited to the tournament again the next year, Paul had the

distinctly eerie experience of being partnered with his father's old friend and frequent playing partner Al Balding, with whom the elder Knudson had won the team title at the 1968 World Cup in Rome. This time Paul was braced for the reaction of the gallery and got off to a sizzling start. He dropped a 30-foot putt for a birdie on the opening hole, following that with a 40-footer for another bird on the second.

A startled Balding looked at him and said, "You didn't learn to putt like that from your old man."

"I always say that, genetically, I wasn't given my dad's swing, but I also wasn't given his putting stroke," Paul said with a chuckle. "Ever since I was a kid, the putter has been the best club in my bag."

When his father died, Paul's inheritance included George's last set of golf clubs. He tried to use them at first but found them heavy and too exacting for his swing. Now they're carefully tucked away with a few of his dad's trophies. During his lifetime, George never bothered much about the glories of the past. Paul remembered that in the basement of the family home there was a whole closet filled with tarnished and forgotten awards. Over the years George gave away many of his cups and old golf clubs to friends. Much of what remained in the family has been donated to the Canadian Golf Hall of Fame and Canada's Sports Hall of Fame.

Paul also owns tapes of old *Shell's Wonderful World of Golf* broadcasts that featured his father, as well as one of George making his famous run at the 1969 Masters. "The tapes are a great luxury," Paul said. "They mean that for my entire family his memory will never die. Even Janice, who never knew him, almost feels like he's still with us."

Like anyone who loses a parent too soon, Paul has often

wondered how things would have turned out if his father had lived. "He would have been 63 now," Paul said. "Knowing how keen he was to get out on the Senior Tour, I think he'd definitely have done that for a few years. I'm also pretty certain he'd have kept teaching, at least part-time, trying to spread his message."

Mostly, though, Paul thought his father would have been quietly savouring the rewards of a richly deserved retirement. He pictured his father and mother, who has never remarried, beachcombing on a tropical island. "Dad loved that type of thing but hardly ever got the chance to relax when he was alive," Paul said. "The big money wasn't there when he played. Most of the time my parents were together, his golf clubs were always going, except for maybe one or two weeks during our annual family vacation."

A devoted family man who regretted every moment away from Shirley and the kids, George would have doted on his first grandchild, Cypress, named after his favourite golf course in the world, Cypress Point. She was born in March 2000 in Vancouver, where Kevin, the eldest Knudson boy, is a commercial airline pilot. Dean, the youngest, works for the federal government in Ottawa.

Trying to give meaning to George's death, the family founded the George Knudson Memorial Pro-Am in 1990, with all proceeds going toward financing a physician or scientist for one or two years of specialized training in cancer research at Toronto's Princess Margaret Hospital. Every year Paul represents his family in the event that has so far raised more than $2 million.

PAUL TOLD ME THAT of all his memories of his father, one had stuck so solidly with him that he recalled it almost every time he walked onto a golf course.

It was of the gorgeous late-summer day in 1988 when he and George played what would prove to be their last round of golf together. That outing at the Cambridge Golf and Country Club was his father's idea. The elder Knudson knew that in a few days Paul would be taking the playing portion of his CPGA eligibility test at the course. Paul, having firmly decided to pursue a career in golf, needed to score 81 or better in each of two rounds to qualify. That piece of paper would permit him to start teaching students at the golf range he had leased with his friend. More than that, Paul had to have it if he were ever to emerge from his father's shadow and make a life for himself in the game.

His dad was there, as Paul remembered, "to hold my hand. To walk me through it. He knew how nervous I was and how much it meant to me."

George had just returned from Austin, Texas, where he had played in his first Senior PGA Tour event. Cancer treatments had robbed him of all his hair, and at Cambridge he wore a Tilley hat to protect his bald head from the sun. But George, his cancer in remission, looked and felt better than he had in months. Paul had rarely seen his father in a better mood.

There'll be lots more of this, Paul remembered thinking during their round together. "I was just so happy to be there with him. To have gone through all that and to now see my father so full of life and confidence. It was an incredible feeling."

Paul was amazed by how living with the disease had transformed his father's personality. George had been an excruciatingly intense competitor during his playing days, his nerves strung so tightly that he often vomited before an important match. Despite his success, George felt convinced that he hadn't lived up to his potential. So gifted a ball striker should have won even more.

Yet all this seemed far in the past that sunny day in Cambridge. "He was like a new man," Paul said. "Cancer changed everything for him. Suddenly he realized that there was nothing to get uptight about. He had a greater appreciation for everything he did."

Even George's putting had dramatically improved with his new attitude. "You have to be relaxed to putt well," said Paul. "It wasn't life and death to him any more. He knew exactly where it fitted in the whole scheme of things. Putting was just putting."

And golf, after all, is just a game.

That was the all-important message George passed on to his son in Cambridge. "Not by anything he said," remembered Paul, "but by the man he had become."

CHAPTER 11

CADDYSHACK

"SOMETIMES IT FEELS LIKE I've been fighting power carts my entire life," said Rob McDannold, the Hamilton Golf and Country Club's head pro. "I don't think I could hate those damn things any more than I do."

McDannold is the leader of a stubborn resistance movement aimed at derailing the golf cart steamroller and keeping caddy programs part of the Canadian game. The historic Hamilton club, where golf-bag-toting youngsters have served in the ranks for better than 80 years, supports what is by far the largest of the country's 14 or so remaining caddy programs. Every spring as many as 300 new enlistees between the ages of 11 and 18 sign on. About 50 diehards will put in enough rounds to receive an invitation to the annual caddy banquet at season's end.

I had arrived at the club, located in the town of Ancaster, just outside Hamilton city limits, shortly after the break of dawn, keen to do my small part for the cause by serving as a caddy for the day. Since then I'd been hanging out with the handful of kids gathered inside the caddyshack, which resembles a concrete carport attached to the rear of the pro shop. Business being slow, the boys and I idled the time away tossing pennies and playing an ingenious game known as Caddy Golf, in which you use your cupped hand to direct a golf ball off the shack's interior walls and benches toward the hole, which is really just a large crack in the asphalt floor.

By the time Rob McDannold called me into his office for a talk, the little devils had taken me for almost $2. I felt lucky to escape still wearing my prized Banff Springs golf jacket, which I'd noticed the boys eyeing covetously.

"Golf is losing out in so many ways by permitting caddy programs to disappear," McDannold, a solidly built man of 45 with a hero's chiseled profile, told me in explanation of the fight he had been waging ever since joining the Hamilton club as head pro in 1990. "What people don't realize is that caddies have always been the lifeblood of the game."

Most clubs once enthusiastically supported caddy programs not just as a membership service but because they knew of no better way to introduce youngsters to golf. Caddying instilled in kids the discipline to show up for work at daybreak and helped them grow straight and strong in the fresh air. Club members, many of whom were community leaders, frequently became role models and mentors. Most important of all, those golden caddyshack summers sparked a lifelong passion for golf that would lead many former caddies to one day apply for club memberships of their own, thus ensuring the game's continued growth.

McDannold had himself started out as a caddy in his hometown of Napanee, Ontario. Indeed, as he pointed out, many of golf's most illustrious figures entered the game through the caddyshack door. Canadian icons George Knudson, Marlene Stewart Streit and Stanley Thompson all began as club bearers. So did Ben Hogan, Byron Nelson, Sam Snead, Lee Trevino and Arnold Palmer, among dozens of other outstanding players.

By the mid-1960s, the age of the caddy was rapidly passing. Golf clubs turned handsome profits renting carts to golfers who had decided they would rather ride than walk. Caddy programs, meanwhile, almost always operated at a loss, and caddies required time-consuming training. By the 1980s, except for during tournaments, caddies had almost disappeared from the nation's fairways.

Mostly, Rob McDannold blamed his fellow club pros for the near extinction of caddy programs. "Even though many of them got their start in the game as caddies, pros haven't been nearly active enough in keeping the programs going," he said forcefully. "Maybe they don't want to be bothered with the extra work. Or maybe they're under pressure to keep the cart revenue flowing in."

McDannold told me that every year he receives about a dozen calls from fellow club professionals inquiring about his program. Most tell him they're determined to follow his model at their own courses and that they'll keep in touch. Few ever bother to call again.

When McDannold first came to the Hamilton Golf and Country Club, its caddy program was also dying. "We were doing about 2,000 rounds annually, not quite half the current total of just over

4,000 rounds," he remembered. "The first thing I had to do was convince the membership to recommit itself to the program."

Like many resistance leaders, McDannold has a charismatic gift for making his message heard. Though the caddy program represents a $20,000 annual hit to the club's general revenue, the 750 club members have unhesitatingly supported it ever since his arrival. In 2000, during the summer of my visit, more than 60 per cent of the membership took a caddy out for at least one round. Even when members choose to ride rather than walk, a contribution of $1 is taken from their cart rental fee and put into a caddy bonus fund.

"There's no longer any question about whether we should carry on with the program," McDannold said. "The club benefits, the kids benefit. Some kids who never saw a golf course before coming here stay with us forever, moving on to the pro shop or the grounds crew. Quite a few of our members started in the caddyshack. I know they're never going to doubt what we're trying to do."

"WE'VE GOT A FOURSOME GOING out," said Cal Armstrong, Hamilton's caddy master and back-shop overseer. "A member and three guests. You'll be sharing a bag with young Mike here."

Cal, a popular fellow of 65 who has been a club fixture for 20 years, put a fatherly hand on the shoulder of my grinning partner.

"Mike's one of our top caddies," Cal said warmly. "You couldn't be in better hands."

A tall, brown-haired 16-year-old with the first hint of peach-fuzz on his cheeks, Mike obligingly helped me into my caddy's bib, a heavy apron with extra large pockets to accommodate towels and golf balls. Together we headed out to Hamilton's first tee, where the other caddies in our group were already waiting. Each of them was a new face to me, having arrived at the club while I was talking with Rob McDannold.

Mike introduced me to Grant, a diminutive, bushy-browed 15-year-old in a floppy hat emblazoned with a Blue Jays insignia. The chatty B-rated caddy (caddies are designated C to AA, based on experience and performance) told me he was in his third summer at the club.

"He's not good enough to be an A caddy," teased Todd, a cocky, muscular 18-year-old in our group.

Todd, who rakishly sported a single dangling gold earring, was one of the oldest caddies at the club, with five years on the job. Like my partner, Mike, he was rated AA.

Finally, there was Eric, a sharp-featured 15-year-old who, like Grant, was impatiently awaiting a growth spurt. Also an AA, with four years' experience, Eric kept his thoughts mostly to himself during our round together.

The night before, I had crammed hard for my day as a caddy by studying the *PGA Junior Golf Foundation Caddie Guide*, which is considered the bag-carriers' bible. But the 78 detailed tips and guidelines quickly overloaded my ageing circuitry: "Memorize the yardage of all holes on the course. . . . Always hand a club to your player grip end toward him. . . . Never lean on the golf bag or clubs. . . . Walk with a hand over the clubheads, so irons cannot rattle. . . . Clean dirt off clubhead before returning club to bag. . . . Hold the bag by its rim square in front of you. . . . Don't stand where your long shadow will bother the players. . . ."

"I'll never be able to remember all that stuff," I said nervously to Mike while we waited at the first tee.

After a brief huddle, the boys and I unanimously agreed that my best approach was to adopt the timeworn caddy adage, "Show up, keep up and shut up."

"That's usually the best way," said Grant. "Especially your first time."

"The main thing is to anticipate," offered Todd. "At the tee, have the golfer's driver ready. If he's in the sand, pull out the sand wedge. Hand him his putter when he's walking up to the green. It's pretty basic."

Soon the middle-aged foursome we'd be carrying for arrived at the tee and began stretching and taking warm-up swings. The host, the only one of them familiar with the course, sidled up to us and whispered, "I usually play from the white tees, but my friends are insisting on the blues. I'm not so sure it's a good idea."

The boys and I shared the club member's misgivings after all three of his guests hit feeble drives on the par-four opening hole. Playing from the blues would stretch the challenge of an already difficult course to 6,667 yards, which seemed a little long for these fellows. The only one to get off a solid wallop was the host, whose bag I shared with Mike.

As we trailed after him in the sunshine, our employer for the afternoon, a congenial man of about my own age, turned back to me and said, "I've been a member here for three years and I still have to pinch myself every time I play the course. It's always a thrill."

Ranked fifth in *Score* magazine's 2000 listing of Canada's top 100 golf courses, Hamilton was laid out in 1914 by the renowned British-born architect Harry Colt. The original course (an additional nine designed by Robbie Robinson opened in 1975), which is what we were walking, still plays much as it did in Colt's day but looks far better. One of Colt's greatest strengths was his uncanny ability to foresee exactly how a course would look and play once the trees he planted grew to full maturity. Originally almost bare farm fields, Hamilton now appears to have been carved out of a thick, rolling forest.

Twice Hamilton hosted the Canadian Open, in 1919 and in 1930, when Tommy Armour set the course record of 64 en route to victory. That mark was equalled by Jim Nelford in 1977 and broken by Warren Sye with a 62 in the 1991 Ontario Amateur Championship. The ladies' record of 68 was set by Marlene Stewart Streit in 1968.

The golf club is also remembered as the longtime professional home of Nicol Thompson, the eldest brother of Stanley Thompson. Nicol, who twice finished as runner-up in the Canadian Open, served as Hamilton's head pro for 47 years until his retirement in 1945.

On the second hole, a tricky dogleg par four, Mike and I headed into the woods to help search for a misfired tee shot off the driver of one of the guests, an exercise we would doggedly repeat a half-dozen or more times through the afternoon. While we were scanning the forest floor, I asked my partner what had first attracted him to caddying.

"Some kids think of it as just a job," answered Mike, who had been looping, as caddying is popularly known, for four years. "But for me it's definitely the golf. I play here every chance I get, as well as at the club in Hamilton my dad and I belong to. Maybe a total of 10 rounds a week."

In addition to a series of five complimentary golf lessons offered by McDannold and his staff, caddies graded B and higher are given the opportunity to play the course Monday mornings before 8:15, and Saturday and Sunday afternoons after 6 p.m.

A gifted all-round athlete who was named junior athlete of the year at his high school, Mike told me he hoped to start a golf team when he began Grade 11 in the fall. Already playing to a five handicap, his ultimate goal was a golf scholarship at an American college.

Earlier I'd heard talk in the caddyshack about the annual caddy tournament held a couple of weeks before.

"I don't want to talk about that," Mike said stubbornly. "Everyone expected me to win, but I played the worst golf of my life. It was horrible!"

With just one exception, the golfers in our group struck me as pleasant fellows. I took them for business associates who, though not particularly close friends, felt themselves fortunate to escape their offices for an afternoon on a superb golf course. If they had a deal cooking, they didn't talk of it in front of us.

The golfer the boys and I all took an immediate dislike to was a red-faced little man with tight curly hair, a receding chin and a perpetually pinched expression. Early in the round, he complained that there were too many of us standing around the green watching him putt. Obviously, he had never before played in the company of caddies. And like a lot of golfers, he felt embarrassed and more than a little intimidated.

"I've had golfers who apologized even before teeing off about how bad they were going to play," said Grant.

"I caddied for a guy who said 'Sorry' after every lousy shot," Mike added. "Finally, I said, 'Mister, don't worry about it. I've seen lots worse than this.'"

Rob McDannold had told me that fighting back such feelings of inadequacy is the biggest hurdle golfers have to overcome the first few times they go out with a caddy. Reared in the age of two-cart foursomes, they find the sudden lack of privacy unnerving.

As the author John Updike, a passionate golfer, once wrote, "My golf is so delicate, so tenuously wired together with silent inward prayers, exhortations, and unstable visualizations, that the sheer pressure of an additional pair of eyes crumbles the whole structure into rubble."

Our red-faced golfer had ample reason to feel self-conscious. His swing surely had to be one of the ugliest I'd ever seen. Every shot he hit performed a funky little duck hook at the highest point of its arc, airborne one second, plunging to the earth the next.

"He's a jerk," said Todd, who was carrying his bag. "Did you guys see him throw his club at me?"

Todd's complaint came after he, Eric, Mike and I had carried the bags on ahead to the next tee, leaving only Grant behind to man the pin while our foursome putted out. We made this a habit after the red-faced golfer's grouse about there being too many people around the green. At any rate, he was right that there was no point in all of us standing around.

"You're full of it," Mike shot back at Todd. "He never threw his club at you."

No doubt Todd was exaggerating, but his imagination had been understandably stirred. In the caddyshack all the kids were talking about how, a week or so before, one of the Hamilton club's most notoriously hot-tempered golfers had whipped his putter into a water hazard, narrowly missing his caddy's head. Or so it was claimed.

Rob McDannold had also told me during our interview that if given the opportunity to help, veteran caddies like Todd, Mike, Grant and Eric could each shave five strokes or more off their player's final score. They had all walked the course hundreds of times and come to know it like their own backyards. The boys could have helped with club selection, in the reading of greens and by providing exact yardage to the pins from any-where on the course.

But not one of our golfers ever asked, which was a crying shame since they needed all the help they could get.

With the exception of the host, who wisely pulled out his 3-wood on narrower fairways, they insisted on using their drivers at the tee of every par four and par five. Yet none of them had the ability to hit the fairway better than once out of every three or four tries.

"I'd tell all of them to put their drivers away," Mike whispered to me. "Everyone knows it's the hardest club in the bag to control."

At the game's highest levels, caddies are considered vital to a golfer's success. Lorie Kane has often described her caddy, former Canadian Tour pro Danny Sharp, as more of a partner than an employee. In fact, before Kane finally broke into the winners' circle during the 2000 season, she was often criticized for relying too heavily on his judgment, the suggestion being that Sharp served as her emotional crutch.

When PGA Tour rookie Rich Beem won his first tourney in 1999, his Canadian caddy Steve Duplantis received a large measure of the credit from onlookers. Duplantis inspired his golfer with frequent pep talks, soothingly patted his shoulder before important tee shots and aggressively guided Beem around the golf course, convincing him that every hole loomed as large as a garbage can. "One of the great caddying performances of all time," enthused CBS golf analyst Ken Venturi.

A handful of caddies have become stars in their own right. Mike "Fluff" Cowan rated a *Sports Illustrated* profile and was recognized by more fans than most PGA Tour players during his days looping for Tiger Woods. Angelo Argea, with his trademark grey Afro, reigned supreme alongside his golfer, Jack Nicklaus, during the 1970s. And the late Jeff "Squeeky" Medlin, one of the most beloved of caddies, shot to fame in 1991 when with icy calm he steered the volatile John Daly to the PGA Championship.

As we made our way through Hamilton's front nine, we five neglected caddies, inspired by our disdain for the red-faced golfer, compared notes about the least likeable golfers we had ever known.

"There's a guy here at the club who's famous for going berserk and throwing his clubs up trees," Grant said. "One time he heaved his sand wedge at least 20 yards up into the branches. Then he threw another club trying to get the first one to come down. Then another. By the time he was finally done, he had something like three wedges, a driver and his putter caught in the tree."

"Yeah," Mike added. "Almost every time he plays, the grounds-keepers have to bring out the ladders."

That same golfer, clearly a troubled individual in desperate need of anger-management counselling, once broke an expensive new driver over his knee, then threw it deep into the woods. That evening his enterprising caddy went back and found the club head. The next day, after having it reshafted, the caddy sold the driver for $200.

Todd, Mike, Grant and Eric were seasoned loopers who could shrug off the occasional foul moods and tantrums of club members as all part of the caddy experience. It should be noted that the boys agreed that most golfers treat them with only respect and solicitude. "What's your name?" club members almost always ask. "What school do you go to?" "Are you a golfer?" "What are your hopes for the future?" Some members have become friends who make a point of asking for them on a regular basis. Almost all, by any criteria, are excellent role models.

But for youngsters just starting out, some of them as young

as 11, that first encounter with a temporarily deranged golfer can be life-altering. "Early this season one of the new C caddies went out with a member who's always swearing and freaking out," Todd remembered with a laugh. "After about three holes, the kid was so terrified he dropped his bag and ran all the way home. We haven't seen him since."

It has long been an accepted truth that a golfer's treatment of his caddy is a reflection of his own psyche. The selfish golfer speaks scarcely a word to his. The insecure player becomes even more diffident and apologetic. The dishonest golfer blames a bad shot on the caddy's advice—or lack of it. And the egomaniac practically begs for compliments.

I asked the boys about this last character trait. I'd noticed that none of them—including Mike, who was carrying for a decent player—had uttered even a single "Good shot" since we'd set out from the first tee.

"Too risky," said Mike. "What we think is a good shot, they might not be happy with. A drive could land nice and straight down the fairway. But maybe the golfer has been working on trying to get more distance, so he's not totally happy with it. Unless you can see that your golfer is really excited about a shot, it's safer just to keep quiet."

"Some golfers are also kind of suspicious," said Eric, speaking up at last. "I guess those would be the insecure ones. They're wondering if we really mean it when we say 'Good shot,' like we're being sarcastic or something."

AH, THE EAGERLY ANTICIPATED Caddy Special—the hot dog and cold drink combo that is every caddy's reward after having lugged the bags over Hamilton's front nine. Tradition dictates that no club member, no matter how miserly or soured in disposition, can refuse to buy his caddy this treat during the stopover at the snack bar near the 10th tee. All beef, thick and juicy, the dogs were tube-steak heaven.

While we were polishing off our snack, I wondered aloud about caddy initiation rites. I'd read somewhere that back in the golden age, when thousands of caddies worked at courses all across Canada, newcomers were subjected to everything from water torture to head shavings to being tied to trees with a garden hose and left out overnight.

"Never heard of anything like that," Todd said, belching loudly. "We usually just beat the hell out of the new kids."

If anything, our golfers played even worse on the back nine. With the exception of their host, they were almost constantly in either the tall grass or the woods. And yet still they stubbornly pulled out the drivers for every tee shot.

One of the other caddies I had talked to early that morning confessed to occasionally taking pity on terrible golfers by kicking their balls into better positions when no one was looking.

Mike, a boy of strong character of whom any parents would be proud, expressed surprise and alarm that a fellow caddy could sink so low.

"If that does happen it's only during casual matches," Mike said emphatically. "No caddy would ever think of doing that during a club tournament or if they knew members had money riding on who won their game."

Just as at any golf club, there are players at Hamilton who haven't played from a bad lie in years. The boys agreed that during casual play a caddy must learn to turn a blind eye to even the most blatant rule infractions.

They nodded and laughed appreciatively at a hoary old caddy

tale I had come across about the unscrupulous golfer whose shot had landed deep in the rough. While pretending to search for it, the golfer stomped down all the grass in the vicinity of his ball. Finally, he asked his caddy, "Do you think I can reach the green with a 4-wood?"

"No, sir," the caddy replied. "It'll take at least three more stomps for a 4-wood."

Though Mike had been doing most of the carrying—well, truthfully, he had been doing *all* the carrying since the third hole, leaving me free to take notes—I started to break a heavy sweat by the 14th tee. It was a languid, typically humid Southern Ontario August day, and I could see that the boys were beginning to wilt under their loads. When asked how heavy his bag is, a PGA Tour caddy will typically respond, "That depends on how many under or over par my boss is." Judged by that criterion, each of the boys, except for Mike, was hauling a psychological ton.

Fully loaded for tournament play, a tour pro's bag tips the scales at around 40 pounds. That includes the regulation 14 clubs, a bare minimum of a dozen balls, rainwear and an umbrella, tees, a half-dozen gloves and such personal items as a wallet, a watch and often nowadays a cellphone. During practice rounds, when many players pack extra clubs they're considering using on that particular course, the bag gets even heavier. Caddies also add to their load during these preliminary outings by carrying laser range finders to measure yardages.

Occasionally, caddy master Cal Armstrong will deem a bag too heavy for his young caddies to shoulder. Unzipped, the bags have been known to spill forth everything from a hundred or more practice balls to a 26-ouncer of Glenfiddich to whole boxes of atrophied chocolate bars. Cal will give the bag his nod of approval only after all non-essential items have been removed.

It is, however, an imperfect system, and offending bags frequently slip through. Not long before we met, Mike had looped for a club member who owned a humungous tour bag dreaded by the caddies for its great weight. Aside from the usual assortment of clubs and paraphernalia, the custom-made bag, which featured five storage shelves, contained a radio, a battery outlet and space for an ice-cream maker, which the owner had only reluctantly removed two days before.

Though he had planned to work two rounds that day, Mike—a sturdy lad who is, remember, an all-star athlete—felt so bushed after 18 holes that he went home and collapsed in bed. "My shoulder was killing me," he complained.

I was relieved to learn that Hamilton's youngest and smallest caddies are encouraged to use pull carts, thus avoiding untimely collapses and the early onset of an affliction known as caddy shoulder. This pronounced droop, which was common during the golden age, is still frequently seen among professional bag carriers.

CAREFREE STROLLS DOWN EMERALD fairways without even the weight of a single club in their hands, never having to rake a bunker or search for a ball—I envied Hamilton golfers the purity of the caddy experience. When the game is stripped to its essence, its attractions become more distinct. The presence of a caddy allows the serious golfer to focus on improving, affords nature lovers more time to admire the scenery and offers everyone the rare gift, if only for 18 holes, of freedom from the mundane.

One persistent knock against caddy programs has long been that walking a course, rather than riding in a cart, slows the pace of play. Yet Rob McDannold informed me that club members who employ caddies on weekend mornings average rounds of three hours and 45 minutes, which is fast by any measure. In fact, it can be argued that caddies actually help speed up the game. A golfer can already be at his ball while another player is hitting his, ready to play instead of having to wait and ride over in the cart.

Despite the heat and a few bug bites and scratches suffered while looking for lost balls in the woods, I was in no hurry to see our round end. It was fun hanging out with the boys, sharing their jokes and for a few hours pretending to be a teenager again.

For Mike the allure of caddying was the opportunity to be close to the game he loved. Todd, who also worked nights in the local Purolator warehouse, said he did it for the chance to be outdoors and get some exercise. Both Grant and Eric said they were in it mostly for the money.

"What other jobs are there for kids our age?" a 14-year-old caddy had asked me that morning. "It's not like we have a lot of choices."

Depending on their rating, Hamilton caddies are paid between $12 and $20 for each round. A bonus of $1 per round is awarded to kids who caddy a minimum of 40 times a season. As well, show money, ranging from $8 to $11, is given to caddies who show up at peak times and wait around for a minimum of three and a half hours without getting a bag.

Although strictly forbidden by club policy, tipping is commonplace at the club. In the caddyshack that morning I had heard talk of a high roller who had recently tipped a boy $50. More often the rewards are in the $5 to $15 range.

The goal of almost every caddy I spoke to was to one day be promoted by Cal Armstrong to service in the back shop: cleaning and storing clubs, washing the fleet of electric carts, picking up at the practice range. Back-shop employment offers prestige, better pay and regular hours. Not quite as glamorous, though still considered a step up from caddying, is a position with the groundskeeping crew.

By this point late in the summer only the most enthusiastic caddies still turned up for work every day. Each of them was determined to complete the 40 rounds required to receive his invitation to the annual caddy banquet. Every autumn on this gala night, some 50 kids dressed in their Sunday best are ushered into the swank dining room of Hamilton's clubhouse. It's their one chance to check out the inside of the stately ivy-covered mansion, for entry is forbidden to them the rest of the year.

After speeches and a full-course dinner, bonus cheques, awards (including Caddy of the Year) and other prizes are handed out. Piled high near the head table is an almost overwhelming assortment of booty, including clubs, golf bags, shirts, caps and gloves.

"Sure, it's a good party," said a jaded Todd, the longest-serving caddy in our group. "But if you've been to one, you've been to them all."

TODD, ESPECIALLY, HAD A HARD time keeping a straight face when the red-faced golfer's tee shot on the 18th hole richocheted off a nearby tree and landed smack in the middle of the parallel-running 17th fairway. Fighting back the giggles, the rest of us sneaked a grin at Todd, who had set out after his golfer on one final detour.

"I've never seen a group play this badly," confided Mike as we walked the home hole. "Not in all my rounds of caddying."

Minutes later we dropped our golfers off at the clubhouse side door. They all politely offered their thanks to the boys, including the red-faced golfer, who handed Todd a generous tip. But had he done that from generosity of spirit or simply because he felt it was expected? Could it be, we all wondered guiltily, that we'd misjudged him?

Before heading home, I stopped in to see Rob McDannold to compliment him on the course and his caddy program.

"As long as I'm the head pro here, there'll always be at least one club in Canada where kids can find summer jobs as caddies," said McDannold, ready to go to the barricades to keep his dream alive. "This caddy program is part of our mission statement."

CHAPTER 12

ISLAND DESTINATION

"HERE'S ONE I BET YOU HAVEN'T heard before," Vic
Clayton insisted in his husky, basso profundo growl while we
waited on the 17th tee of Cape Breton's Dundee Resort and Golf
Club. His eyes shining with pleasure, Dundee's course marshal, a
gregarious transplanted Torontonian who in a previous life was a
linebacker with the CFL Toronto Argonauts, knew his material
cold and by now felt certain of his audience's reception. Vic's was
the confidence of a born comic who had worked the room—or in
this case, the tees and sloping fairways of Dundee—a thousand
times before.

"A woman is having a heart-to-heart talk with her husband," Vic began, his voice rumbling like distant thunder.

"'If I die will you remarry?' she asks him.

"'Yes, I think I probably will,' her husband answers after a moment's pause.

"'Will you give her my clothes?' she asks.

"'Yes,' he says. 'It would be a shame to see them go to waste.'

"'Will you give her my golf clubs?' she demands with growing concern.

"'No, don't be silly,' he answers firmly. 'She's a lefty!'"

The Dundee course, part of a family resort complex near the village of West Bay, just over the Canso Causeway that joins mainland Nova Scotia with Cape Breton, was my first stop on an autumn tour of this ruggedly beautiful island (no less an authority than *Condé Nast Traveller* magazine has called it the world's most scenic isle) that is busily remaking itself into one of North America's premier golf destinations. Right now there are four public courses — dubbed the Fab Four by Nova Scotia's tourism marketers — drawing the attention of ever-increasing numbers of golfers. West Bay's Dundee and Le Portage Golf Club in the picturesque Acadian village of Chéticamp are both demanding and rewarding layouts. But what has really created a buzz in the golf community is the one-two knockout punch of newcomer Bell Bay Golf Club in the booming tourist town of Baddeck, and recently restored Highlands Links in Cape Breton Highlands National Park, two world-class courses situated less than an hour's drive apart on the famed Cabot Trail. Designed by Toronto's Tom McBroom, Bell Bay was voted Canada's best new course of 1998 by *Golf Digest*. And following a $4-million facelift, Highlands Links, a Stanley Thompson gem opened in 1941, was ranked the world's 57th best course by *GOLF Magazine* in 1999, the highest rating given any Canadian layout.

"When you're driving up the road to the course, it's like driving up to heaven," George Knudson enthused of Highlands after playing a "Shell's Wonderful World of Golf" television exhibition against fellow Canadian Al Balding there in 1965. "There's not a better walk in golf."

At Highlands, thanks to a by now well-worn videotape I'd managed to acquire of the Knudson-Balding match, I would for the first time be able to literally golf in George Knudson's spikeprints, imagining myself in my hero's company throughout a complete round of play. I'd been eagerly anticipating the experience for months.

Golf is helping revitalize the economy of an island hit hard in recent years by the near-collapse of coal mining and the exhaustion of Atlantic fishing stocks, industries that had sustained Cape Breton for decades. Highlands Links and Bell Bay in particular are drawing golfers who just a few years ago would never for a moment have considered a golf junket to Nova Scotia's backwoods. The opening of three more courses still on the drawing boards during the time of my visit can only enhance the island's reputation and attract even more visitors. There's Ben Eoin, another Tom McBroom project, located a 25-minute drive out of Sydney; Inverness, a links-style course by Montreal architect Graham Cooke, who oversaw the Highlands' restoration; and Whycocomagh, designed by Michigan architect Rick Smith on land owned by a local Mi'kmaq band.

Certainly my new friend Vic Clayton was convinced of the charms of Cape Breton golf.

"Just look at that," he said with the hint of an island inflection he had picked up during his five years in the West Bay area, sweeping his beefy arm over the distant horizon of Bras d'Or Lake after stopping our cart midway up the 17th fairway. Almost every hole at Dundee, which has been chiselled into the side of South Mountain above the resort's main lodge and rental cottages, offers panoramic views of the southern shore of the world's largest saltwater lake. The vista that spread before us on this crisp and gloriously sunny day in early October, the leaves a crimson and yellow blaze of colour, was nothing short of breathtaking.

Vic pointed to an eagle lazily circling high over the lake. "You won't see anything like that in Toronto, will you, boy?"

From the moment of his arrival after marrying a native Cape Bretoner and moving east, the 61-year-old former footballer and retired Toronto firefighter had fallen under the spell of the still largely unspoiled island explorer John Cabot first set foot on five centuries ago. Today, three distinct ethnic cultures thrive in Cape Breton. The original inhabitants, the Mi'kmaq, have five First Nations on the island. The Acadians of Cape Breton arrived in the 1700s. And in the early 1800s, Gaelic settlers came in force from the highlands and islands of Scotland, bringing with them the language, customs and music of a culture that remains stubbornly intact to this day. Traditional Scottish singing and fiddling is as ubiquitous in Cape Breton as reggae is in Jamaica and has provided the inspiration for such Canadian recording stars as Natalie MacMaster, Ashley MacIsaac and the Rankins.

Vic and I had been getting on like a couple of old teammates ever since discovering on the first tee that we had attended the same public school in Toronto's suburban west end, good old Maple Leaf P.S. He went on to play two seasons as a second-string defensive lineman for the Toronto Argonauts in 1959–60, back in the heyday of the CFL when 30,000 to 40,000 fans routinely turned out for games at CNE Stadium.

Football left Vic with two wrecked knees and a convenient excuse whenever he shanked or sliced a ball during our round together. He grumbled loudly about not being able to get a good turn on his swing, cursing the fates that had led him to a career on the gridiron.

"Jesus, Mary and Joseph!" he howled after an errant drive.

"Get up there, you bastard!" he roared like a wounded bear when his approach shot quit on him just short of the green.

Between the end of his football days and the start of a 30-year career with the Toronto Fire Department, Vic caddied for a variety of top Ontario professional golfers. He'd been in love with the game ever since taking it up as a teenager at the Oakdale Golf and Country Club, George Knudson's first Toronto home.

When he told me he'd carried Knudson's bag in several Ontario tournaments, our bond of friendship was permanently sealed.

"Man, old George could really smack that ball," Vic remembered fondly. "He hit them so hard he used to crack the wood of his drivers right around the hosel."

Knudson was at his peak then, Canada's most admired golfer, and the crowds turned out in force to follow him. "He'd take a divot and before I could replace it, the crowd would almost trample me, taking off after George," Vic said. "I'd have to ask a straggler in the crowd to replace it for me just to keep up.

"He was such a terrific guy," Vic said of George. "We'd pass the beer tent after the ninth hole and he'd look over at me lugging his big bag of clubs in the heat, smile and say, 'Give that boy a brew.'"

Vic recalled a miraculous recovery shot he saw Knudson make after my hero had pulled his drive deep into the woods on a tricky par five during an Ontario Open played at Toronto's Islington Golf Club.

"Well, sir," said Vic. "George goes in there and finds his ball buried in just a terrible spot—in heavy brush, twigs all around. But he says, 'I can make this.' He pulls out an iron and hits a shot that soars over a old spruce tree and drops onto the green no more than five feet from the pin. Then George drops the putt for an eagle. I'd never seen anything like it."

Knudson went on to win that tourney (one of five Ontario Open titles he captured) and paid Vic a princely $50 for his labours, the standard 10 per cent of his winnings.

"Easy money," Vic told me with a smile. "I would have carried George Knudson's bags for free."

Vic greeted by name most of the golfers we encountered during our weekday morning round at Dundee. In October, almost everyone who plays the course from Monday to Friday is a local. When he let a solo player, the captain of an oil tanker, play through, I asked him about the role of a course marshal, a thankless but increasingly vital job in these days of bumper-to-bumper traffic and the ugly rise of what has become known as "golf rage" on public courses across North America.

Though golf is still generally the most civilized of sports, where tradition is revered and praise and sympathy are offered to an opponent as generously as to a partner, many veteran golfers are gnashing their teeth at the interminable delays during their rounds. Sometimes it seems that *everybody* is playing golf—young, old, middle-aged, male, female. According to the Royal Canadian Golf Association, Canada has by far the highest participation rate in the world. In 1998, the year of the RCGA's last survey, 5.2 million Canadians, or a whopping 20.5 per cent of the population, played golf at least once.

A big part of the frustration stems from the difficulty in getting tee times at public courses, where 70 per cent of all golfers take their divots. Many courses further aggravate the problem by greedily bunching groups too closely together, making it all but impossible for play to flow smoothly. When golfers finally do get onto the course, a round can easily stretch longer than five hours. This in a sport in which a round of three and a half hours has long been considered the ideal.

Fisticuffs have been known to break out when frustrated golfers deliberately hit into a slower group ahead to hurry them along.

Perhaps Canada's most notorious case of golf rage erupted in the summer of 1999 when a burly 33-year-old Guelph, Ontario, golfer grabbed an older man by the neck and punched him four or five times in the face. The younger golfer, who outweighed his opponent by 70 pounds, lost his temper after learning that the fellow's group had hit six shots into another foursome that included his brother, 12-year-old nephew and a friend. An Ontario Court judge sentenced the attacker to three months of house arrest and 18 months of probation.

I'd heard the role of a public course marshal compared to that of an overworked air controller trying to juggle arrivals and departures at a stacked-up metropolitan airport, and to a cowboy rounding up resisting stray cattle and herding them back home to the corral before nightfall.

When I suggested this last analogy to Vic, he snorted loudly and said, "More like a mule driver, you mean! Some golfers I've seen have about as much sense."

Even more than the overwhelming increase in golfers vying for tee times, Vic blamed the epidemic of slow play on TV. "People watch Tiger Woods and the other big stars on television deliberate over every shot and then figure that's the way it's done," he said. "But what they forget is that those guys are playing for millions of dollars in prizes and endorsements. I see players who've maybe been out twice in their lives throwing grass in the air to see which way the wind is blowing, pacing off yardage like a goddamned football referee and checking the green from every which angle to try to get a read on their putts. Then, after all that, they usually muff the shot anyway.

"Good players are almost always fast players," Vic was convinced. "It's the 25 handicapper who drives you crazy."

As a resort course, Dundee gets more than its fair share of newcomers to the game. It's always a dead giveaway a player is a novice if he asks about renting golf shoes at the pro shop. Another sure tip-off is when a husband and wife arrive with the kids and a picnic lunch.

In truth, Dundee is one of the last courses on which any novice golfer's soft spikes should tread. Designed by Canadian Robert Moote, another of the many architects who got their start as an apprentice to Stanley Thompson, the 17-year-old course's Slope Rating of 132 is second on the island only to Highlands Links' 141. Dundee's narrow landing areas and fiendishly tiered and sloped greens can send frustrated duffers into club-throwing fits of frenzy.

It's Vic's job to gently hurry slowpokes up, as well as to listen patiently to the complaints of the golfers playing behind them who are fuming over the delays. Like all successful course marshals, Vic is a master of diplomacy. Often he dips into his vast catalogue of jokes to break the tension when he's forced to push the plodders along. The old gladiator will also ease his aching knees out of his cart to help golfers look for lost balls, or offer them a used one to keep things moving. The idea is to establish such rapport with the customers they don't realize they're being managed.

Sometimes, though, Vic has to bite his tongue to keep from

telling a customer what he really thinks. He gets particularly infuriated by golfers who hold up traffic to take business calls on their cellphones. The reason Vic fled the big city was to find a simpler way of life in Cape Breton. He hunts and fishes and strings traps for beaver, fox and coyote, every day spending as many hours as he can outdoors. He can't understand the minds of people who are supposed to be enjoying a relaxing game but who will stand there talking business, oblivious to the impatience of their partners and everyone playing behind them. Before the coming of cellphones, the golf course was a refuge of tranquillity.

Unfortunately, jokes and kid-glove diplomacy don't always work. Course marshals collect horror stories about golfers so wilfully ignorant of the game's rules of etiquette—or even seemingly of how to behave in civilized society—that no amount of cajoling can get them to change their ways.

"Company tournaments are the worst," Vic complained with a groan. "Some guys at company outings practically have A.H. tattooed on their foreheads. They're out for a good time and couldn't care less about the consequences. I've seen men puking in bushes at these events and getting so drunk that for a lark they try to plough their carts through sand traps."

Even sober, golfers frequently treat their carts like bumper cars on a carnival midway. At courses with water hazards, people inevitably drive into them at least once a season. Carts overturn when drivers attempt to scale steep hills; they're smashed into trees and sunk in swamps. One fellow at Dundee sent his cart hurtling down a drainage ditch with a 10-foot drop.

In extreme cases, Vic will revoke a golfer's playing privileges on the spot, offering a full refund to avoid as much unpleasantness as possible. Players who are guilty of nothing more than persistent dawdling are given at least two warnings before finally being told to pick up and go home.

What the owners of Dundee and other public golf courses are starting to realize is that slow play costs them money. With new courses opening at a rate of better than one a day across North America, competition is stiffer than ever. No course that wants to reach its full profitability can afford to be known as a safe haven for dawdlers.

Many golf courses have started posting playing tips on golf carts to encourage golfers to get moving. Some nine-hole courses that never bothered with marshals before have now seen the wisdom of always having one on the grounds, while better 18-hole tracks frequently employ two marshals at all times. One increasingly popular innovation is the flying of flags from marshals' carts to let everyone know at a glance how things are moving along: red means there's a gap and everyone should step it up; green means play is proceeding apace. Courses have also taken to posting clocks every few holes to let groups know how fast they're playing in relation to their starting times, with "time pars" noted on the scorecard for each hole.

Vic offered the sensible suggestion that many players, particularly novices, might enjoy the game more if they played best ball or broke into teams for match play, where the defeated twosome picks up once the hole is lost or conceded. "How much fun can it be to look at your scorecard at the end of the day and see you've shot 120 or something horrible like that?" he asked. "With best ball or match play they'll go away remembering only their good shots."

He felt certain that if only golfers would lighten up a bit and not take the game so seriously that every shot seems like a matter of life or death, pace of play would naturally pick up.

"We had a guy around here who got so frustrated with himself that he was always throwing his clubs and cursing a blue streak," Vic recalled. "Then I overheard someone tell him one of the wisest things I've ever heard on a golf course. 'I don't know why you get mad,' this fellow said. 'You're not good enough to get mad.'

"Think about that," Vic went on. "Most people never practise, maybe play once a week at best and then when they get on a golf course they expect to play well. It doesn't make sense. Golf is a lot more difficult than that."

Vic paused for a beat, timing a punchline that served as a fitting endnote to a frustrating but otherwise splendid day during which we'd both muffed more than our share.

"You know why they call it golf, don't you?" Vic asked, enjoying himself. "Because every other four-letter word was taken."

IN PINNING ITS HOPES ON golf tourism to bolster the island's economy, Cape Breton is following the path first blazed by its Maritimes cousin, Prince Edward Island.

Back in the early 1990s, the 10 courses then open for business in Canada's smallest province banded together to form Golf PEI, an organization whose sole purpose was the marketing of Prince Edward Island as a travel destination for golf-loving outlanders. The gist of their pitch was that even if golfers came for only three or four days, they could easily play as many as five courses within the island's cosy confines.

Marketers set up toll-free reservation lines, bought advertising space in golf magazines and other publications and took booths at golf shows across North America. The results were almost instantaneous. Bookings for golf throughout the province jumped dramatically and continue to climb to this day, with economic benefits plain for all to see. Golf grew to a $70-million industry in 2000 from about $17 million just five or six years before. More than 10 new courses — including such showpieces as the Links at Crowbush Cove and Dundarave — have opened since the formation of Golf PEI and still more are on the way.

None too surprisingly, other regions of the country were quick to jump on the destination-golf bandwagon. Wherever a tourism industry existed in combination with a handful or more nearby courses, a promotional net was cast to entice golfers to come partly to play the game they love and partly to see the local sights. Marketing groups formed among pay-for-play courses in the Whistler, Vancouver, Kamloops and Okanagan regions of British Columbia; in the Alberta Rockies around Banff; the Toronto, Muskoka and Niagara areas of Ontario; Montreal and the Laurentians in Quebec; as well as in several other parts of the country.

Cape Breton's Fab Four is a consortium of local courses formed in 1998 to chase after the mushrooming national and international golf market. Also pitching in with funding was the province's tourism department.

Today, Nova Scotia attracts most of its golfers from Quebec and Ontario, but increasing numbers are arriving from the United States and Europe as word spreads about Highlands Links, Bell Bay and such top mainland courses as Glen Arbour and the Pines. And almost always golfers come prepared to spend freely. According to provincial tourism officials, the average visitor spends about $1,500. The average golfer, however, spends at least 35 per cent more than that.

Certainly the next stop on my tour of the Fab Four, Le Portage

Golf Club in the Acadian village of Chéticamp, has made every effort to get its share of the loot being tossed around by golfing tourists. An expansion from nine holes to 18 was completed in 1998, just in time to reap the first rewards of the Fab Four's marketing campaign.

Improvements included a new clubhouse and a subtle reworking of the original nine holes designed by Robert Moote (also the architect of Dundee) and opened in 1981. This time the designer was Moote's son, David, which seemed entirely appropriate at a course that has always operated as something of a family affair. Many of Chéticamp's tradesmen, who like most citizens of the town can trace their local roots back a dozen generations, worked on the community-owned course not for money but for memberships.

The result of their labours is a par-72, 6,751-yard layout offering a stiff test of every aspect of a golfer's game. Best of all is the setting at the foot of the rolling Highlands on a plateau overlooking the harbour and historic St. Peter's Church. It's said that on a clear day from certain vantage points on the course golfers can see Pillar Rock and the Presqu'ile headland far up the coast in Cape Breton Highlands National Park.

Sadly, the afternoon I played, Pillar Rock might well have been a world away. Near hurricane-force storms were battering Canada's Atlantic coast. For the first— and I knew very likely the last—time in my life I had a golf course entirely to myself. So unusual was the opportunity that through a driving downpour and bone-chilling winds I played on, too stubborn or too stupid to come in out of the rain.

Afterwards, I sat in the clubhouse warming myself with a bowl of the house specialty, a spicy tomato-and-macaroni soup. Toe-tapping Acadian fiddle music, also good for the circulation, poured forth from the sound system.

Wet but happy, I for once refused to even consider adding up my score.

THERE'S A POPULAR SAYING in the Maritimes: "If you don't like the weather, wait five minutes and it'll change."

Yet the unrelenting late-autumn rain dogged me across the island from Chéticamp to the Bell Bay Golf Club in the resort town of Baddeck, situated at the eastern extreme of the Cabot Trail. No stranger to the vagaries of the local weather, Bell Bay saw its grand opening delayed by six months after Hurricane Hortense raged through the region in September 1996, washing away $750,000 worth of choice topsoil and several tons of bent-grass seed.

From the moment Bell Bay finally opened the following autumn, Cape Breton golf was forever changed. Here, at last, was a worthy partner to venerable Highlands Links. On its own, Highlands had never been enough of a draw to lure large numbers of golfers to the island. But a restored Highlands in combination with the newcomer *Golf Digest* named Canada's best new course of 1998 was a rare treat guaranteed to make golfers sit up and take notice.

Twice before in his better than 15 years as a designer, Tom McBroom's courses had been singled out in the same category by *Golf Digest*. He also won in 1994 for the Links at Crowbush Cove in Prince Edward Island, the course most often credited with pro-pelling that province's golf boom, and again in 1997 for the Lake Joseph Club in Ontario. As well, McBroom has designed such lauded courses as Le Géant at Mont Tremblant in Quebec, Heron Point in Ontario and Morgan Creek in British Columbia.

There are, however, knowledgeable observers who believe that

McBroom has done his best work here in Baddeck on a rugged jut of land set amidst rolling highlands on the eastern shore of the Bras d'Or.

Bell Bay, named for telephone inventor Alexander Graham Bell who spent the last 37 summers of his life across the bay in a hilltop mansion named Beinn Bhreagh (Gaelic for "beautiful mountain"), is a marvellously scenic, painstakingly thought out design with plush fairways lined with towering stands of birch and pine trees, boldly moulded bunkers and velvet greens. McBroom has emphasized strategy, shot-making and playability over the raw power demanded by so many modern courses. Four sets of tees stretch the challenge from a starting point of 5,165 yards to 7,037 at the tips. Even a rank duffer, provided that he acknowledges his limitations and chooses the sensible tee, should walk away with pride intact.

About two-thirds of the $8 million raised by four local businessmen to build Bell Bay was provided by loans from the federal and provincial governments. To ensure that the golf course became a vital part of the community, the developers purchased land just a 10-minute walk from a quaint downtown lined with craft shops, cafés and inns that had long relied almost entirely on the town's connection with Alexander Graham Bell to bring the tourists in. Anchoring one end of Baddeck is a museum dedicated to telling the story of the inventor's life and his work, which annually attracts more than 120,000 visitors.

Now, suddenly, Baddeck had two major tourist attractions. New jobs were created in a community that, like most of Cape Breton, needed them desperately. It has been estimated that the golf course and the visitors it attracts annually inject more than $4 million into the local economy.

Encouraged by what would sadly prove to be only a temporary

lull in the downpour, I donned my rain gear and ventured out into the heavy mist to play Tom McBroom's masterwork. Accompanying me was Bell Bay's assistant pro, Stu Musgrave, a sweet-natured, towering 28-year-old whose praises I had heard sung ever since I'd first set foot on the island. Stu had recently returned in triumph from the Canadian Tour's fall qualifying school. Starting the next spring, he would become the first native Cape Bretoner ever to play on the national tour.

Though I could make out nothing in the mist beyond a few hundred yards, Stu informed me that usually visible on the far headland across the bay from the first tee is Alexander Graham Bell's mansion, a property that holds the gravesites of Bell and his wife, Mabel, and is owned by the family to this day. Indeed, every hole on the front nine of Bell Bay affords stunning vistas — not that I was able to personally confirm this — of the bay and Beinn Bhreagh.

History has been made on these salty waters. Casey Baldwin's giant hydrofoil set the world's water-speed record just below Bell Bay's fairways, and from its frozen surface the Silver Dart made the first successful airplane flight in the British Empire. Alexander Graham Bell occupied his summers in Baddeck tinkering with everything from radar and rocket propulsion to sonar, the iron lung, airscrews and airships.

Even the names given to Bell Bay's 18 holes reflect the past. Banshee, Golden Arm, Highland Lassie . . . each was the name of a ship built locally and that once called this port home.

So pleased was Stu to escape his duties in the pro shop and be out on the course that he hardly seemed to notice the driving rain that started up again by the third hole. Our round was but a prelude to the 250 or so balls he would hit later that afternoon, rain or shine, on the practice range.

"I've played in a lot worse than this," Stu told me, glancing dismissively at the darkening sky after driving his ball 260 yards or so down the soggy fairway. Like all Maritimers, he had a horde of stories about past storms that, by comparison, made the current conditions seem like a passing sunshower.

His biggest scare in bad weather, he told me as we squished along, came when he was 18 and a member of Nova Scotia's junior golf team. Returning home by ferry after a competition in Newfoundland, Stu and his teammates ran straight into the eye of a major storm. Though ordered below, the boys snuck back on deck, splashing and sliding and having a wonderful time until one of them slipped and barely managed to grab on to a railing before going overboard.

"How do you tell your coach you've lost one of your teammates?" Stu asked with a grim smile. "We pulled him back and went below without another word. We were all so frightened that no one dared come back on deck until the ferry docked."

Stu got his start at a nine-hole course called the Seaview Golf and Country Club in his hometown of North Sydney. Though a natural lefty, the future pride of Cape Breton golf learned to play right-handed with a set of clubs that had mysteriously found its way into the family garage—though no one in his family had ever played the game.

"Some things are simply meant to be, I guess," Stu said with a shrug. "I played soccer and baseball every summer, too, but from the moment I picked up a golf club everything else took a back seat."

At Seaview, Stu was taught by Lorne Jennex, the club's head pro and the father of Stu's best friend, Lorne Jr. Spending time with Jennex, to whom Stu still went for swing advice, made him realize he might also be able to make a future for himself in the game as a club pro or even, in his wildest dreams, a playing professional.

He started competing in tournaments when he was 11, though without notable success. When he was growing up, there were always other young players who routinely outplayed him or seemingly possessed more talent. Stu was the slow and steady type, every year getting a little better and growing more confident in his game. And just in case the career in golf didn't pan out, he made certain he got a solid education, first earning an arts degree from Quebec's Bishop's University and then adding a bachelor of business administration from the University College of Cape Breton. Only then, at the relatively ripe old age of 24, did Stu trust in his future enough to turn professional.

For two years he worked off-island as an assistant pro at the Belvedere Golf Club in Charlottetown, PEI, the home course of LPGA Tour star Lorie Kane. Canada's top female golfer, a famously good-natured and down-to-earth woman, was quick to offer Stu her advice and friendship.

"I think the best advice Lorie gave me was to not worry about what other golfers are doing, but to just play the golf course," Stu remembered. "I've found that's a great way to stay focused."

Stu continued his steady improvement by winning or placing well in a variety of local tournaments. In 1998, his game took a giant leap forward when he finished 22nd at the Canadian Tour's New Brunswick Open in Moncton after being given one of several spots left open for local players. His sizzling final-round 63 included three eagles.

That round, easily the best of his life either in casual or competitive play, gave Stu the confidence to try for his Canadian Tour playing card at the qualifying school held that fall in Ontario. But hampered by a severe case of tennis elbow, he finished a distant

42nd in the gruelling four-day showdown where only the top 15 finishers receive full playing privileges.

"I was reliving shots for months afterwards, thinking I should have done this differently, or if only I could have a particular shot back," Stu said. "But I'm an optimist by nature. A younger guy could end up wrecking his career from disappointment. But I was a little older and ready to learn from it."

Rather than worry that at age 27 time was running out for him to start a successful playing career, Stu took heart knowing that his friend Lorie Kane was 28 when she turned professional on the du Maurier Series, Canada's national women's tour, and that Mike Weir, the brilliant lefty from Bright's Grove, Ontario, was the same age when he finally earned his PGA Tour card after graduating from the Canadian Tour.

Whatever it took, Stu stood ready to make the sacrifice. He finally got serious about a weight problem he had mostly managed to ignore ever since he was a child. At one point he tipped the scales at 340 pounds. Being big-boned and six foot one helped him carry the extra weight with a minimum of self-consciousness, but he knew it had to be hurting his golf game. After months of rigorous workouts and faithful attendance at Weight Watchers, Stu got down to a comparatively svelte 260 pounds and felt stronger and more flexible than ever. His swing felt more rhythmical, and his drives carried an extra few yards.

Before the start of the 1999 season, Stu made the switch from Belvedere to Bell Bay, where the owners, proud Cape Bretoners all, offered the local boy the freedom to pursue his dream of a playing career. He competed throughout the Maritimes that summer, winning four tournaments and finishing near the top in several more. By autumn, Stu felt ready to try his luck once again at the Canadian Tour's Q-school, held at the Thunderbird Golf Club in Whitby, Ontario.

Like everyone else, I'd heard the horror stories about the six-round, 108-hole death march the final qualifiers are forced to endure for a shot at playing privileges on the world's premier professional circuit, the PGA Tour. But I'd heard barely a whisper about the Canadian Tour's Q-school. Was the pressure anything like that of the American version, where golfers have been known to vomit in the bushes between shots, break out in cold sweats and chills, endure sleepless nights of uncertainty and generally suffer through the most miserable few days of their entire careers, if not their lives?

Of course, I realized that among the world's professional circuits Canada's stands at least three or four very significant rungs down the ladder from the PGA Tour. Still, the Canadian Tour is respected as arguably the world's top developmental tour, an essential training ground where young players from around the globe gain competitive experience in preparation for an eventual leap to golf's big time.

More than 38 PGA Tour events have been won by Canadian Tour alumni. Prominent graduates include Mike Weir, Notah Begay III, Stuart Appleby, Scott Dunlap, Tim Herron, Stephen Ames, Dennis Paulson, Steve Stricker and Grant Waite.

So one would imagine that the emotional strain on Stu and the other hopefuls who try their luck at the tour's Q-School has to be intense. Failure, after all, means the almost certain death of the dreams of glory they've all been nurturing since the first day they picked up a golf club. This is their chance—maybe their last chance—to prove to themselves and to the golfing world that they have what it takes to be the next Weir or Appleby.

"Canadian Tour Q-school is four rounds of sheer hell for every golfer there," Stu readily agreed as we played on in the rain at Bell Bay. "Maybe the strangest thing, especially for golfers who've always had a lot of success, is to suddenly realize that the most talented players don't always win. It's the ones who handle the pressure best who make it through. Q-school is the survival of the mentally fittest."

The starting field that included Stu and 126 other golfers at Thunderbird would be reduced to the top 90 players and ties after the second round. The top 70 and ties would survive the third day, leaving the survivors to fight it out for 15 full tour cards in the stress-filled final round. Golfers finishing 16th to 25th receive conditional cards, which earn them entry into about half the tournaments. They have the opportunity to play their way into others during pre-qualifying rounds.

Stu told me of his disappointment after shooting 75 to finish the opening round in 28th spot, far back in the pack. His confidence level, though, remained high. Except for one bad hole, he played strongly on a blustery day that saw most golfers struggle.

One significant difference this year was the presence of his fiancée, Erin, whom Stu had met during his time in Prince Edward Island. Erin, a nurse, took time off from work to go to Whitby with Stu and serve as his caddy. If Stu got his card, she hoped to travel across Canada with him the next summer. Stu shyly confessed to me that he found the presence of the woman he loved calming and possibly even inspiring during the trial by fire of Q-school.

While we talked about Erin and their future together, I described for Stu an extraordinary group photograph of the wives of the American Ryder Cup team that had recently appeared in newspapers. Dressed in identical outfits for the opening ceremonies, each was a leggy, buxom, gorgeous, conspicuously blond Stepford wife clone of the next. The overwhelming impression left by the photo was that brunettes or redheads need not apply. They'd never survive the qualifying rounds.

"Then I guess it's just as well I'm not American," Stu said with mock sadness. "I couldn't even dream of making the team. Erin's gorgeous, but she's a brunette."

"Like Mike Weir's wife," I put in.

"Must be a Canadian thing," Stu said, chuckling.

For a competitive athlete, nothing is more emotionally draining than the countdown to the opening kickoff or the faceoff or the tee-off. All agree that once the battle has been entered most of the pressure instantly lifts.

A long rain delay tested Stu's calm on the second day of Q-school. After several hours spent anxiously pacing the clubhouse, he completed just 13 holes before darkness suspended play. The next day, following a restless night, he returned to finish his second round, waited impatiently a couple more hours and then played a full 18. "It was 13 hours of hard slogging, from sun-up to sundown," Stu grimly recounted. "Now that's nerve-racking, because you can't get into your normal rhythm the way you would in a regular tournament. All day I felt like I was playing hurry-up golf."

He told me he'd never forget the spooky silence that fell over the course from the second round on. Everyone was so intently focused on his game that Stu could almost hear the bent grass grow beneath his feet. The hush unnerved him. A self-described "yapper," Stu finds talking to his partner when he plays helps him stay loose. But this day the dagger-sharp looks of annoyance he got whenever he opened his mouth kept him unusually and uncomfortably quiet.

Despite the strangeness of the situation, Stu shot a 72 during his rain-delayed second round, a score strong enough to vault him into 17th place, only two spots short of the top-15 finish that would earn him his playing card.

Unfortunately, the rest of the day didn't go nearly so well. Growing fatigue quickly led to panic as Stu helplessly watched his game fall apart during the third round. A miserable score of 79 dropped him like a dud bomb to 38th in the field. With just one more round to go, Stu saw his chances as somewhere between hopeless and slim.

"That night Erin and I were emotional wrecks," Stu confided. "We sat talking and worrying for hours. We'd planned to go to Florida so I could work on my game. But suddenly it looked like we'd be spending another cold winter at home. Everything depended on me getting that card."

After talking in circles for hours, Stu finally told Erin he didn't want to discuss it any more. He knew in his heart he could compete with anyone in the field. Lying in bed late that night, he calmed his mind by focusing on memories of his final-round score of 63 the year before at the New Brunswick Open, the golden round that convinced him he had a future as a playing professional. He knew he'd have to play that well again to succeed the next day. No negative thoughts, he told himself over and over before he finally drifted off to sleep. No doubts.

The next morning Stu awoke in a strangely heightened state of calm. "Maybe I'd learned something from having been at Q-school before," he reflected. The most important thing he'd learned was that many players wilt under the intense pressure of the final round, and so scores typically go higher. "Pars are usually pretty good even when you're trying to make up ground," Stu said. "If I managed to play better than that, I still had a chance."

Through the first nine holes Stu reached deep down and played some of the best and smartest golf of his life. On the par-five opening hole, he resisted the temptation to try a risky second shot to the green. Instead, he layed up, then pitched to within 10 feet and sank his putt for birdie.

Fighting gusting winds, Stu just missed chipping in for another birdie on the second hole, settling for par. He went on to birdie the third, eighth and ninth holes, parring everything else on the front nine to make the turn at four-under.

A pair of bogeys on Thunderbird's tough back nine left Stu at two-under for his round as he prepared to hit his drive on the par-four 18th hole. "I had no idea where I stood in the field," Stu said. "But I thought I must be getting close to one of the final cards. Most important, I still felt calm and in control. Even the two bogeys hadn't changed that."

A strong tee shot found the middle of the fairway. Then, pumped with adrenaline, Stu sent his approach shot skidding 40 feet past the pin to the fringe of a wickedly difficult two-tiered green.

Stu's putting stroke had gone missing for most of the season. But he'd recently returned home to North Sydney for a putting session with his old coach Lorne Jennex, and that had seemed to help. Still, he was hardly brimming with confidence as he set up over his ball. All he hoped was to get it close enough to the hole for a chance at par and a score of 70. Three-putting this hole, which was all too easy to do, could prove disastrous to his chances.

He breathed deeply, stroked and then lifted his head to watch his ball on a journey that seemed to take hours rather than seconds. "As it got closer I saw it had a chance," Stu recounted. "When it dropped I could hardly believe it. A 40-footer for birdie! That had to be the greatest putt—heck, the greatest shot—of my life. What an awesome feeling!"

Looking on at Thunderbird's 18th green was Canadian Tour commissioner Jacques Burelle, who saluted Stu with a hearty round of applause as he walked from the green.

Stu had played to his full potential and even beyond when it mattered most. His score of 69 would equal the low round of the week. But was it enough? Golfers would still be on the course for another two hours. At least half of them had placed ahead of Stu after three rounds.

He felt hungry, but he was too nervous to eat. All around him stressed-out golfers awaited word of their fate. Some sat despondent, heads in their hands, knowing or fearing they had blown it on the final day. A few were openly crying. At the PGA Tour's Q-school, a sports psychologist stands beside the final green waiting to help distraught young men pick up the pieces. No such service is offered by the Canadian Tour.

For the next two hours, Stu's eyes never strayed from the leader board. He and six other players were tied at 295, seven over par for the four rounds. It looked as though there might have to be a playoff to decide who got in.

At last, word came that Stu had made it. He had jumped from 38th place after the third round into a tie for eighth at the end. Even so, there had been scant room for error. A score of 296 got the last card. "If I'd two-putted the 18th, I still would have been safe," Stu recalled. "But a three-putt would only have been good for a conditional card."

Commissioner Burelle sought him out in the crowd to offer his congratulations. "Well, I guess you really did need that putt," he said with a smile.

"I was just so relieved that after all that hard work, I had finally gotten it done," Stu told me. "Then I got on the phone to tell everyone back home the news.

"I can still hardly believe it," he said as we played on in the rain at Bell Bay. "I can't wait to get started."

A few weeks later he would be off to Florida to hone his game in preparation for his rookie campaign. In the meantime, he'd be working feverishly to raise the sponsorship money he needed to finance his new life as a playing professional. Not a few tour pros are children of affluence, their careers initially financed by rich fathers or friends among the country club set. Stu, whose background is working class, would have to raise the cash himself.

Canadian Tour players enjoy discounted rates at some hotels and often receive free balls and other gear from equipment manufacturers. All that helps. But players haven't a prayer of breaking even for the year unless they finish in the top 10 on the Order of Merit. During the 2000 season, tournament winners took home between $22,500 and $36,000, not even one-tenth the first-place payouts on the PGA Tour. Mike Weir, whose success Stu hoped to emulate, earned just $80,000 when he topped the Canadian Tour's Order of Merit in 1997.

Stu held no illusions about how difficult his adjustment to the pro playing ranks was likely to be. Like most newcomers, he was bound to struggle both financially and on the course for at least a season or two. He conservatively estimated it would cost $70,000—for travel, hotel rooms, food and other expenses—to keep him afloat on the tour during his rookie campaign. Realistically, he might earn only a fraction of that back in purses.

For years now, his mind set firmly on the goal of a playing career, Stu had been a tireless self-promoter. That his name was known in golfing circles not only in Nova Scotia but throughout the Maritimes was largely a credit to his talents as a public-relations flack.

"People often come up to me and say, 'Gee, I just saw your name in the paper,'" Stu said, laughing. "I've even had people razz me about being a media darling. What they don't know is that I was planting most of the stories myself, especially this past summer when I knew I was going to be looking for sponsors for next season. Whenever I did well in a tournament, I'd call in the results right away."

Several Cape Breton companies as well as the Fab Four consortium had already stepped forward to offer Stu sponsorship money. In return for help from the latter, Stu agreed to spread the word about the pleasures of golf in Cape Breton during his travels across Canada. At each stop on the tour, he'd distribute brochures and make a point of contacting the press with story ideas.

Stu genuinely appreciated all the local support. He'd courted it like a lover and he knew how much he would continue to rely on it while he chased his dream. But as we reluctantly cut short our round after the ninth hole, the slate grey sky still drenching Bell Bay without hope of reprieve, he confessed that sometimes he almost wished for the relative anonymity afforded most freshman pros.

"What if I don't make it?" Stu asked darkly, the expectations of all Cape Breton suddenly heavy on his shoulders. "I'd sure hate to let everybody down. That would be the worst thing of all."

OF HIGHLANDS LINKS, THE eagerly awaited final stop of my Cape Breton tour, George Knudson once raved, "This is the Cypress Point of Canada for sheer beauty. Take a box lunch, go out for 18 holes and you're gone for the day."

And yet despite the endorsement of our top professional golfer, the rise to prominence of Highlands Links was long delayed. In the first years after it opened in 1941, Highlands went largely overlooked mostly due to its distant location in Cape Breton Highlands National Park, far removed from the eyes of the majority of the nation's golfers. Even more damaging to its reputation was the utterly shameful long-term neglect by the federal government, which quickly lost interest after building Highlands as an adornment to stately Keltic Lodge on the same property. Year after year the feds stubbornly refused to spend the money needed to properly maintain a championship course.

Hardly noticeable at first, the decay deepened with the passing decades. Groundskeepers pinched pennies by ordering bunkers filled in and by using fertilizer only sparingly, if at all. Fairways grew thick with weeds, and the greens were notoriously bumpy and unkempt. When it rained, bunkers went undrained. The pro shop was barely more than a shed heated by a pot-bellied stove.

By the early 1990s, Highlands had been reduced to a pathetic shadow of the Stanley Thompson jewel George Knudson had once so admired. Indeed, the very nature of the golf course had changed. Built beside rugged oceanside cliffs, Highlands was once the closest thing to a true links course found in Canada. But over the years the forests that lined the fairways had been allowed to grow unchecked. Branches and new growth reached out to block many of the views Thompson had painstakingly cut through the trees to reveal the ocean and the surrounding mountains. In a few spots, the overgrowth was so pronounced that golfers playing from the back tees actually found their shots blocked.

Finally, as word spread of the course's decline, the federal government felt shamed into action. In 1994, under the direction of architect Graham Cooke, work began on a three-year, $4-million rescue operation that saw the character and beauty of Highlands Links fully restored.

Undone was the sacrilege that saw some 40 of Thompson's famously imaginative bunkers sodded over. The drainage system in the bunkers was rebuilt and a new irrigation system installed. With the permission of Parks Canada, Cooke ordered overgrown branches that cut off strategic views pruned back, and he had scrub and more than 4,000 dead trees removed from the course. Forward tees were also introduced, making Highlands more playable for women and seniors in particular. A handsome new clubhouse with central heating went up. And cart paths were routed close to the edge of the woods, then hidden from view wherever possible by rocks and tall earth mounds.

In combination with Nova Scotia's emergence as a golf destination of international stature, the restoration focused the world's attention on a course that had for too long gone ignored. In 1998, Highlands' first full year of operation following completion of the work, U.S.-based *GOLF Magazine* ranked it the world's 75th best golf course. The same publication promoted it to 57th the next year. A truly remarkable turnaround was capped in the summer of 2000 when, for the first time, Canada's own *Score* magazine rated Highlands the country's number-one course.

Still more proof of the economic impact of golf tourism can be seen in the constantly growing numbers of golfers flocking to the Highlands. Course officials, expecting momentum to build gradually, originally projected that by the year 2002 some 23,000 rounds would be played there annually. But that number was bettered by more than a thousand rounds as early as 1997. In 2000, an unprecedented 27,000 rounds of golf were played at the Highlands.

The citizens of Ingonish, the quiet north shore community

that borders Cape Breton Highlands National Park near the golf course, have gratefully seen their tourist season stretched by several weeks. Cottage, motel and hotel rentals have increased by as much as 60 per cent, with the most pronounced jump coming in spring and fall, precisely when it's most needed.

Golfers return home from Highlands dazzled by one of the most perfectly suited natural settings ever given to a Canadian golf course. Mountains, the tallest in Nova Scotia, loom over rough-and-tumble terrain ranging from a pine-edged valley floor cut by the charging Clyburn River to rocky outcrops and seaside marshes.

Stanley Thompson was said to have been astonished by the site's potential when Parks Canada hired him for the job in the late 1930s. By then Thompson's reputation as Canada's premier course designer had been firmly established with his work in Banff and Jasper and at Vancouver's Capilano, each of those courses carved from terrain as rugged as this. For a fee of $55,000, Thompson was to design and build a nine-hole course.

He set to work with a small crew, a team of horses and just two pieces of heavy equipment (an excavator and a small bulldozer) on open farmland close to the ocean shore. It is here on these original nine holes — today's 1 to 4 and 14 to 18 — with their rolling fairways and greens open at the front that Highlands most resembles a classic links course. When he was done, Thompson paused just long enough to convince Parks Canada to add nine more holes for a full 18. These he cut through the pine forest of the Clyburn Valley, making strategic use of the winding river in his design.

Adding still more charm to the setting is Keltic Lodge, a provincially operated 104-room resort dating from 1940 that lies just a few hundred yards away at the end of a long birch-lined drive. Constructed in the grand style, with a red-tiled roof and white clapboard siding, the lodge offers panoramic views of the ocean and Cape Smokey across the bay.

It was from this popular hostelry that I emerged on a cool and grey late-autumn morning to at last join my boyhood hero for a round of golf.

By now every detail of George Knudson's match here against Al Balding had been indelibly transferred from scratchy videotape to my memory. The 1965 *Shell's Wonderful World of Golf* telecast pitted Canada's two most accomplished professional golfers in a stroke-play, 18-hole showdown. The winner would take home $3,000, the loser pocketing $2,000. In the event of a tie, Balding and George would divide the $5,000 purse equally.

Balding, it need hardly be said, was a more than worthy opponent. He won four times on the PGA Tour, including three events in 1957 when he placed sixth on the tour's money list, the highest finish by a Canadian until Mike Weir equalled his mark in 2000. Balding went on to capture the 1968 World Cup individual title while joining with Knudson to win team honours. Together, the two friends would be inducted into the Canadian Golf Hall of Fame in 1985.

I found it easy to imagine myself standing between Knudson and Balding in front of the rickety old clubhouse while the show's co-hosts, golf immortal Gene Sarazen, who was gaily clad in his trademark plus fours, and announcer George Rogers conducted a brief interview.

Warily surveying the sky after the gallery of about 200 had followed us to the first tee, Rogers whispered to Sarazen, "I think it's going to be a little bit rugged out there, Gene. It's really blowing." The day had dawned blustery and overcast, following a night that had seen heavy rains soak the fairways and slow the greens.

After winning the toss, Balding, tall and lean and wearing a boldly striped cardigan against the chill off the Atlantic, stroked a strong drive hard into the gusting wind, his ball coming to rest about 230 yards down the fairway of the 415-yard straightaway par-four opening hole.

With rapt attention, I watched while George, nattily dressed in a black sweater and tan pants, set up. He sneaked a quick last look down the fairway, then swung through with a flawless stroke that sent his ball straight down the fairway's heart, about the same distance as Balding's drive.

Other than on the tee boxes, the luxury of a level lie would seldom be ours the rest of the day. Highlands' fairways pitch and roll, as Gene Sarazen wryly observed, "like the deck of a battleship." During construction, the shaping of each hole required the excavation of hundreds of sizeable granite boulders. But rather than hide them in the bush, Stanley Thompson cleverly had his workers pile the boulders on the fairways and then cover them with just enough soil to grow grass.

The difficulty of playing from these giant moguls — which have been likened to the humped backs of an army of rampaging elephants — largely explains why a course measuring only 6,592 yards from the back tees has been awarded a Slope Rating of 141, the highest in the province.

Both men chose 2-irons for their second shots, leaving their balls just short of the green. George pitched on to within five feet of the pin. Balding put his even closer with an 8-iron — or it might have been a 9-iron, Sarazen wasn't sure and I couldn't tell either. Both George and Al dropped their putts for par.

Even before George retrieved his ball from the cup, I saw him reach for his smouldering cigarette, which he'd flung, almost disdainfully, to the grass just seconds before. Through the entire afternoon he was never without a cigarette, lighting one on the butt of another, then carefully cupping it in his right hand against the wind.

With a perpetually dour, almost pained expression, George went on to par the second hole, a descending dogleg par four, grabbing a one-stroke lead when Balding missed a five-foot putt. Then George picked up another stroke when Al bogeyed the third hole, a par three over a pond to a heavily bunkered rolling green.

By the fifth hole, George had already built up a three-stroke advantage and was playing confident, almost flawless golf. On the sixth, a 565-yard par-five dogleg to the right, Knudson astonished even Sarazen by walloping his drive 300 yards. For his second shot, George chose a 3-wood and proceeded to play a lovely left-to-right cut shot from a tight lie that landed just feet from the front of the green.

"I want to tell you those are two of the longest shots under the conditions I've ever seen," Sarazen told George admiringly, pulling him aside after he'd putted out for a birdie to open up a four-stroke lead over the struggling Balding.

"How could you get 565 yards with a drive and a three-wood?"

"I don't know," answered a bemused Knudson, a golfer of usually only average length off the tee. "I think the wind helped me quite a bit."

In keeping with Cape Breton's Scottish heritage, each hole at Highlands has been given a Gaelic name reflecting its character. The second hole, for instance, is called Tam O'Shanter, since the shape of the green recalls that of a Scot's bonnet. The fourth hole, an uphill par four boobytrapped with two water hazards and greenside bunkers that feast on wayward approach shots, is aptly titled Heich O'Fash, which means "heap of trouble."

Then there's George's favourite hole at Highlands, the par-five seventh, known locally as Killer, although its given name is Killiecrankie, meaning "a long and narrow pass," notorious in reputation. Unquestionably the most difficult hole on the course, the double-dogleg to the right stretches 585 yards through a tight valley bounded by towering maples. Knudson managed par here, and walked away calling the seventh one of the most magnificent par fives he'd ever seen.

While I looked on with open admiration, George parred the next two holes, making the turn with a score of 34, two-under and still four strokes better than his opponent.

With the exception of the transparently unhappy Balding, we were enjoying a magnificent nature walk that had so far taken us from the coastal plane deep into the backwoods. In true links fashion, Highlands' seven-mile routing is nine holes out from the clubhouse and nine back, making this an inconvenient course for anyone contemplating just playing nine.

I would have loved to talk to George during our round together, asking him for his impressions of Stanley Thompson's course. But knowing how focused and aloof he always was when he played, I didn't dare risk breaking his concentration.

Our long trek between the 12th green and the 13th tee, nearly a third of a mile in length, led us down a sylvan path beside the wide and crystal clear Clyburn River. Moose, accustomed to human contact, are often seen here munching on sweet roots. Also making frequent appearances on the course are red foxes, who brazenly position themselves alongside fairways to better steal golf balls. A bald eagle makes its home in a tree over the tee box on the fourth hole.

Though putting was easily the weakest part of his game, Knudson had been dropping them like Billy Casper all day —

eight-footers, 10-footers, even a 12-footer on greens large and rolling and made treacherous by Thompson's distinctive hollows and bumps.

Not until the par-five 13th (today a par four), did George misjudge a putt, just missing a five-footer for a birdie. This provided the opening Balding had been impatiently awaiting. He holed a twisting 20-foot putt for an eagle to slash Knudson's advantage to just two strokes.

When both men bogeyed the par-four 14th, I wondered if George was feeling the pressure. But his face, covered in red blotches from a summer in the sun, was an impenetrable mask of furrowed concentration. Those blotches worried me, knowing that a decade later he would develop skin cancer. This day, though, it was too cloudy to do him much harm.

On the next hole, George padded his lead by a stroke when his par trumped Al's bogey. Balding then blew his last best chance against my unflappable idol. En route to the 16th tee, Al unwittingly marched right past St. Paul's Church, where locals seeking divine assistance down the stretch have been known to stop and dip their golf balls in holy water. I suppose I could have told him.

George and Al matched pars on the 16th and 17th, bringing us to the par-four, 420-yard final hole, or Hame Noo, Gaelic for "home now," with George still enjoying a commanding three-stroke lead.

The roiling, gun-metal grey ocean beyond the distant green provided a dramatic backdrop for Knudson's final tee-shot of the day—another distinguished blast, this one 275 yards. Three more shots, including a superb 20-foot downhill putt that left him with a tap-in for par, saw George home with a score of 70, two-under par and three strokes better than Balding.

Moments later he was standing in front of the old clubhouse, smiling his familiar little grin and accepting the winner's cheque for $3,000 from Sarazen and Rogers.

My fantasy video still unreeling, I imagined that George and I sat in the lounge at Keltic Lodge that night, laughing, talking golf and celebrating his victory. We'd invited Balding to join us, but Al was in no fit mood for company.

Knudson, I discovered to my delight, was a different man away from the pressure of competition, witty and charming and making every effort to put me at my ease. Before long I felt familiar enough to start calling him Georgie and Knudie, just like all his closest friends.

"I heard a good one a couple of days ago from an old pal of yours at Dundee," I said to him, deep into the hilarity of our evening together. "'If I die, will you remarry?' a woman asks her golfer husband. . . . "

Knudson loved Vic's joke, practically busting his gut at the "No, she's a lefty" punchline.

At any rate, that's how I'll always remember my visit to Highlands Links. George Knudson and I, golf buddies forever.

AFTERWORD

DURING THE TWO SEASONS of my *Northern Links* adventure, I often found my thoughts returning to the golfers I had left behind. I wondered if Brian McCann, the likeable young pro from the Oakville golf dome, would succeed in his Canadian Tour comeback. Could Bill Hardwick fight off the march of time and extend his career on the European Senior Tour? Would Cape Breton's Stu Musgrave make the giant leap from local to national hero? Before signing off on the project, I decided to retrace my tracks across the country for the latest news.

I began with a call to Marlene Stewart Streit, who had suffered through a difficult time since our round at Lambton. In July 2000, John Douglas Streit, Marlene's husband of 43 years, passed away following a stroke.

Using golf to help her through her grief, Marlene advanced that autumn to the third round of the U.S. Senior Women's Amateur, the prestigious event she had won twice before. Marlene told me that she still dreamed of extending her string of national championships into a sixth successive decade. "Don't bet against it," she said with a girlish laugh. "There's a lot of golf left in me yet."

Despite the frequent disappointments that are part of the nature of the game, every golfer I met who had known success in the past shared Marlene's unshakeable belief that somehow they would overcome all obstacles.

When I last saw Brian McCann in the late winter of 2000, the former top-ranked amateur was optimistically preparing for the Canadian Tour's spring Q-school following a disastrous rookie season that saw him miss 14 cuts in the 14 tournaments he entered. Brian, though still working out the kinks in his swing, managed to win a conditional card at Q-school. By mid-summer all his hard work finally started to pay off. Playing better every week, he entered the final event of the year needing only to make the cut to ensure at least his conditional card for the 2001 season.

"You won't believe what happened then," Brian told me. "During the fourth round, having already guaranteed my card by making the cut, I got angry after a bad shot and bent my 3-wood over my shoulders. But the damage to the club was so slight that I didn't realize it was bent until after I hit another shot with it two holes later."

Brian knew there was a penalty for playing with a bent club. "I figured one or at most two strokes," he remembered. "Then a rules official said to me, 'I'm sorry to have to tell you this, but you're disqualified.'"

One rash, reflex act destroyed Brian's entire season. The disqualification dropped him too far down the Order of Merit to earn even a conditional card. Never in all his life had he felt so low. Still reeling emotionally a few weeks later when he attended the tour's autumn Q-school, Brian played miserably and went away empty-handed.

So now, once again, all his efforts were aimed at the spring Q-school, his last chance to get back on tour for the 2001 season. "I'm not too worried," Brian said bravely. "My swing is looking really good. I'm confident I'll make it."

The other Canadian Tour hopeful I had met, Cape Breton's Stu Musgrave, also experienced a rocky start to his 2000 campaign. Hampered by tendinitis in one elbow, the tour rookie missed the cut in his first five tournaments. By the time his game finally got back on track it was too late to make an impact. Stu finished a distant 91st on the Order of Merit and that autumn had to return to Q-school, where he tied for 20th to earn a conditional card for the 2001 season.

"The Canadian Tour was a little tougher than I'd imagined," admitted Stu, whose winnings totalled just $3,877. "But I won't really know where I stack up until I play a full season in good health. It's still not time to panic."

One young man whose destiny was unfolding exactly as he'd hoped was Chris Miranda, who had served eight memorable months as the first head pro of Egypt's Royal Valley Golf Club. Chris took the job in Luxor hoping that his experience there would put his career on the fast track. After two summers back home in Ontario, Chris called in January 2001 to tell me that he had just been named head pro at Savannah Golf Links in Cambridge, a busy public course not far from his hometown of Stoney Creek.

"The funny thing is, they never even asked about my Egyptian experience," Chris said. "But they did like my ideas about marketing and customer service, two things I had learned a lot about in Luxor. I got the impression they thought I was a guy who could think on his feet. There's no question Egypt helped me to do that."

Of all the professional golfers I met, easily the two I most identified with were Bill Hardwick and Doug Robb, who were living out every middle-aged duffer's fantasies on the European Senior Tour.

As planned, Doug Robb began winding down his career in 2000 by entering only about half of the tour's events. "We had a wonderful time," he recalled. "Adeline and I rented a car in England, drove to Ireland and then across to Switzerland, Germany and France. I made $11,000 in winnings, about enough to pay our way. Next year I'll probably only play in three or four tournaments."

Bill Hardwick, who at age 60 is five years older than Doug, had invested too much sweat and emotion in his senior golf career to consider making his exit even a moment too soon. In 2000, Bill enjoyed one of his best seasons yet, leaping to 30th on the Order of Merit from 41st the season before, with official winnings of approximately $82,000. In his last two tournaments of the season, the former Toronto businessman finished sixth and fifth respectively, giving hope that his second tour victory may still lie ahead.

"I never stopped believing," Bill told me early in 2001. "The way I'm playing, I can hardly wait to get out there again this spring. Who knows? Maybe the best is yet to come."

ACKNOWLEDGEMENTS

LIKE MOST BOOKS, THIS ONE would never have been published without the enthusiastic help of an editor who promoted the project from the start. Fortunately, I found such an ally in Scott Sellers, who worked with me on *Northern Links* until leaving Penguin Books Canada for another publishing company. Then, my luck still holding, I had the pleasure of working with the talented Michael Schellenberg, whose patience and encouragement were always appreciated.

Two others at Penguin Canada must also be thanked: art director Martin Gould, a tremendously gifted designer, and president and publisher Cynthia Good, an old friend and mentor who gave the project the go-ahead.

There were many people who helped speed and smooth this duffer's unforgettable journey through the world of Canadian golf. I am deeply indebted to them all, but especially to Irene Khatter, the promotional whiz behind the success of Cape Breton's Fab Four; Holly J. Wood, the director of public relations at the Banff Springs Hotel; David Merry, a golf pro, professional comedian and all-round great guy; my good friend Bernard Dunn, whose counsel was invaluable; and Bill Steinburg, the former editor of *Golf Canada* magazine.

Most works of non-fiction are built at least in part on the hard work of journalists who have gone before. In particular, I owe thanks to golf historian James A. Barclay for his *Golf in Canada: A History* (McClelland & Stewart, 1992), a ground-breaking work that has become an essential resource for anyone writing on almost any subject related to Canadian golf. Another book I found myself reaching for time and again was *The Architects of Golf* by Geoffrey S. Cornish and Ronald E. Whitten (Harper-Collins, 1993), a title regarded as the bible on golf course design. And when writing about the colourful history of the Banff Springs Golf Course, I relied heavily on E.J. Hart's thoroughly researched and entertaining *Banff Springs Golf* (EJH Literary Enterprises).

Finally, I would like to express my heartfelt appreciation to copy editor Mary Adachi, who is both a pleasure to work with and a consummate pro. May she go on forever.